Noir,
Now and Then

Recent Titles in
Contributions to the Study of Popular Culture

Noir,
Now and Then

Film Noir Originals and Remakes
(1944–1999)

RONALD SCHWARTZ

Contributions to the Study of Popular Culture, Number 72

GREENWOOD PRESS
Westport, Connecticut • London

Library of Congress Cataloging-in-Publication Data

Schwartz, Ronald, 1937–
  Noir, now and then : film noir originals and remakes (1944–1999) / Ronald
Schwartz.
    p. cm.—(Contributions to the study of popular culture, ISSN 0198–9871 ; no. 72)
  Includes bibliographical references and index.
  ISBN 0–313–30893–4 (alk. paper)
    1. Film noir—United States—History and criticism. I. Title. II. Series.
  PN1995.9.F54 S39   2001
  791.43'655—dc21   00–049505

British Library Cataloguing in Publication Data is available.

Library of Congress Catalog Card Number: 00–049505
ISBN: 0–313–30893–4
ISSN: 0198–9871

First published in 2001

Greenwood Press, 88 Post Road West, Westport, CT 06881
An imprint of Greenwood Publishing Group, Inc.
www.greenwood.com

Printed in the United States of America

∞

The paper used in this book complies with the
Permanent Paper Standard issued by the National
Information Standards Organization (Z39.48–1984).

10 9 8 7 6 5 4 3 2

Copyright Acknowledgment

The author and publisher gratefully acknowledge permission for the use of the following
material:

From Lawrence Russell's review of *The Asphalt Jungle*, as posted in Film Court
(www.culturecourt.com). Reprinted by permission of the author.

For Amelia,
both a film noir and a neo-noir femme fatale.

Contents

Acknowledgments

I must thank my friends Jeff Leibowitz, Ray Meola, and Charles Mitchell for their ongoing dialogues with me about noir and neo-noir. I also cherish my argument with Paul Shrader at a film conference that led me to write this book. Martin Scorsese's book and video *A Personal Journey Through American Movies* prompted me to do this volume, and Foster Hirsch's *Detours and Lost Highways* provided much inspiration.

Fred MacMurray and Barbara Stanwyck in a scene from *Double Indemnity* (1944). Reproduced from the author's collection.

Introduction

Film noir and neo-noir are cinema styles that date as early as the 1940s and continue into the twenty-first century. *Noir* is a French word meaning "black," and although "film noir" literally means "black film," it refers to the mood of the films made between 1940 and 1959 on black-and-white film stock, in which a male protagonist is usually led to his destruction by a femme fatale and winds up getting neither the money nor the dame.

The French critic Nino Frank coined the term "film noir" in 1946, and the French authors Raymond Borde and Etienne Chaumenton, in their seminal critical work *Panorama du film noir américain*, used "noir" to describe the films in a particular sort of American cinema produced in the United States from just before and after World War II until the late 1950s.

Some American critics cite *The Maltese Falcon* (1941) as the first real "film noir," but I prefer to think of *Citizen Kane* and *Stranger on the Third Floor* (both 1940 productions) as the real start of American noir (with many pre-noir antecedents dating back to the early 1930s, such as *Scarface*, and/or either *Odds Against Tomorrow* or *Touch of Evil* (both 1958 productions) as noir's terminal signpost. It must be said that no American director during that period ever used the word "noir," nor did he or she set out to create a style or genre. It was the French critics who applied the term "noir" to this group of films that shared a similar photographic, artistic, and thematic style. Therefore, noir is not a genre, but an unconscious stylistic movement shared by many directors in 1940s and 1950s Hollywood.

It is also certain that societal influences contributed to the design of these particular films. Their thematic pessimism can be attributed to the post–World War II disillusionment of returning servicemen on a variety of issues, such as their replacement by women in the workforce and their lack of adjustment to postwar values. Coincidentally, there was a rise of acceptance of the "hard-boiled" school of writers, whose escapist, masculine themes provided entertainment during the war years. The novels of James M. Cain, Raymond Chandler, David Goodis, Dashiell Hammett, and Cornell Woolrich were widely read and provided the "raw material" for films noirs. Also, because of the use of new high-speed film stock and the ease of photographing outside of the studio (on location), real people and streets were used in a great number of films of the period. And, finally, many émigrés from France and Germany, who filmed in Hollywood and on locations, brought with them a style of "expressionist" cinema that developed in Europe in the early 1930s and reached its fulfillment in the films noirs of the 1940s and 50s.

There are many qualities and characteristics of film noir: chiaroscuro lighting (or low-key lighting); screenplays set in urban milieus filmed mostly at night; frequent images of water and reflections of street life; inverted frames (cameras held diagonally and/or vertically), reflecting the inner thoughts of the protagonist; and very complex and convoluted plots, usually expressed in a voice-over by a central character or a detective or a femme fatale who "flashes back" to the past. There is much violence and crime; eroticism and hetero- and homosexuality abound. Characters share obsessive behavior, males are generally untrusting and misogynistic, and become victims of their own paranoia. All of the aforementioned characteristics are framed in a pervasive darkness; photographers combine low-key lighting with deep focus shots that provide a claustrophobic ambience. The viewer is constantly jarred by the editing of the film, always surprised by the asymmetrical compositions within the frame of the camera, the mystery of the plot, the xenophobia of the characters as they move through the darkness toward an unknown conclusion.

Neo-noir, the "new noir," is a direct outgrowth of the film noir style. Although most American film critics feel that either *Harper* (1966) or *Chinatown* (1974) was the first signpost for the emergence of the new noir, I feel it is Alfred Hitchcock's seminal film *Psycho* (1960), in which the reemergence of film noir begins, but with several new spins. Still a style and definitely NOT a genre, neo-noir has taken advantage of color, the latest in projection technology (CinemaScope and the like), and the less restrictive rating system that allows greater violence, nudity, and harsher themes to be presented on screen. Of course the real imitators—like Lawrence Kasdan, whose neo-noir *Body Heat* (1981) is a true rip-off of Billy Wilder's *Double Indemnity* (1944)—are the conscious auteurs/

directors who set out to revive the film noir in the 1980s by making it more violent, sexually graphic, and truthful, the subject of my opening chapter on remakes.

And remakes continue to be made from the old hard-boiled school of detective fiction (compare the two versions of *The Big Sleep* or *Farewell, My Lovely*), but with new writers who, instead of singling out the good-bad detectives, are writing and filming screenplays about the good-bad cops or the emergence of the serial killer. Film noir always dealt with con artists, petty gangsters, and psychopaths. Now these characters have been upgraded to grifters, techno-noir gangsters, and sci-fi psychopaths in a variety of new noir labelings that boggle the mind, such as "future noir," "agrarian noir," "techno noir," "parody noir." But all new noirs contain many of the old elements of the 1940s and 50s films, updating them from the 1960s onward. Charles Mitchell published a wonderful article in *Big Reel Magazine* in May 1999, "The Film Noir Alphabet," in which he describes and names the A to Z of noir—from Amnesia Noir, Boxing Noir, and Communist Noir to Xenophobic Noir, Youth Noir, and Zen Noir—placing the films in their respective categories and giving the thematic reasons for the assignment of each film to a particular group. Mitchell neglected to include New Noir/Neo-Noir/Film Après Noir/Noveau Noir; under "N" he placed Nazi Noir.

My mission in this book is not to redefine film noir or come up with a new definition of the continually emerging neo-noir, but to examine the thirty-five pairs of films that had their origins in noir, the originals and the remakes. I will judge the critical worth of these transpositions of art, from one style to another, and provide some entertaining perceptions and reading for our journey, from 1944 to 1999, to gauge an awareness of the changes in American social mores through these two unique styles of peculiarly American cinema.

One additional comment. Throughout the research for this book, it became apparent that no two film critics chose the same signposts for the beginning and end of film noir. The French critic Patric Brion, in his wonderful text *Le Film Noir* (1991), begins his appraisal of the style in 1940 with Alfred Hitchcock's *Rebecca* and ends it in 1958 with Nicholas Ray's color and CinemaScope *Party Girl*. Most American critics would begin with John Huston's 1941 film of Dashiell Hammett's *The Maltese Falcon*, and some might start with Boris Ingster's *The Stranger on the Third Floor* (1940). Because my book deals with films noirs and their remakes, I decided to add two appendixes, the first listing the mysteries, melodramas, thrillers, or pre-noir movies that were remade into real "films noirs"; the second, discussing the new noir films from 1960 on and their remakes through 1999, in an effort to provide as complete a picture as possible of the film noir and neo-noir remakes to date.

It is also appropriate to state why I began my book on film noir remakes with *Double Indemnity* (1944) rather than a predecessor like *The Letter* or *Rebecca* (both 1940) or especially *The Maltese Falcon* (1941). I would agree with most film critics that all three films have "noirish" stylistic elements, but with *Double Indemnity*, all of the stylistic characteristics basic to noir came together in a whole that identifies this particular kind of cinema. *Rebecca* is more of a "gothic romance" with noirish elements; *The Letter* is a story of adultery and murder with a noirish lighting style but is not true noir. *The Maltese Falcon* does have many noir elements, but it is a studio-filmed Warner Brothers "film gris"—a gray film, not a true noir, because many of its best moments are played "offstage." It is too cerebral a film, lacking in sexuality and sensuality. Only *Double Indemnity*, despite production code adherence, portrays the sexual and sensual "frissons" in its ambience and the motivations of its characters. This 1944 film captures the true meaning of "noir."

NOTE

Credits for films in each chapter are presented in the following format: Title of film, year released, (d.) director, studio, running time, b&w/ color, special format (CinemaScope, VistaVision, etc.), (sc.) screenplay, (ph.) photography, (m.) music, (v.) video. ("Video" refers to VHS format only. Although laser, DVD, and Super VHS versions of films may exist, VHS is still the most popular and accessible format in the United States.)

THE FILMS

Double Indemnity (1944, 1954 [TV], 1960 [TV], 1973 [TV]), and Body Heat (1981)

DOUBLE INDEMNITY (1944)

"From the moment they met, it was murder!" This is the infamous tag line for Billy Wilder's most trenchant film noir, *Double Indemnity*, although in 1944, when it was first released in New York on September 11, *Times* critic Bosley Crowther referred to it as a "melodrama," "a long dose of calculated suspense," "with a realism reminiscent of past French films [poetic realism of the 1930s]," with characters as tough, "hard and inflexible as steel."

Although James M. Cain is credited with the original novel and Raymond Chandler and Billy Wilder share screenplay credit, the film is actually based on the case of Ruth Snyder, a convicted murderess who died in the electric chair on January 13, 1928. Aided by Miklos Rozsa's pounding film score and John Seitz's expressionistic black-and-white photography, Wilder had no real idea he was filming in a style called "noir"; he discovered this many years later, to his great surprise.

In *Double Indemnity*, Walter Neff (Fred MacMurray), a somewhat cute but dim insurance agent, falls prey to the charms of a teasing blonde, Phyllis Dietrieckson. (Barbara Stanwyck), an anklet-wearing femme fatale/housewife. She wants him to kill her husband in a "railroad accident" that would net her a double indemnity insurance payment. What makes this film a fabulous example of the culture and style of film noir is that, as dictated by the movie production code of the period, jealousy enters Walter's relationship with Phyllis after he commits the crime. Believing she has another, much younger lover, he murders her in a fit of jealousy, then probably bleeds to death from a shot fired by the dying Phyllis, having first dictated the entire story of the film in a two-hour flashback. (In the original novel, Walter and Phyllis go off together on a cruise, happily reunited.) In keeping with the "crime doesn't pay" morality of the period, Billy Wilder even added a scene of Neff dying in the San Quentin gas chamber, but felt the film played better with the film ending as Neff hears police and/or ambulance sirens in the distance. *Double Indemnity* is the best example of a noir film to date: tough as nails, with acid, wrenching dialogue and realistic sets. Watch Walter and Phyllis as they meet in a gleaming white southern California supermarket, wearing dark glasses, not shopping or even looking at each other while firming up plans for a murder. And those fabulous lines: "There was no way in the world I could have known that murder sometimes can smell like honeysuckle," or "I couldn't hear my footsteps. It was the walk of a dead man," or "Yes, I killed him for money and for a woman. I didn't get the money and I didn't get the woman. Pretty, isn't it?"

Double Indemnity also has a homoerotic relationship between Walter Neff and Barton Keyes (Edward G. Robinson), the claims investigator who suspects Phyllis, but not Walter, of the crime. Wilder downplayed the father-son relationship as well as the "police procedural" element that could have made his film a "detective story" rather than a twisty noir, which is what it really is. Wilder took the focus off Robinson's role and humanized his outlook, in contrast to the many detective films of the period that originated in novels of Raymond Chandler, his coscenarist. By fashioning *Double Indemnity* into a murderous melodrama with sexual innuendo, Wilder created a realistic crime triumph.

TELEVISION VERSIONS OF *DOUBLE INDEMNITY*
(1954, 1960, 1973)

It was more than fifteen years before *Double Indemnity* was filmed for television. In the interim there were two television specials. *The Lux Video Theatre* did a live broadcast with Frank Lovejoy, Laraine Day, and Ray Collins in the roles of Walter, Phyllis, and Keyes in December 1954; it received fairly good reviews crediting much to Buzz Kulik's direction, Laraine Day's underplaying of the femme fatale, and Ray Collins' tough guy insurance investigator. In Great Britain, Granada TV did a filmed "Play of the Week" special in 1960 with William Sylvester, Madeleine Sherwood, and Donald Pleasence playing the three key roles and directed by Gerald Savory. Television critics were not too kind to the performers because Sylvester and Sherwood didn't strike any sparks at their initial meeting (remember the anklet scene in the MacMurray-Stanwyck version?) and the underscore was too insistent, especially during the murder scene. But Sylvester and Sherwood played their roles competently.

The most recent totally filmed version, the most faithful remake, was a flattish copy of the original film scene for scene that contained at least 98 percent of the original dialogue. Directed by Jack Smight and starring Richard Crenna as Walter Neff, Samantha Eggar as Phyllis Dietrickson, and Lee J. Cobb as Barton Keyes, this ABC color television special produced at Universal is a pale imitation. Although writing credit is given to Steven Bochco, creator of the popular television series *NYPD Blue*, and inspiration is credited to Cain, Chandler, and Wilder, color obfuscates the noirish aspects of Phyllis and Walter, and Eggar cannot generate the sexual heat that Barbara Stanwyck did in the original.

Howard Thompson, in a *New York Times* review of December 13, 1973, said, "Eggars patters through her part . . . like a cast-iron daffodil with a wide-eyed petulance [and] . . . Crenna settles for arched eyebrows and a tired jauntiness. The best is Lee J. Cobb . . . [in] a sensible reprise of Edward G. Robinson's insurance-claims bulldog." The real oxygen is that Chandler dialogue!

So why the remake? Perhaps Jack Smight and ABC executives thought he could do a better film for television than Billy Wilder's Paramount original, since there was now a more permissive production code regarding sexuality on screen. No matter. *Body Heat* is the real remake of *Double Indemnity*, definitely in color and for the CinemaScope screen.

BODY HEAT (1981)

"As the temperature rises, the suspense begins." "They called it love. The D.A. called it murder." *Body Heat* is the best example of a neo-noir film derived from *Double Indemnity* the great James M. Cain novel of the 1930s, but its source goes uncredited. *Body Heat* is *Double Indemnity* with explicit sexual scenes added because of the loosening of production codes in the 1980s. The fundamental story of *Body Heat* parallels its predecessor: for love and money, a dazzlingly attractive redhead uses her wits and sexuality to ensnare a weak-willed, easily dominated male, whom she convinces to murder her wealthy husband. Of course, the deluded male is tricked and ends up with neither the money nor the dame. In *Body Heat*, spiderous but hot-blooded Matty Walker (Kathleen Turner), "whose body temperature runs a few degrees above normal," traps Ned Racine (William Hurt), a not-so-bright and easily corrupted lawyer, into killing her husband, Edmund Walker (Richard Crenna), in a deserted country house, then setting a fire to cover up the murder after changing the husband's will. Like Phyllis in *Double Indemnity*, Matty is trapped in a loveless marriage and seeks to dissolve the union through murder. But the men in both versions, Walter and Ned are also greedy—

each wants the money and the woman. Walter and Ned want to manipulate their lovers and reap their fortunes, but poor Walter dies, probably
of blood loss, and Ned winds up in jail while Matty finds new lovers on
a faraway tropical isle.

The updated story of *Body Heat* is a true neo-noir because Ned is manipulated by the shrewd (and shrewish) Matty into a position of culpa-
bility and the possibility of capital punishment. Ned is imprisoned for
killing her husband and is led to believe Matty died in an accidental
bombing. The Lawrence Kasdan script trumps the original Chandler
screenplay by killing off a substitute character (the "real" Matty Walker)
and having the black widow flee to some far-off island with her husband's fortune. Meanwhile, Ned, sentenced to life in prison, realizes too
late that he has been the dupe, the true victim, of a very, very unscru-
pulous woman.

In 1980s neo-noir, the male characters are more vulnerable than their
female counterparts. In the 1940s, male protagonists were a lot simpler;
sex and money are their only objectives. Compare Fred MacMurray's
role in *Double Indemnity* with Burt Lancaster's in Robert Siodmak's *The
Killers* (1946) or *Criss Cross* (1948). Both men are naive and vulnerable,
and end up dying because they are trapped by vicious females—Barbara
Stanwyck, Ava Gardner, and Yvonne De Carlo, respectively.

In 1940s noir, the plots of the films are less tortuous and convoluted.
In 1980s neo-noir, there are many plot twists that dazzle and leave the
audience limp and breathless. During the 1930s and '40s, crime did not
pay and punishment was meted out accordingly . . . the deleted gas-
chamber scene from *Double Indemnity*. As we moved into the 1950s
through the late '90s, the rules and morality depicted changed quite dras-
tically. World War II, the "red scare" era, McCarthyism, and Watergate
all caused a decay of the American dream. Consequently the portrayal
of American society in films, especially relationships between the sexes,
changed radically.

In addition to the great work of the leading actors, *Body Heat* contains
some excellent performances by Ted Danson, as a "dancing" district attorney, and Mickey Rourke, in his screen debut as a "bomber" who aids
Ned in the cover up of Edmund Walker's murder.

Obviously, the 1980s femme fatale has triumphed; she has got the
money and it is probable that she will hunt for another male victim.
Notice the resemblance between Turner's character and Theresa Russell's
in Bob Rafelson's 1987 film, *Black Widow*. Ned Racine's betrayal is classic,
a pure noir experience because viewers watch his downfall. What makes
Body Heat a true neo-noir film are its use of color and CinemaScope, the
femme fatale cleverer than every male (or female) who crosses her path,
and her triumph over everyone.

Compare other neo-noir women like Linda Fiorentino in John Dahl's

The Last Seduction (1994) or Theresa Russell in *Black Widow*. These women take no prisoners. They will go on using their sexuality and their murderous ways until they are trapped by the law. Curiously, these women themselves commit murder to keep their illegal gains. Bill Pullman is tied up and lethally gassed by Linda Fiorentino, and Nicol Williamson is murdered by Theresa Russell—two examples of vulnerable men. In the 1940s men were simpler—sex and money were their only objectives. They were drawn to their mates, and the spider women did them in sexually after getting them to commit murder for them. In the 1980s, women are fully emancipated from traditional roles and a neo-noir icon like Matty Walker (Kathleen Turner), who has become a lethal antagonist in '90's noir, is the equal or the better of any male counterpart.

Body Heat also benefited from a terrific "noir-sounding" film score by John Barry, punctuating the visuals with sensuality, and the Miami Beach locale was adoringly photographed with all of its luxurious, languorous, and sultry beauty by Richard H. Kline. But where *Double Indemnity* only suggested the "sexual liaison" between Walter and Phyllis, Matty's seduction of Ned takes place in three "explicitly sexual scenes," especially one in a bathtub that leaves little to the imagination. One decided advantage to neo-noir, then, is the revelation of sexuality as the true core of the motives for the protagonists to commit their crimes. Because of the relaxation of the production code and the new rating system, neo-noir is definitely here to stay.

FILMOGRAPHY

Double Indemnity (1944), d. Billy Wilder, Paramount, 107min., b&w, sc. Billy Wilder and Raymond Chandler from the novel by James M. Cain, ph. John Seitz, m. Miklos Rozsa, v. MCA.

Double Indemnity (1954 [TV]), d. Buzz Kulik, NBC Television, teleplay based on the Raymond Chandler original film script from the James M. Cain novel, shown live nationally on December 24, 1954.

Double Indemnity (1960 [TV]), d. Gerald Savory, Granada Television-London, teleplay based on the original film script, shown live in Great Britain throughout the year.

Double Indemnity (1973 [TV]), d. Jack Smight, Universal Television, 105 min., color, sc. Steven Bochco based on the novel *Double Indemnity* in the James M. Cain collection *Three of a Kind* and the 1944 screenplay by Raymond Chandler and Billy Wilder, ph. Haskell B. Boggs, m. Billy Goldenberg, v. not available.

Body Heat (1981), d. Lawrence Kasdan, Warner Bros., 113 min., color, CinemaScope, sc. Lawrence Kasdan, ph. Richard H. Kline, m. John Barry, v. Warner Bros.

2

Murder, My Sweet (1944) and Farewell, My Lovely (1975)

MURDER, MY SWEET (1944)

"I caught the blackjack right behind my ear. A black pool opened up at my feet. I dived in. It had no bottom." In a voice-over that plunges Raymond Chandler's famous detective, Philip Marlowe, into a whirlpool of unconsciousness, director Edward Dmytryk utilizes Harry J. Wild's sparsely lit expressionistic camera to tell his crime story, full of blackmail and murder, in a taut ninety-five minutes.

Murder, My Sweet stars former singing star Dick Powell as the famous detective Chandler created in *Farewell, My Lovely*, the original novel that *Murder* is based upon. However, the 1944 version is the "second" translation of *Farewell, My Lovely* to the screen. The first was the 1942 RKO film *The Falcon Takes Over* a "B" feature starring George Sanders as Gay Stanhope, otherwise known as "The Falcon." Costarring Lynn Bari as his sidekick reporter/girlfriend, *The Falcon* follows Chandler's plot to its stunning conclusion, but as a mystery/melodrama/whodunit without any pretensions of noir style. (See Appendix A for further discussion.)

Murder, My Sweet recycles the intriguing plot of *The Falcon*, in a hauntingly stylish manner. We first encounter Marlowe in his seedy Los Angeles office, hired by ex-thug Moose Malloy (former wrestler Mike Mazurki in his breakthrough role) to find a "hostess" in a dance hall/nightclub he frequented before he served a prison term. She is his former girlfriend, Velma, whom he describes "as cute as lace panties." Marlowe is also hired at about the same time by Judge Grayle (Miles Mander) to pay off some petty thieves who have stolen his wife's valuable jade necklace. Unknown to Marlowe, the judge is married to the former Velma, a blonde femme fatale half his age, who has a comely daughter by a first marriage (Ann, played by Anne Shirley). There are so many twists and turns in the plots of both cases that viewers sometimes wonder where the film is going. Marlowe relates the film's entire story in flashback, his eyes covered (powder burns from a gun fired too close to his face), in an office at a police precinct. Finding Moose Malloy's former "dancer girlfriend" and buying back the stolen jade necklace, with Marlowe acting as a bodyguard, are the two plot elements that finally dovetail, leading us to the film's memorable conclusion.

Several murders are committed: first is Marriot (played by Douglas Walton), a gay consort of Mrs. Grayle, hired to recoup the stolen necklace. Then Mrs. Florian (played by Esther Howard), Velma's former employer, who has a photo of her before she married Judge Grayle. And there are subplots involving Jules Amthor, a psychiatrist of dubious repute who runs a sanatorium and sequesters Marlowe, feeding him drugs that propel him to escape, but not before revealing his "hallucinatory images" that are the real essence of this film noir. Marlowe is also a suspect in several of the murders, but all comes right when he discovers Mrs. Grayle's true identity (Claire Trevor in her best role as a bewitchingly blonde femme fatale). As she tries to use her sexual charms to persuade Marlowe to forget what he knows, she is killed by her jealous husband, who in turn is shot to death by Moose Malloy, who later dies at the hands of the police. The only truly winning performance is given by Anne Shirley, who, in sharp contrast to the predatory Claire Trevor, is the soft, righteous daughter caught in the crossfire of her father's weakness and lust and her young stepmother's wiliness and greed. In fact, after the police believe Marlowe's tale and set him free, it is Ann Grayle who goes off with him in a police car, to tend his wounds.

Murder, My Sweet is a tough, taut thriller. It's as smart as it is gripping, with ace direction, fine camera work, and top performances. Your interest never flags, nor does the mystery, with all of its convolutions, ever overwhelm the viewer. That punchy, dramatic conclusion is worth the wait. *Murder, My Sweet* is pure Chandler, pure entertainment, pure noir.

FAREWELL, MY LOVELY (1975)

Farewell, My Lovely (1975) is the neo-noir color remake of the original 1944 film, using the original title of the book. Directed by Dick Richards, it stars Robert Mitchum in the title role of Marlowe. The film has not been updated to the 1970s, but Marlowe is a good deal older than the Philip Marlowe played by Dick Powell in the 1944 version. (Powell wanted out of playing juvenile leads in 1930s Warner Bros. musical entertainments.) Mitchum plays Marlowe with a cigarette dangling out of the side of his mouth; his eyelids are droopy; he has a slight paunch; and he is always tired. All of the plot elements are exactly the same, but more truthful in this new noir. That is, when Marlowe is tracking down the elusive "brunette" Velma (actually, he says her hair is the color of "old gold"), he visits a Los Angeles brothel where the girls are photographed in the nude, an episode that doubtless gave the film its "R" rating. In the 1944 version, Velma worked in a dance hall/nightclub; in the 1975 one, she is apparently a prostitute who works for Frances Amthor, a grotesquely fat woman reminiscent of Hope Emerson's masseuse in Robert Siodmak's *Cry of the City* (1948) and Eleanor Parker's prison warden in *Caged* (1950). It is she who injects Marlowe with drugs that lead him on a downward spiral to noirish depths. The 1944 version's spiral was closer to RKO's dream sequence in Boris Ingster's *Stranger on the Third Floor* (1940), perhaps the real beginning of the film noir style.

In the 1975 version Marlowe looks more like a seedy Humphrey Bogart (via *The Big Sleep*, 1946) than a youthful Dick Powell. Charlotte Rampling plays the Claire Trevor role of Mrs. Grayle as a Lauren Bacall look-alike, right down to her 1940s hair styles and delivery of her lines. (One wonders if this is what director Dick Richards really had in mind.) Sylvia Miles strays from her usual campiness in Andy Warhol films in her sympathetic role as the brothel madam, Mrs. Florian. But, in a more comely interpretation for the 1970s, Jack O'Halloran puts a new spin on Moose Malloy, trumping Mike Mazurki when he utters the line about what Velma was like—"Cute, cute as lace panties." Said *New York Times* critic Richard Eder, "His lips and neck quiver with the effort and triumph of finding a verbal equivalent for the delicate memory that torments his great bulk."

Farewell, My Lovely certainly does not avoid the sleazier parts of the original novel, as its predecessor did. But Mitchum is a bit too old for the role, and Rampling is extremely wooden as the femme fatale. And the excellent actor John Ireland is relegated to the minor role of Nulty, a cop. Anthony Zerbe brings some life to Brunetti, a new role from the original novel. He plays a gambling kingpin who owns a small yacht on which illegal gaming takes place. The yacht is the site of the finale of the film. Instead of Judge Grayle shooting his wife, it is Marlowe who does Velma in, after she shoots Moose Molloy, her former lover. (Apparently Molloy went to jail for a bank robbery, but before he did so, he gave Velma some $80,000, which he wanted to reclaim, along with her "love.")

In smaller roles, Harry Dean Stanton and John O'Leary are wasted, respectively, in the minor roles of Nulty's sidekick cop and Marriot, the gay intermediary who is killed early on while trying to retrieve the jade necklace that was never really stolen but served as a plot device, much like Alfred Hitchcock's famous "McGuffin." But there is one great surprise: mystery writer and neo-noir stylist Jim Thompson, author of *After*

Dark, My Sweet and *The Hot Spot*, plays the role of Judge Grayle very, very capably. His face, wrinkled from life's experiences and abuse, is a mask of revelation, especially when he is required to watch his young wife betraying him with Marlowe. "He's old. What can he expect?" she warbles as she grabs Marlowe in a tight embrace. This was Jim Thompson's only film performance.

On a lesser note, *Farewell, My Lovely* marked the debut of a former porn actor, Sylvester Stallone, playing a thug. A year later he began his ascent to stardom, writing and starring in his own *Rocky* series. Stallone is caught in bed with one of Frances Amthor's best prostitutes. Amthor beats the woman silly, and Stallone shoots the bulky Amthor in a bloody scene.

If *Farewell, My Lovely* (1975) belongs in the pantheon of neo-noir remakes, it is because Dick Richards, the director, has given a great amount of attention to carefully following the Chandler original, including racism, the consequences of intermarriage (a white musician married to a black woman is killed because he tried to cover up Velma's true identity by giving Marlowe a bogus photograph), and the realism of the "black" sections of Los Angeles, where life is cheap. "What's another dead nigger, more or less?" asks Marlowe in one breath, and in the next breath, referring to Marriot, "He was a fairy, anyway"—assuming that the death of each of these men means little in a white, straight world.

Once again, relaxation of Production Code rulings makes for more truthful cinema. Despite the lack of original noir style, Richards opted for his own, realistic, authentic interpretation of the Chandler novel. Nevertheless, I believe *Murder, My Sweet* is the superior film because of its style, photographic inventiveness, lighting, performances, and demands on the imaginations of its viewers. Although the critic, Judith Crist, called *Farewell* "a moody, bluesy, boozy re-creation of Marlowe's tacky, neon-filled Los Angeles of the early forties," and Michael Billington called it "a delicious remake with a nice, smoky forties atmosphere," *Farewell* is just too matter-of-fact, colorful, and nostalgic, yet realistic and out of joint with the mysteries of the 1930s and '40s. One great advantage of the 1975 version was the excellent, moody, bluesy score written by David Shire (although Roy Webb's score for the 1944 entry was equally appealing, but in a less sexy manner). But the urge to redo and update Chandler is always there among film directors. Let's see if Michael Winner accomplished his goals in the 1978 color version of *The Big Sleep*, transposed to a "British" setting!

FILMOGRAPHY

Murder, My Sweet (1944), d. Edward Dmytryk, RKO, 95 min., b&w, sc. John Paxton, based on the Raymond Chandler novel *Farewell, My Lovely*, ph. Harry J.

Wild, m. Roy Webb, v. Nostalgia Merchant and RKO/Turner Home Entertainment.

Farewell, My Lovely (1975), d. Dick Richards, Avco/Embassy, 97 min., color, sc. David Zelag Goodman, based on the original Raymond Chandler novel, ph. John A. Alonso, M. David Shire, v. Avco/Embassy.

3

Detour (1945, 1992)

DETOUR (1945)

"That's life. Whichever way you turn, fate sticks out a foot to trip you."
A great line spoken by Tom Neal in *Detour*, Edgar Ulmer's classic B-film
noir. Tom plays Al Roberts, a talented pianist working in a dive, the
Break-of Dawn nightclub in Manhattan, circa 1942. His girlfriend, Sue
Harvey, the principal singer at the same club, whose rendition of "I Can't
Believe That You're in Love with Me" permeates the musical score (written by Erdody), decides to leave for California to make it big in Hollywood as a leading chanteuse. Al wants to marry her but resigns himself
to her departure. When Al decides to quit the club to reunite with Sue
(played by Claudia Drake), the film really gets going. Al's hitchhiking
through the American West is the principal story of the film and what
finally does him in physically and spiritually.

In the Mojave Desert, Al meets Charles Haskell (played by Edmund
MacDonald), who is driving to Los Angeles in a white '42 Packard convertible. They take turns driving and have supper in a local diner. Al
notices Charlie's right hand has several deep claw marks, and Charlie
tells him, leeringly, it was a female hitchhiker who got away. While they
are crossing the desert at night, a sudden rainstorm forces Al to put up
the roof of the convertible. Charlie falls into a deep sleep, and as Al tries
to wake him up for his turn at driving, Charlie falls out the passenger's
side door and strikes his head on a rock. Al checks his pulse, but Charlie
is a goner. It could have been a heart attack, or the fall from the car, but

Al takes no chances. He hides the body far from the road, takes Charlie's wallet and clothes, and assumes his identity. Al then goes to a motel to shower and get a good night's sleep. He is wearing striped pajamas that symbolically imprison him in the motel. As the sun comes up the next morning, rays of light through the blinds cast horizontal bars across Al as he gets up to leave.

On the road once more, he stops for gas and picks up a woman thumbing a ride. He thinks, "She's beautiful, but she looks like she's been thrown off a freight train." After a short nap, hatchet-faced Vera (played fiercely by the underrated B-actress Ann Savage) accuses Al of murdering Haskell and tells him she is the woman who gave Charlie those scratches on his hand and rode with him from Louisiana through Texas.

The rest of the film is the tale of Al and Vera's ride together to Los Angeles, his wimpiness, her aggressive taunting of him. Along the way, Al wants to sell the car and Vera almost lets him do it, but she finds a packet of money in the glove compartment and reads a newspaper article about the death of Charles Haskell, Sr. Vera wants Al to pass himself off as Haskell, Jr., so that they can collect the inheritance. She tries to persuade him by coming on sexually to him, but he will have none of it. They get a bit drunk together, and Vera threatens to call the police and say Al was responsible for Haskell's death. She grabs the telephone, which has an unusually long cord, and runs into the bedroom. After locking the door, she accidentally wraps the cord around her neck as she telephones the police. Al tries to stop her, pulling on the cord with all of his strength. When Vera doesn't answer, he breaks into the bedroom and finds her, strangled, on the bed. Of course, the police would not believe Al's story; he looks responsible for two accidental deaths. Al has narrated all these events in flashback as he is drinking his coffee in the Nevada Diner. He realizes his life with Sue is finished, and as he steps out of the diner to hitch a ride east, a police car picks him up.

Al portrays himself as a total loser tripped up by fate. On the sound track, one can hear the strains of Chopin and the popular song written from his music, "I'm Always Chasing Rainbows." The predecessor of all those "road" movies, Al's journey has come to its abysmal end. Although the tag line for the film was "He went searching for love . . . but Fate forced a DETOUR to Revelry . . . Violence . . . Mystery!," Al's story is far more painful than the advertising lets on. Al is a morally bankrupt person, undeserving of Sue; he is one of the weakest cynics of all cinema, perhaps deserving his fate. The film was supposedly shot in six days by Edgar G. Ulmer, a schlockmeister of Hollywood's Poverty Row. Both Ulmer and Tom Neal have achieved cult status today, and it is still amazing that *Detour*, for all of its sixty-nine minutes, still packs a hell of a wallop as the embodiment of the guilty soul of film noir.

DETOUR (1992)

Wade Williams's color production of *Detour* (1992) is the neo-noir remake of the 1945 Ulmer film down to use of the exact script with a few added scenes that bring it to a feature length of eighty-nine minutes. Although Williams credits himself and Roger Hull with the screenplay based upon Martin Goldsmith's original short story, much of the dialogue of the 1945 version is lifted directly from the original screenplay by Goldsmith. To add authenticity to this remake, Williams tracked down the original Packard used in the first version and starred Tom Neal, Jr., in the role his father played some forty-seven years earlier.

Tom Neal, Jr., looks very much like his father, but unfortunately does not possess the raw masculinity and acting ability that made Tom Neal, Sr., so convincing in the role of Al Roberts, although he gives screen acting a good first try. More capable is Lea Lavish in the role of Vera. She plays Vera just as harshly but not as memorably as her predecessor, Ann Savage. Savage's Vera was evil incarnate, predestined to die from consumption, a hard dame who has scratched her way through the world but has come up empty. Lavish is a pretty version of Vera whose careful good looks and lithe body are sexually provocative. In fact, in the new version, Vera makes a pass at Al and he begins to respond, holding her, kissing her face, arms, neck, breast, but to no avail. Roberts does not even *touch* Vera in the first version.

A very big difference in the 1992 version is added scenes in Hollywood, restored from the original short story. Sue (played by Erin McGrane) has arrived in Hollywood, lives in a boardinghouse run by Evvy (played by 1940s actress Susannah Foster), and works in a drivein. Realizing her singing career is getting nowhere, she takes up with a cowpuncher-cum-actor working for Monogram studios, sleeps with him, and even proposes marriage to him after dumping him in an earlier scene where she accuses him of being a poor bed partner. When she discovers the cowboy (played effectively by Brad Bittiker) is no longer working for Monogram after an injury, she dumps him and returns to her dull life in the boardinghouse (actually a brothel) and the drive-in. Evvy reads Sue the notice of Al's death (actually Haskell's body found with Al's clothes and identification), but Sue is totally unmoved. "Everyone dies," she says.

One interesting but important detail. At the film's conclusion, Al finishes his coffee, leaves the Nevada Diner, and disappears into the darkness, using the same voice-over about fate as in the 1945 version. But no police car picks him up, and there is no resolution to his wandering. In 1992, Al Roberts is not charged with two accidental deaths and, like Albert Camus's protagonist in *The Stranger*, wanders the world, a prisoner of his conscience.

Another difference between the films is the music. Whereas "I Can't Believe That You're in Love with Me" is entwined in themes of Chopin and "I'm Always Chasing Rainbows" in the 1945 version, Williams opts for a new ballad, "Careless," sung at the piano by Al in the Break-of-Dawn Club just before he is fired by the owner. In the earlier film Al just "decides" to leave for California after talking long-distance to Sue on the telephone. Minor but important plot differences. The earlier Al decides his own fate by hitchhiking, whereas the later Al is forced onto the street and has no choice except to hitchhike to California.

Although most critics felt the 1992 *Detour* was a disappointment, I rather liked Williams's re-creation of the 1940s ambience—in fact, a title card informs the audience that it is, indeed, 1942! Director of cinematography Jeff Richardson did a terrific job of lighting the sets, especially using pulsating red neon during Vera's accidental strangling. He also integrated some excellent color stock footage of New York and Los Angeles of the 1940s. Unlike Ulmer, who used fog machines to photograph New York streets, Williams did not spare any expense for location shots, vintage cars, and period clothes, furniture, and settings. Although *Variety* panned the film, saying "This [version] provides a textbook lesson in how NOT to remake a memorable B-movie," I believe Williams's film adds new life and stature to the neo-noir movement. Like the original, this new *Detour* is full of personal betrayals, intended and accidental crimes committed by an antihero who relates the story in flashback, showing his isolation in society.

FILMOGRAPHY

Detour (1945), d. Edgar G. Ulmer, PRC (Producers' Releasing Corp.), 69 min., b&w, sc. Martin Goldsmith, based on his short story, ph. Benjamin H. Kline, m. Erdody, v. Admit One.

Detour (1992), d. Wade Williams, 89 min., Deluxe Color, sc. Williams and Roger Hull, based on Martin Goldsmith's short story, ph. Jeff Richardson, m. Bill Crain, v. Evergreen.

4

The Big Sleep (1945/1946, 1978)

THE BIG SLEEP (1945/1946)

There are two versions of Howard Hawks's *The Big Sleep* that can now be considered critically because the earlier one was released by Turner Classic Movies in 1998. Robert Gitt, a preservation officer at the UCLA Film and Television Archives, made a short film of thirty-six minutes that identified scenes in the 1945 prerelease version that the public never saw, and showed fifteen minutes added to the 1946 version shot by Howard Hawks before the definitive second version was released in August 1946. Two chief reasons for the additional scenes were (1) to enhance the performance of Lauren Bacall, considered a hot new property by Warner Bros., and (2) Warners was anxious to release all of its war-themed films made just before World War II ended in 1945, and thus held back the original detective film, finished early in 1945, releasing it with Bacall's additional scenes late in 1946.

The Big Sleep was, in reality, Bacall's second film for Warner Bros., but when the actress received such bad reviews for *Confidential Agent*, her third film (based on a Graham Greene novel and costarring Charles Boyer), Jack L. Warner, the studio head, took the advice of Charles K. Feldman, Bacall's agent, and shot additional scenes to insure his investment in Bacall. Director Howard Hawks recaptured Bacall's insolence, admirably displayed in her first film with Humphrey Bogart, *To Have and Have Not*, made in 1944. Howard Hawks had no idea he was making what proved to be a classic film noir of the mid-1940s.

Shot with low-key lighting in black and white by Sid Hickox, *The Big Sleep* was adapted for the screen from the Raymond Chandler novel by William Faulkner, Leigh Brackett, and Jules Furthman, and with an excellent score by Max Steiner. It has six murders, and the sophisticated team of Humphrey Bogart and Lauren Bacall lead Philip Marlowe's investigation into the mayhem. At the beginning, Marlowe is invited by General Sternwood (Charles Waldron) to resolve a blackmail situation involving his daughter Carmen, beautifully played by Martha Vickers, who eclipses Bacall in almost every scene. Carmen loves to drink, use drugs, and gamble heavily, and is possibly a nymphomaniac. There are incriminating photographs and IOUs held by a book dealer, Arthur Guinn Geiger (Theodore von Eltz). Marlowe is hired to retrieve these documents, but before he can do so, Geiger is found shot in a country house in a Los Angeles suburb, and Carmen is found drugged and incoherent. What starts out as an attempt to end a blackmail scheme triggers other murders and introduces other characters into a muddle of events in an almost incomprehensible plot at whose center is the team of Bogart and Bacall (Philip Marlowe, detective, and Vivian Sternwood, Marlowe's love interest and protective sister of Carmen).

First, Sean Regan, General Sternwood's drinking buddy, supposedly runs off with the wife of gambling kingpin Eddie Mars. Then Owen Taylor, the Sternwood chauffeur, is found dead, apparently having driven the Sternwood limousine off a dock into the Pacific Ocean. Then Arthur Geiger, the blackmailer, is found shot. We later learn that Joe Brody (played by Louis Jean Heydt) has the photos of Carmen and is trying to shake down the family. He is shot by Carol Lundgren (Tom Rafferty), Geiger's chauffeur and sometime lover. Then Joe Brody's girlfriend, Agnes Lozell (played hard as nails by Sonia Darrin), uses her boyfriend, Harry Jones (beautifully played by the eternal loser, Elisha Cook, Jr.), in an attempt to blackmail the Sternwoods once again. But Jones is poisoned by a thug named Lash Canino (icily and memorably played by former western star Bob Steele) after Jones gives Canino the wrong address for Agnes. Marlowe finally tracks down Agnes and gets the incriminating documents. Then, just when we think the case is over, the disappearance of Sean Regan pops up again.

There are many sidetracks to solving the Regan mystery. One is Marlowe's visit to Eddie Mars's gambling house. Eddie is capably played by the wonderful supporting actor John Ridgely, a member of the Warner Bros. stable of players who appeared in many 1940s and '50s films for the company. Marlowe watches Bacall sing, wins thousands of dollars at roulette, and interrupts an attempted theft of Bacall's money. Bacall refuses to tell why she is a shill for Eddie. Marlowe's investigation, through a tip from Agnes (who apparently had seen Eddie Mars's wife driving on the outskirts of Los Angeles), leads him to a house where

Marlowe is captured by Canino and he finally meets the elusive Mona Mars, icily played by Peggy Knudsen. Mona doesn't believe her husband could be the mastermind behind Sean Regan's possible murder and the Sternwood blackmail scheme.

Realizing he will be murdered, Vivian unties Marlowe, who shoots Canino and lays a trap for Eddie Mars. Having arranged to meet Eddie at Geiger's country house, Marlowe and Vivan get there before he does. Mars is the true villain, having murdered Sean Regan (we never see him or the crime), blackmailed the Sternwoods, and covered up Carmen's drug abuse, nymphomania, and a possible murder. He is now set up by Marlowe's clever planning. Eddie arrives with three thugs whom he orders to shoot anyone coming out the front door of Geiger's house. After Mars realizes he has been outsmarted and explains his role as the "eminence grise" behind all of the murders, Marlowe forces him out the front door, to die in a hail of bullets from the guns of his own men. Marlowe and Vivian look adoringly at one another as we listen to the sounds of wailing police sirens and the film closes on a title card showing two lighted cigarettes burning in an ash tray and THE END, accompanied by the windup of Max Steiner's sensational musical score.

It is a great pity that the scenes cut from the 1945 version were not included in the 1946 film, because they tend to make the screenplay more comprehensible. We miss James Flavin as Captain Cronjager, who is out to jail Marlowe and revoke his license for not reporting two earlier murders. Flavin's scenes in the District Attorney's office help to explain the motivation behind many of the crimes committed in the film. Also, most of the scenes of Officer Bernie Ohls (ably played by character actor Regis Toomey), Marlowe's friend and contact who puts him on the Sternwood case, unfortunately wound up on the cutting room floor. The reshooting also amplified Bacall's role as well as that of Norris, the butler (capably played by Charles D. Brown), and provided Peggy Knudsen (who replaced another minor actress) with her opportunity to appear in an A-production, as Mona Mars.

Director Howard Hawks insisted on keeping a small gem of a scene between Humphrey Bogart and Dorothy Malone. Malone plays a bookstore proprietor who has a sexual interlude with Marlowe during a rainstorm as he waits to follow Geiger to his hideout. This totally underplayed scene gave Malone a gloss as a sexy icemaiden, one that she revived for Douglas Sirk and that won her the Best Supporting Actress Oscar for in the 1956 Universal film *Written on the Wind*. Ironically, she once again played against Lauren Bacall in the lead. Malone's transformation from moth into butterfly gave *The Big Sleep* of 1946 a peripheral jolt that spiced up the action and added a human dimension not seen in the film until after retakes were done. Hawks was glad he insisted on following his intuition.

THE BIG SLEEP (1978)

The tag line for *The Big Sleep* (1946) was "The Violence-Screen's All-Time Rocker-Shocker"; the British revival made in 1978 used "Some days business is good—and some days it's murder!" in its advertising. An older, grayer Robert Mitchum reprises his role as Philip Marlowe in this new color and wide-screen version of Chandler's 1939 novel that was shot in and around London three years after Mitchum's first outing as Marlowe in Dick Richards's *Farewell, My Lovely* (1975). Although this British version is handsomely mounted, transferring Chandler's Los Angeles of the 1940s to London of the late 1970s, and the plot is more faithful to the Chandler novel than the Faulkner-Brackett-Furthman screenplay, fidelity to the novel may be this updated neo-noir's sole virtue. Producer Elliot Kastner and director Michael Winner concocted a colorful, panoramic new version of the old story, but without much spark or sparkle despite a knockout British cast.

There are few nighttime scenes, no shadows, no rain-swept streets, no confusing mystery to follow, as in 1940s noir. Mitchum announces how well his shirt, tie, and suit are color coordinated, and we watch him move through a series of set pieces: the Sternwood mansion, gambling casinos, antiques shops. Gone are the Los Angeles seediness, the pulp fiction voice-over, the gaudiness of 1940s costuming—replaced by sunny skies, green lawns, manicured driveways, smashing Rolls Royces, Mary Quant couture, and unbelievably vulgar villains.

As in the 1946 version, General Sternwood (this time played by a doddering James Stewart) hires Marlowe to foil a blackmail scheme of Arthur Gwynn Geiger (played absentmindedly by John Justin). Geiger owns a bookstore that is a cover for pornographic photos and materials. Agnes, played by Joan Collins, works for Geiger but is in league with Joe Brody (Edward Fox) and, later, Harry Jones (Colin Blakely). Brody dies at the hands of Karl Lundgren, Geiger's lover (Simon Turner), and Harry Jones is poisoned by Lash Canino (heavily played by American actor Richard Boone).

The blackmail scheme is really a cover story for the General Sternwood's actual intention: to discover the whereabouts of Rusty Regan (apparently married to Charlotte Sternwood, Sarah Miles in this version; Vivian Rutledge [née Sternwood] in the 1946 screenplay). Apparently Regan was a drinking buddy of Sternwood's who was in love with a singer, Mona Grant (Diana Quick), but married Charlotte on the rebound because Mona preferred gangster kingpin Eddie Mars (overbearingly played by Oliver Reed). Actually, Mona was hiding out in a suburb of London, but not with Rusty. Mona is really in love with Eddie Mars, unaware of his underworld activities and his hiring of Canino to murder Harry Jones.

The real culprit in this version is Candy Clark, who gives the best performance of her career as nymphet Camilla Sternwood (changed from Carmen in the 1946 version). Camilla reveals her uncontrollable sexuality when she uses her playful nudity to entice a tired Marlowe into bed. Marlowe guesses she is responsible for the demise of Rusty in a shooting practice scene near an old ruin that we see in flashback. When Marlowe exposes the cover-up to Charlotte, she admits the truth and reveals that Eddie Mars and Canino disposed of Regan's corpse in a nearby lake. "This is what Mars has got on you," Marlowe repeats over and over. Expecting to be blackmailed by Marlowe, Charlotte is amazed by his ethical behavior and recommends that Camilla be sent to an institution, where she may possibly be cured of her murderous practices.

Mitchum intones the last lines of the original Chandler novel, about how everyone at one time or another sleeps "the big sleep," and the films end in the sunshine as Mitchum drives away from the Sternwood mansion and we watch the credits roll up. No big deal. Porno rings are not necessarily scabrous business in modern London; wise-guy detectives are no longer the rage of the 1970s and have been rendered moot by time. Nymphomania and epilepsy are now more easily treated by a combination of psychiatry and chemicals than they were in pre–World War II America. But the glaring failure of this neo-noir remake is that there is no sense of humor or real humanity portrayed by its actors. Sara Miles as Charlotte comes off sexy but lewd. Oliver Reed as Eddie Mars is overblown, fat, even foppish. Richard Boone as Canino is as unbelievable as a murderer as he is loud. No sexual banter or humor here. Gone is the bookstore proprietor so capably played by Dorothy Malone. Except for Candy Clark, who plays Camilla with a certain spontaneity and naïveté (especially in her nude scenes), the film has no real spark. Fidelity to the novel is not enough. One devastated viewer called this version "the big mistake." Chandler and the actors deserved much better treatment.

FILMOGRAPHY

The Big Sleep (1946), d. Howard Hawks, Warner Bros., 114 min., b&w, sc. William Faulkner, Leigh Brackett, and Jules Furthman, based on Raymond Chandler's novel, ph. Sid Hickox, m. Max Steiner, v. MGM/UA Home Video.

The Big Sleep (1978), d. Michael Winner, United Artists, 100 min., DeLuxe Color, sc. Michael Winner adaptation of Chandler's novel, ph. Robert Paynter, m. Jerry Fielding, v. ITC Entertainment.

5

Notorious (1946, 1992 [TV])

NOTORIOUS (1946)

"Notorious woman of the world . . . Adventurous man of the world!" This is the tag line from Alfred Hitchcock's glorious film noir *Notorious*, starring Cary Grant as Devlin, an FBI agent seeking to recruit Ingrid Bergman as Alicia Huberman, daughter of a convicted American spy working for the Nazis during World War II. After Alicia's father is sentenced to life imprisonment, she throws an elegant party in Miami Beach, at which she meets "Dev," falls in love with him, and then is convinced to travel to Rio de Janeiro and infiltrate a Nazi group. The pair is assigned to renew acquaintances with a former friend of Alicia's father, Alexander Sebastian (Claude Rains in one of his most elegant roles); his mother (Leopoldine Konstantin in one of her most elegant Nazi dowager roles); and other Nazi agents, Eric Mathis (Ivan Triesault) and Mr. Anderson, a bubble-headed scientist who lives in the Sebastian mansion, the center of Rio's covert Nazi spy activities.

Alicia's mission is to enter the house, find out what is going on, and report all activities to Devlin at weekly meetings. After Devlin arranges an "accidental" reunion of Alicia and Alex, Alex is so taken with Alicia's beauty that he asks her to marry him. The FBI gives its consent (what incredible sacrifices a woman will make for her country), and Alicia weds a man twenty-five years her senior in order to maintain her cover.

After a European honeymoon, Alicia suggests they give a huge party for all their Rio friends. She is aware of some nefarious activity in the wine cellar and arranges for Dev to find out the secret of the wine bottles. In one of the two most memorable visual shots in the film, Bergman is standing in the foyer, greeting her guests with Rains next to her. She slips the key to the wine cellar off her husband's keychain and holds it in her right hand. A crane shot starting high over the couple works its way down from the ceiling to Bergman's hand holding the "Unica" key. When Dev greets her, she slips him the key as he kisses her hand. Fabulous photography! (The other singularly fascinating shot in the film comes at the very beginning, when Alicia, held in Dev's arms, nibbles on a chicken drumstick and Dev's ear at the same time, as the camera circles their bliss. This shot also contains the longest kiss in the history of cinema, though in fact it is not a single kiss, which could not last for more than three seconds, but a series of kisses and nibbles that passed censorship review.)

Alicia and Dev slip away from the guests. Alex misses his wife and begins to look for her. While Alex searches for Alicia, Joseph, the butler (perfectly played by Alex Miotis in a gem of a supporting role), is keeping an eye on the few bottles of champagne left and asks Alex for the wine cellar key. Alex looks, realizes it is missing, and orders Joseph to serve hard liquor for the rest of the evening. He heads for the cellar and sees Bergman and Grant in an embrace outside the cellar door. Devlin makes an excuse about meeting Alicia first, then adds, "You won her" and goes off, pretending to be drunk. Alex does not know that the lovers spent a good ten minutes in the wine cellar, and during that time accidentally knocked over a bottle containing pitchblende (uranium ore), an ingredient for the atom bomb. Devlin managed to scrape some into a handkerchief in his breast pocket before leaving.

Later that evening, Alex awakes from sleep, looks at his key chain, and notices the "Unica" key has been replaced. He goes to the wine cellar and finds glass and a label with black dust on it under a wine rack. Immediately he goes upstairs to his mother. They commiserate, then Alex announces, "Mother, I married an American agent!" The two devise a plan to poison Bergman slowly, giving her some unnamed substance (probably arsenic) in her daily coffee.

In her weekly meetings with Dev, Alicia appears weakened, but he attributes it to her high living, alcohol, and extramarital sex. One of the greatest problems the lovers face is their own love-hate relationship. Dev didn't want Alicia to marry Alex because he really loved her and wanted her for himself. Alicia really wanted Dev for herself but had to play the role of whore for the FBI. The acting team handles this complicated plot with utmost Hitchcockian sophistication. Louis Calhern, playing an FBI go-between named Paul Prescott, realizes Alicia is in danger. Dev is not put off by excuses of ill health and the like, bypasses the butler, and goes directly to Alicia's bedroom. She tells him she is being poisoned slowly, a conclusion she reached after Mr. Anderson almost took her coffee by mistake and the others were so upset that the conversation was disrupted. Dev carries Alicia out of the house, followed by Alex, who is afraid to give Alicia up to the Nazis because he would be blamed for marrying an American agent who now knows about the pitchblende and its source in Brazil. After Dev securely places Alicia in the car, pretending he is taking her to the hospital, Alex returns to the house, awaiting the "interrogation" of his Nazi cohorts. This is Hitchcock's most perfect ending. One of the Nazi agents says to Sebastian, "Alex, will you come in, please? I wish to talk to you," and you know Alex will never come out alive. The mansion door slams behind Alex as Dev and Alicia drive off to the ominous strains of Roy Webb's wonderful noir score.

Hitchcock's *Notorious* is a taut noir romantic melodrama with beautiful chiaroscuro lighting and terrific camera work by Ted Tetzlaff that contains many velvety smooth dramatic moments set in sophisticated upper-class Rio in the mid-1940s. Bergman plays Alicia, a woman of dubious morals, with a certain edge that shows her vulnerability and great acting skill. Grant may be lacerated inside, but projects only wooden reaction until the moment he saves Alicia and takes her in his arms. We must credit Ben Hecht with a wonderfully intelligent script that keeps the viewer working to discover the realities of the plot and the dangers therein. And Claude Rains, as the anguished Alex, gives one of the best performances of his career, not saying too much but looking worried. We will never know his fate, and Hitchcock will not show us the obvious. That's why *Notorious* is such a classy, sophisticated film noir. Its dialogue and visual imagery sparkle like diamonds in the darkness.

NOTORIOUS (1992)

The remake, *Notorious* (1992), made for Lifetime Cable in color, filmed in Paris and directed by Colin Bucksey, starring John Shea as Dev, Jenny Robertson as Alicia, and Jean-Pierre Cassel as Alex, is *not* a reprise of the 1946 production. Although John Shea may be dimpled like Cary Grant, the resemblance ends there. Updated as an agent of the CIA, he is supposed to lure Alicia into spying for the United States. By having Alicia marry (if need be) an arms dealer illegally selling weapons to the Soviet Union, this 1992 *Notorious* uses the same device to get her into Alex's mansion, but this time the enemy is the Communists.

John Shea goes through Cary Grant-like pangs of emotion for Alicia when she marries Alex, and snatches her away just before the Commies find out her double-agent role. The former lovers reunite in a wonderful bedroom with a view of the entire city of Paris—in fact, Paris is the real star of this production. Forget espionage, adultery, alcoholism, despair. As Van Gordon Sauter put it in *Variety Television Reviews* on January 28,

1992, "Forget Alfred Hitchcock and Ben Hecht—this remake of their popular romantic thriller bears the far stronger genetic footprints of the French Board of Tourism, Piper Heidsieck champagne and a racy Harlequin romance."

When this Lifetime Cable film ends, you don't care about the characters, the plot, or the film. Paris survives, as do John Shea, Jenny Robertson (less so), and Jean-Pierre Cassel, who look none the worse for wear. So why remake the wonderful 1946 *Notorious*, giving credit to Ben Hecht for the original screenplay, when none of the original noirish elements survive in this 1992 production? This new film is clearly not a revival of noir, nor does it have either the charisma of the original actors or the maximum suspense of the 1946 version. The camera work is neither inventive nor inspiring, the director is lackluster, and the actors (Shea from a *Superman* TV series), with the exception of Cassel (who is no Claude Rains), are generally uncharismatic. So why a made-for-television movie with the original *Notorious* as its source? Obviously, there is a great lack of inspiration or creativity among the producers, who wanted to recycle the original Hitchcock film and perhaps do something better. However, when the net result is patently so bad, not even imitative (compare the 1960 version of *Psycho* and its 1998 production by Gus Van Sant), one realizes it is useless to try to improve upon an original classic. If only the 1992 *Notorious* were enjoyable, or sophisticated, or witty—not the banal hodgepodge it turned out to be! Perhaps one should never attempt to remake a classic! Future chapters will reveal the truth or falsity of this statement. As for *Notorious* 1992, this production was clearly an egregious and irreversible error in creative judgment. May its limited reruns prove this singular truth.

FILMOGRAPHY

Notorious (1946), d. Alfred Hitchcock, RKO, 101 min., b&w, sc. Ben Hecht, ph. Ted Tetzlaff, m. Roy Webb, v. Key Video/Fox Video.

Notorious (1992), d. Colin Bucksey, Lifetime Cable-Hamster-ABC Productions, 80 min., CFI Color, sc. Douglas Lloyd McIntosh, based on a screenplay by Ben Hecht, ph. Peter Sinclair, m. Don Davis, v. Blockbuster.

6

The Postman Always Rings Twice
(1946, 1981)

THE POSTMAN ALWAYS RINGS TWICE (1946)

"Their love was a flame that destroyed!" This was the tag line for the 1946 version that flooded American screens, starring luscious Lana Turner as Cora and macho John Garfield as the drifter Frank Chambers. Made by Metro-Goldwyn-Mayer, this film clearly was not intended for the "family entertainment" audience, but for the postwar public seeking escapist film fare.

The first version of *Postman, Le Dernier Tournant* (The Last Turning), was made in France by director Pierre Chenal in 1939. It was based upon the 1934 novel by James M. Cain and starred Corrine Luchaire and Fernand Gravey as the doomed lovers. The second version, in the United States; filmed in Italy in 1942 by Luchino Visconti, did not give screen credit for the Cain novel; it starred Clara Calamai and Massimo Girotti as the lovers. The French and Italian versions have hardly ever been shown in the United States; the latter can be found on video with English subtitles and the new title *Ossessione* (Obsession). It is still an unofficial remake without copyright authorization.

Of the two versions in English, *Postman* (1946) is superior to the Bob Rafelson 1981 version, although both have their strong points. Many critics have called *Postman* (1946) a "film gris" (gray film) because of its obvious M-G-M glossy studio sheen. Turner and Garfield project so much vivid sexuality that the screen burns with their heat, though the actions stays within the limit of the Motion Picture Production Code of the era. But it is the same story whichever version you watch.

Drifter Frank Chambers stops in at the Twin Oaks Diner, run by Nick Papadakis, for a burger. Nick's curvaceous wife, Cora, stops Frank's wanderings. Nick is a good twenty-five years older than Cora, so it is only natural that she and Frank feel a sexual attraction. Cora uses that attraction to inveigle Frank into murdering her husband, using ball bearings, water in a bathtub, and a downed electric wire to electrocute the old man while he is taking a bath. Unfortunately, a cat steps on the wire and triggers a blackout, leaving Nick momentarily knocked out but breathing. After a brief sojourn in the hospital, Nick returns. But while he is away, Frank and Cora have been swimming together nightly, and probably have shared a bed (offscreen). Because of the accident, Nick decides to sell the diner, move to northern Canada, and have Cora take care of his invalid sister.

When the sale is almost final, Cora and Frank decide to celebrate in Los Angeles, where they drink heavily. Much like the murder scene in *Double Indemnity*, when Cora stops driving and pulls over to the side of the road, Frank beats Nick to death with a bottle. Frank and Cora push the car over a cliff, but the auto gets stuck. They scramble down to finish the job, and Frank is caught in the back seat as he dislodges the car. Nick is dead, Frank has a broken leg, and Cora fights her way through brambles back to the main road, seeking help. There she encounters the local district attorney.

The rest of the film is rather anticlimactic. Frank and Cora are arrested. Frank is pressured into signing a statement indicating Cora's guilt, and Cora gives her confession to a court stenographer (really an employee of their own lawyer). Both are freed because there is no substantial evidence or eyewitnesses to convict them. Cora gives the $10,000 insurance on Nick's life to their attorney and the lovers start anew—with one basic difference. Cora forgives Frank for his duplicity, but she is now pregnant. In the 1946 version, Cora gives Frank the option to leave her, swimming out too far to return to shore alone, if Frank should want to leave her. But Frank, too, has changed. He really loves Cora, and on the way home, they plan to be married. Kissing while driving, Frank narrowly misses an oncoming car and Cora is killed. Frank is convicted of her "murder," and as he awaits his death in the gas chamber, he confesses this entire story to a priest.

There are two stunning scenes in the 1946 version. The first is at the very beginning, when Frank first sees Cora. She drops her lipstick. We hear it fall, but we do not see Cora. The lipstick rolls toward Frank. He picks it up, and we follow his eyes (the camera) from Cora's white slippers all the way up her legs, thighs, waist, breasts, hands holding her

compact. She is dressed in a white top and shorts, and has a white ban-
dana in her hair. Cora says "Thank you" to Frank, and we watch her
apply lipstick to her gorgeous lips. An absolutely sensual introduction!
Lana Turner wears white throughout the film except for a brief scene
where she is dressed in black, on the way to and returning from the
funeral of her mother. When Turner is away, Garfield takes up with a
circus animal trainer (Audrey Totter in the 1946 version; Jack Nicholson
does the same with Angelica Huston in the 1981 film). This interlude
does not advance the plot in any appreciable way, but perhaps underlines the "animal and itinerant behavoir" of Frank.

The other spectacular scene is the one of night swimming. Turner, in
a two-piece white bathing suit and white cap, and Garfield, wearing a
full boxer-type bathing suit, look sensational, wet and dry. We watch
them run into the surf, swim, return, towel off, embrace each other in
beach robes—all very sensual and beautifully photographed by Sidney
Wagner.

Another minor but worthy scene takes place early on, when Nick asks
Frank to dance with Cora, to the music of the jukebox. Turner and Garfield rumba sensuously until Turner gets so physically hot that she pulls
the jukebox plug out of the wall. Generally George Bassman's score for
Postman (1946) has a tinny sound, except for this scene. The better neo-
noir score is Michael Small's for the 1981 *Postman*, directed by Bob Rafelson. Small's score really underlines the darkness of the action and the
motives of the characters. It is a terrific dramatic score on its own. But
in terms of pure cinema and in the opinion of this critic, *Postman* (1946)
is still the superior version.

THE POSTMAN ALWAYS RINGS TWICE (1981)

Bob Rafelson's 1981 version, with a screenplay by David Mamet and
shot in Metrocolor by Sven Nykvist, is more faithful to the original novel.
We watch the same story, set in the mid-1930s, unfold, but with no "Ma-
metian" dialogue—straight Cain. Jack Nicholson acquits himself very
well as the drifter, but Cora, as played by Jessica Lange, strangely seems
out of place in the Twin Oaks Diner kitchen. Although her husband Nick,
marvelously played by John Colicos, is younger, cruder, and more oily
than the benign old man, hardly Greek, played by Cecil Kellaway in the
1946 version. Director Rafelson follows the same trajectory but with some
important differences.

Regarding sexuality, there is more lust, groping for genitals, and animal fighting between the lovers, reflecting the relaxation of the production codes. Although we never see a nude Jessica Lange, we do see Jack
Nicholson lying face down, completely nude, in a bed scene near the
end of the film. You would think nudity would improve the film, but it

is "skin without heat." We do see Nicholson's head between Lange's legs, suggesting cunnilingus, but a scene in Joseph Lewis's *The Big Combo*, where Richard Conte makes love (in black and white) to Jean Wallace, carressing her body with his lips, is far more sensuous because we see his head move down out of the frame as the actress sighs with joy! There is no subtlety in any of the sex scenes—in fact, no real "love" scenes—in Rafelson's *Postman*.

Another important difference is at the conclusion. Whereas Garfield is arrested for Turner's death (not perceived as accidental and following production code rules that crime does not pay) in the 1946 version, after Nicholson sideswipes another vehicle and the pregnant Lange is thrown from the vehicle (no seat belts here), Lange lies on the ground, face up, motionless like a rag doll. Nicholson cries loudly and takes her hand, and the camera holds that last shot on the close-up of Lange's motionless hand. No arrest, no police called; Nicholson is probably on the road again after making funeral arrangements, doing more damage to the women he will meet as he wanders through 1930s California. Certainly another ending without psychological closure for the character and viewers alike.

Although the 1981 version had more "nostalgia" values in terms of set design, antique cars, cigarette brands, 1930s-looking houses, diners, and clothing, what is really missing is the real "smell" of the period. Yes, the players are sweating throughout the film (no air conditioning here), but for all their sexual gropings (especially on that kitchen table covered with flour), they seem curiously deodorized. The 1946 version, albeit without body hair and groping, is far sexier because of its sanitized, white, studio look. However, one scene in the 1981 version is definitely on target. Before Nicholson sends the car down the cliff a second time, Lange is sitting on the cliff side, her nostrils flaring, her legs wide open, whiffing the scent of murder, death, and sexuality. Nicholson takes her then and there, then proceeds to push the car a second time. The thrill of the kill has turned them on sexually and sensually. This is perhaps the most emotionally corrosive scene in the latest *Postman* version. Though faithful to the Cain story and old "noir" stylistics, this last scene reveals a truth that could have occured only on the page, not on the screen. If it were not for the "new noir" style and the new truthfulness found in expressing an author's real meaning, this *Postman* would not deserve another viewing. Happily, it is a very good experience.

One last note regarding the two earlier foreign versions. Because I have never seen *Le Dernier Tournant*, I can offer no critical judgment other than its place in French cinema as belonging to the school of "French poetic realism," a movement of the late 1930s that preceded the eruption of "film noir." The stills I have seen would definitely put it in the pre-

noir category. Visconti's *Ossessione* is another matter. Having seen a restored version at the British Film Institute in the late 1980s, I can say
with authority that if Italian noir exists, this film belongs in that category.
The story is the same as Cain's *Postman*. Clara Calamai and Massimo
Girotti (especially the latter in an athletic shirt covering his hairy chest)
generate such heat with their lovemaking that they practically burn up
the screen. Watching their performances is the best advertisement for the
film. You can also see the beginnings of the Italian neorealism movement
here in the use of location settings and the people of small towns of
southern Italy who make anonymous appearances, as appealing as the
unknowns in Roberto Rossellini's *Open City* or Vittorio De Sica's *Bicycle
Thief*. *Ossessione* is a thrilling black-and-white Italian crime film with sensational performances from two young actors whom we have never seen
in the United States but who deserve international careers. Of course,
Luchino Visconti's films are well known here, especially his *Rocco and
His Brothers* (1960), his second Italian noir after *Ossessione*. "Noir" knows
no geographical boundaries, and Visconti's films are certainly worthwhile contributions to the genre.

FILMOGRAPHY

The Postman Always Rings Twice (1946), d. Tay Garnett, MGM, 113 min., b&w, sc.
Harry Ruskin and Niven Busch, based on the James M. Cain novel, ph. Sidney
Wagner, m. George Bassman, v. MGM/UA.

The Postman Always Rings Twice (1981), d. Bob Rafelson, Paramount, 123 min.,
Metrocolor, sc. David Mamet, based on the James M. Cain novel, ph. Sven Nykvist, m. Michael Small, v. Warner Home Video.

7

The Killers (1946, 1964)

THE KILLERS (1946)

"Tense, taut, terrific! Told the untamed Hemingway way!" and "Every kiss carved his name on another bullet." These were the tag lines for the 1946 version of *The Killers*, the first Hollywood production of producer/ex-newsman Mark Hellinger (also responsible for *The Naked City*) in collaboration with director Robert Siodmak. It was also the debut film for Burt Lancaster, playing Swede, an ex-prize fighter hiding as a gas pump jockey who "did something wrong" and calmly awaiting his murderers.

The opening of the film is pure Hemingway dialogue. The killers, Al and Max, played by Charles McGraw and William Conrad, arrive in a small town; ask for Swede's address; then tie up the owner of the town diner, his counterman, and Nick Adams, Hemingway's famous character who narrates the story behind Swede's murder in flashback. Although the film version uses multiple narrators to explain Swede's past, the tautness of the film's opening, the chiaroscuro lighting, and Miklos Rozsa's dynamically pulsating score (TV's *Dragnet* theme is based upon these opening bars) are the closest to reproducing the first ten minutes of Hemingway's short story on screen.

The Killers is essentially a caper film, mostly narrated by Edmond O'Brien playing an insurance investigator named Riordan who is seeking to pay Swede's insurance policy to a maid at an Atlantic City hotel. He interviews many people before he discovers there was a successful robbery and a double cross that led to Swede's murder. Swede (Burt Lancaster) fell in love with and was betrayed by Kitty Collins (Ava Gardner, in her most sensuous screen siren role), who was secretly married to Colfax (Albert Dekker), the brains behind the scheme. It is Colfax who sends Al and Max to kill Swede, whose death starts Riordan's investigation.

We meet a great number of Universal Studios character actors: thugs like Dum Dum (Jack Lambert) and Blinky (Jeff Corey), who participated in the robbery; cops like Lubinsky (played credibly by Sam Levene); and his wife, Lilly (played by Virgina Christine), who introduced Swede to Kitty Collins. It is Kitty who persuades Swede to take the rap for her. Swede keeps a green silk scarf embroidered with an Irish harp, which she wore, all through his prison term. When he gets out of prison, he takes up again with Kitty and the Colfax mob, only to lose both the money and the dame. He dies with the scarf in his hand.

Riordan tracks down Colfax. After several bursts of gunfire, Dum Dum shoots Colfax, and Kitty pleads with the dying Colfax to spare her from a possible jail term for her complicity in the robbery. Colfax dies, Riordan solves the crimes, the stolen money is recovered, and Kitty goes to prison without an ounce of remorse or a single thought of Swede.

Ava Gardner's shining moment in this film occurs in the nightclub, where she wears a slinky black dress pulled tight over one shoulder and sings, in her own voice, the ballad "The More I Know of Love." When Swede sees her, he becomes enslaved to the sexuality of this femme fatale. Gardner also looks stunning wearing dungarees and a man's shirt, with very little makeup. She truly evolved into a star in this crime film.

Perhaps the real stars of the film are the writers—Richard Brooks and John Huston go uncredited. But the Hemingway story about killers waiting for a man in a diner is the basis for Anthony Veiller's script (with the help of Huston and Brooks) that unfolds this tale of Swede's past in flashback (a real noir style) with voice-over, key lighting, suspenseful music, a double-crossing femme fatale, and a heist that involves the audience. Woody Bredell's sensational camera work in black and white recalls Edwin Hopper's lonely paintings—all-night diners, gas stations, bars. Some scenes even conjure up memories of Wegee photographs of the mid-1940s, especially the scene showing Swede's death. When *The Killers* was released in the summer of 1946, it became an instant hit, mesmerizing critics and audiences alike and definitely displaying all the stylistic elements of crime films we now call "film noir." It also gave Burt Lancaster the opportunity to triumph in other noirs like *I Walk Alone* (1947), *Sorry, Wrong Number* (1948), *Brute Force* (1947), and *Sweet Smell of Success* (1957), in the process becoming noir icon.

THE KILLERS (1964)

"There is more than one way to kill a man!" asserts the tag line from Don Siegel's 1964 remake of the classic Universal film of 1946. Siegel is a practiced professional, familiar with noir style in black and white. That he chose to redo the original script with several important changes, in color and wide screen, was certainly his and screenwriter Gene L. Coon's prerogative. Although the plot specifics are followed with variations, one cannot help noticing the "television" qualities of this version, specifically because it lionizes car racing: John Cassavetes as Johnny North, a racing driver in love with a beautiful woman and having a penchant for getting into trouble. Sounds like a pilot for a television series, something like NBC's *Peter Gunn* of the 1950s.

Although Hemingway's short story is given credit as the inspiration for this film, nothing of Hemingway's dialogue survives, only the bare bones of the original story. In addition, Riordan and Nick Adams are eliminated. Lee Marvin and Clu Gulager play the killers of the title Charlie and Lee, respectively; Charlie wonders why North accepts being shot in a classroom as he teaches automotive skills to blind students. Discovering that North's last contact was his pit man and racing partner Earl Sylvester (Claude Akins), the killers visit Miami, grill Earl, and discover it was a woman, Sheila Farr (ravishingly beautiful Angie Dickinson) who lured North into a mail truck robbery (over $1 million) and then betrayed him. When the killers catch up with Sheila, she tells her story in flashback: how Mr. Brown (Ronald Reagan in his last film role) engineered the entire plot; was forced out of a car by North; and appeared at a motel to reclaim the loot and not split the million dollars with other members of the gang.

North is not killed. When Brown realizes the killers are now after the money, he sets them up and, using a high-powered rifle, kills Lee and wounds Charlie. Charlie arrives at Brown's house as Brown tries to escape with the money and Sheila; he realizes Sheila is Mrs. Brown, and shoots both of them dead. Charlie stumbles out of the house, bleeding profusely, with an empty suitcase, he dies as the police arrive. We see Brown shot, but we never see Sheila fall or hear her cry out, something viewers have waited for since she ordered North's death. Perhaps censorship restrictions caused the elimination of this scene, yet in 1944, when Fred MacMurray kills Barbara Stanwyck in *Double Indemnity*, you see the smoke from the gun and Stanwyck's collapse, dead, into his arms—a realistic, suitable, and justifiable conclusion.

Compared to the 1946 version, this *Killers* is much more violent and sadistic. A blind secretary is throttled by Charlie. Lee, his partner, threatens to tap Earl Sylvester with a lug wrench, and whacks him across the face. The pair threaten to scald Mickey (Norman Fell) to death if he does not reveal the whereabouts of Mr. Brown. When they meet with Sheila to hear her explanation of what happened to the million dollars, she doesn't talk until Lee slaps her hard and they hang her out the hotel window, threatening to let go unless she reveals her part in the robbery. And the final high-powered shoot-out is another part of the violence that makes this film new noir. These killers are cold-blooded, sadistic, intense, histrionic, humorous, edgy, erratic, playful, vengeful, and totally nuts!

Unlike the black-and-white noir original, this 1964 version owes much of its "new noir" style to photographer Richard L. Rawlings, whose distorted camera angles keep the screen alive with variety—tilted camera angles, zoom shots, sudden shifts of movement move the plot along in a breathless and exciting manner. One of the great faults, however, is the use of Pathe Color, which gives the film a yellowish-greenish palette and highlights many pastel colors that seem at odds with the realistic grittiness of the story. And that song by Nancy Wilson in a hotel bar, "Too Little Time," does little to enhance the story line although it is a sweet tune for the lovers, Cassavetes and Dickinson, to hear during one of their trysts. But Johnny Williams's rather undistinguished score is barely noticeable, unlike Miklos Rozsa's masterpiece, which punctuated the action of the 1946 original. Nevertheless, Don Siegel's *Killers* is a successful remake on its own terms—a bit uninspired, yet of great interest to film buffs who want to compare this transposition of art from its earlier version. The 1964 version is not a classic like its predecessor, but it will endure and enhance the reputations of its actors and director.

FILMOGRAPHY

The Killers (1946), d. Robert Siodmak, Universal, 105 min., b&w, sc. Anthony Veiller, from a story by Ernest Hemingway, ph. Woody Bredell, m. Miklos Rozsa, v. Universal/MCA.

The Killers (1964), d. Don Siegel, Universal, 95 min., Color by Pathe, wide screen, sc. Gene L. Coon, based on a story by Ernest Hemingway, ph. Richard L. Rawlings, m. Johnny Williams, v. Universal/MCA.

8

Somewhere in the Night (1946) and The Crooked Way (1949)

SOMEWHERE IN THE NIGHT (1946)

"Somewhere in his mind!" is the tag line from *Somewhere in the Night* (1946), which belongs to a group of films known as "amnesia noir." The hero or heroine usually blacks out because of a trauma, and by the end of the film discovers his (her) true identity and solves the mystery. This is Cornell Woolrich country, and film like *Street of Chance* (1942) and *Black Angel* (1943) are perfect examples. Raymond Chandler also dabbled in amnesia in the film version of his novel *The High Window* (1947), but the two outstanding entries are the films under scrutiny in this chapter. Both concern war veterans in search of their real identities as they unfold their pasts for us and look toward uncertain future.

Somewhere in the Night stars John Hodiak as George Taylor, a World War II Marine veteran stricken with amnesia after receiving multiple injuries. He narrates the entire film, especially while in pain and the camera becomes subjective (his eyes) when nurses talk to him and George tells us of his feelings and eagerness to be discharged. George's only connection with his past is his wallet, which holds a letter from a former girlfriend (who committed suicide while he was at war) that is addressed to "Larry Cravat" and is postmarked San Francisco.

Georges goes to San Francisco (one of the great noir cityscapes) in civilian clothes. While searching for his identity and Larry Cravat, he is hustled, beaten, and shot at as he begins to unravel the mystery, aided by Nancy Guild in her debut role as Christy, a nightclub singer employed by Mel Phillips (Richard Conte in one of his nasty-smoothie roles). Apparently Cravat was a private detective hunting for $2 million that was mysteriously delivered to him on Terminal Dock. There was a murder, and Cravat fled with the money. Other interested parties are Anselmo (played by the great German expressionist actor Fritz Kortner); his companion, Phyllis (Margo Woode), a truly deadly femme fatale; Conroy (Charles Arnt); Conroy's daughter Elizabeth (Josephine Hutchinson in a moving cameo as a lonely spinster); and Lt. Kendall (Lloyd Nolan).

Taylor receives a tip that Conroy, who is in a mental hospital, knows about the murder three years earlier, as well as the whereabouts of the money. As Taylor breaks into the private sanatorium (a big plot device in 1940s noir films), Conroy is mysteriously stabbed, but reveals to George that he hid a suitcase under the dock. George returns to Christy's apartment (she already loves the guy and knows he's incapable of murder), and they go to the dock, find the suitcase loaded with $1000 bills, and retreat to a nearby mission. George's questions go unanswered—who is he, and did he commit murder?

Mel Phillips arrives at the dock, apparently to help them out of this dangerous situation (the couple have been pursued and shot at), and they go for a drink at his nightclub. When they are alone, Mel pulls a gun, admits he murdered the man who delivered the money, and says Cravat ran off, never to be heard of again—until Taylor arrived in San Francisco after spending three years in the Marines. Voilà, Taylor *is* Cravat. Taylor and Christy run out of the nightclub, into the arms of Lt. Kendall, who wounds Mel Phillips. He guessed the whereabouts of Taylor (Cravat) and Christy after they sent the suitcase to him from the mission. The couple leave the police station, destination to the Marriage License Bureau, and the film ends happily. Nancy Guild sings a song, "Middle of Nowhere," which expresses John Hodiak's predicament throughout the film.

Hodiak gives a fine performance—strong, manly, delicate, and sensitive—as the amnesiac seeking to learn about his past. Guild is equally good, as is the roster of minor actors in the film. But the true star is the script by Howard Dimsdale and the director, Joseph Mankiewicz, full of crackling dialogue. The producers wasted no expense on sets, costumes, and noir atmosphere. David Buttolph's score is supportive of this tightly knit, melodramatic film noir. And there are some chillingly realistic moments: when Hodiak searches for Conroy in the sanatorium, and when he is almost killed in front of Conroy's home by a runaway truck. *Somewhere in the Night* is escapist entertainment—not a problem film like *The Best Years of Our Lives* (1946) and *Till the End of Time* (1946), which deal with the "real" problems of servicemen's adjustments. The amnesia noir film will continue to entertain us through the 1990s.

THE CROOKED WAY (1949)

Three years later, United Artists decided to film the radio play *No Blade Too Sharp*, which became *The Crooked Way* (1949), starring John Payne as Eddie Rice (formerly Riccardi), a former Army sergeant who has an irreversible form of amnesia (caused by shrapnel in his brain) that has wiped out his memory. Eddie, is released from an Army hospital and returns to Los Angeles, where he had enlisted. Upon arrival, he is picked up by the local police (Rhys Williams as Lt. Joe Williams) and taken to headquarters. There he is informed that he is a convicted gangster named Eddie Riccardi, and his arch enemy, Vince Alexander (played against type by blonde Sonny Tufts), will murder him on sight, whether he is a war hero with a Silver Star or not, because Eddie turned state's evidence against Vince, who then spent time in prison.

Leaving the police station, Eddie is determined to stay in Los Angeles. He meets Nina Martin (beautifully played by Ellen Drew), who works for Vince. She telephones her boss, who with his thugs goes to Eddie's apartment; they give him a brutal beating. Realizing Nina informed on him, Eddie shows up at her suburban home. She admits the truth, especially working for Vince as a shill at an illegal gambling establishment. In a later scene, when Eddie does not recognize a cigarette case he gave to her, Nina tells him that she was once his wife, but divorced him three years earlier, at the time he disappeared and joined the Army. She urges Eddie to get out of town, but he refuses.

Meanwhile, Vince has a change of heart. He wants Nina to keep Eddie in Los Angeles so he can frame him for a crime he intends to commit. Lt. Williams visits Vince and accuses him of murdering one of his underlings—nail clippings with traces of a medicine Vince uses on a daily basis were found at the scene of the crime. As Williams is about to arrest Vince, Vince kills him. Eddie is brought from Vince's gambling club, the Golden Horn, to Vince's home and is knocked unconscious. He wakes up in an abandoned car with a gun in his hand and Lt. Williams in the driver's seat, slumped dead over the wheel. Having nowhere to turn, Eddie goes to Nina's home, but Vince and his boys arrive. The couple flee and hide out at the apartment of Hazel (Greta Granstedt, playing a shill employed by Vince) until a henchman of Vince's arrives, shoots Nina in the shoulder, and is killed by Eddie in self-defense. Eddie calls a doctor for Nina, who in turn calls the police and a city ambulance. Eddie first threatens the ambulance doctor, but permits his calls to the police and hospital because he is indeed the good Eddie Rice, not the evil Eddie Riccardi.

The finale of the film takes place in a Santa Monica warehouse. Eddie is in search of Petey (played by weasel-wheezing actor Percy Shelton), who saw Vince kill a stool pigeon named Kelly (John Harmon) at the beginning of the film. Vince gets word Eddie will be there, and the two meet and fight with their fists, and guns until Vince throttles Eddie unconscious. When the police arrive, Vince holds a gun to Eddie's head and threatens to kill him unless the police let him go. Meanwhile, Petey (shot by Vince, but not dead) crawls behind Vince, picks up Eddie's gun, and shoots at Vince. Vince shoots Petey, refuses to drop his gun, and begins firing at the police. Vince is killed in a barrage of bullets; Eddie, in bad shape (nearly beaten to death), is visited in the hospital by Nina. They promise to one another to begin a "new life."

Although there is no real mystery about who Eddie really is and no secret treasure to uncover, the film is a gripping example of criminals, caught in their milieus, who are trying to seek a better life. Eddie Rice is a new man, reborn, trying to escape from his past. Nina Martin wants to leave the gambling underworld for a peaceful and secure lifestyle. Their final scene in the hospital room spells the promise of a good future together in post–World War II American society. It is rare that noir couples have a chance to begin again, but Nina and Eddie will survive.

The final shoot-out scene looks contrived, and some of the acting is a bit stilted (scenes where Eddie refuses to leave Los Angeles, for example), and Ellen Drew looks too beautiful and unbattered to be a shill in a gambling casino. However, Sonny Tufts is convincingly irate, evil, and vicious as a mob boss. The true star of this film, however, is John Alton, the photographer. His night-lit scenes are superbly executed, and Louis Forbes's musical score strengthens the realism and vibrancy of this amnesia noir. Though it occasionally affords us too much heavy melodrama and violence in its sometimes illogical plot, *The Crooked Way* is a credible, but not exact, remake of *Somewhere in the Night*. The plight of the ex-soldier returning from the war, the amnesiac discovering his place in postwar society, is certainly the thematic stuff of great noir films. *Somewhere in the Night* totally succeeds and pulls all the plot devices together in a realistic manner. *The Crooked Way* needs tighter plotting and pacing. Although both films were piloted by seasoned directors, Joseph L. Mankiewicz and Robert Florey, and photographed by ace cinematographers, Norbert Brodine and John Alton, the main difficulty with both amnesia noirs is in the writing. Obviously the radio play on which *The Crooked Way* is based did not translate as well to the screen as did Marvin Borowsky's story for *Somewhere in the Night*, rewritten for the screen by Mankiewicz, Howard Dimsdale, and acting coach Lee Strasberg. *Somewhere in the Night* is a truly artful amnesia noir that radiates hope for its protagonists. *The Crooked Way* is less satisfying in its production values, and the future of its noir hero is doubtful.

FILMOGRAPHY

Somewhere in the Night (1946), d. Joseph L. Mankiewicz, 20th Century Fox, 108 min., b&w, sc. Marvin Borowsky (from his story "The Lonely Journey"), Howard Dimsdale, Joseph L. Mankiewicz, and Lee Strasberg, ph. Norbert Brodine, m. David Buttolph, v. not available.

The Crooked Way (1949), d. Robert Florey, United Artists, 90 min., b&w, sc. Richard H. Landau and Robert Monroe from Monroe's radio play *No Blade Too Sharp*, ph. John Alton, m. Louis Forbes, v. not available.

9

Body and Soul (1947, 1981, 1998 [TV])

BODY AND SOUL (1947)

"The story of a guy that women go for!" was the tag line for the 1947 Enterprise Studio production *Body and Soul*, starring John Garfield and Lilli Palmer, written by Abraham Polonsky, and directed by Robert Rossen.

John Garfield had been tied to a Warner Bros. contract since the late 1930s, when he made his film debut in *Four Daughters* (1938). With an occasional loan-out, he started to make more "meaningful," "socially significant" films. A member of the Group Theatre in New York in the early 1930s, Garfield could not forget his poor Bronx-Jewish background. And so he and several partners created Enterprise. *Body and Soul* was its first and most successful project.

Released by United Artists late in 1947, it was not just another "boxing film" in the tradition of Clifford Odets's *Golden Boy* (1939), but contained a subtext relating to freedom of enterprise, corruption in a capitalist system, the rise of a Jewish-American boy from the New York slums, and a critique of the "boxing game," gambling, material benefits of the American dream, debt, greed, exploitation, waste, cynicism ("Everybody dies!"), and ownership by the mob, "body and soul."

Photographed by James Wong Howe in glorious black and white, the film begins with Charlie Davis (John Garfield in the first of his two best roles) waking up on a couch in his country training camp, shouting "Ben!" He then gets into his car and we follow him across the George

Washington Bridge to the Lower East side, where he parks in front of D. Davis, a notions store. Charlie runs up stairs into a tenement and enters an apartment, where his gray-haired mother, Anna (strongly played by Anne Revere), greets him coldly with "What do you want, Charlie? What are you doing here?" Then Peg (beautiful and with a German accent, played by Lilli Palmer) walks in, carrying parcels from food shopping. Charlie embraces her, but she fights him off. Clearly, Charlie is no longer welcomed by his mother or his girlfriend. He leaves the tenement, dashes into his car, and arrives at a nightclub where Alice (Hazel Brooks in her first femme fatale role) is singing. They spend several hours together, drinking and (probably) making love offscreen. The next day Charlie returns to the arena where he is defending his middleweight world championship.

In Charlie's dressing room, we hear his manager, Quinn (William Conrad), talking to Roberts (Lloyd Gough), the gambler financing Charlie's bout. Charlie made a deal to throw the fight because he owed so much money to Roberts—he even bet his own purse (some $65,000) against himself. As Charlie rests on a cot and puffs on a cigarette, the camera moves into his face, the picture blurs, and suddenly we are back several years in time. We hear Charlie repeating the phrase "Everything's gone down the drain" over and over, and suddenly we are at a local restaurant. Apparently Charlie had won a neighborhood bout and, as a prize got a kiss from a local beauty queen (a youthful Lilli Palmer). Charlie's friend and then manager, Shorty (played by soon-to-be Hollywood director Joseph Pevney), introduces his fighter to Quinn, who later gets Charlie a series of fights. Enter Roberts and the mob.

The rest of the film deals with the years Charlie fights for the championship, his victories, his fights with Peg and his mother, his debts, his fast life with Alice (formerly Quinn's girlfriend), his selling out to the mob, and his newfound courage—winning for himself and his community even though he finds himself dead broke and possibly the target of mob brutality. (Robert Wise's 1949 film *The Set-up* dramatically takes us further into the life of a fighter [played by Robert Ryan] who betrays the mob and has his hands broken as a result.) Charlie cynically repeats the phrase "Everybody dies!" to Roberts, and walks to his mother's tenement apartment, hand-in-hand with Lilli Palmer, as the title card "The End" flashes on the screen. Here is a film noir with a happy ending? Perhaps.

There is really only one scene that raises this film noir to artistic heights rather than just pure melodrama. We meet Ben Chapin (Canada Lee in a most affecting role), a former fighter who has a metal plate in his head. Ben worked for Roberts, was a champion, made big money, got hurt, and then was tossed aside by the mob when he was of no further use. When Roberts tries to get rid of Ben and asks Charlie to "pay him off," Charlie refuses. Roberts continues to needle Ben and to

push Charlie to get rid of his sparring partner. One night Ben goes ber-
serk in the deserted ring—punching at the air until he falls dead. Bosley
Crowther said of this scene: "[Ben] . . . shows through great dignity and
reticence the full measure of his scorn for the greed of shrewder men
who have enslaved him, sapped his strength and then tossed him out to
die. The inclusion of this portrait is one of the finer things about this
film" (*New York Times*, Nov. 10, 1947).

This *Body and Soul* benefited from wonderful performances by John
Garfield, Canada Lee, Anne Revere, Lilli Palmer, Lloyd Gough, and Hazel Brooks. Particularly good are the black-and-white fight scenes shot
by James Wong Howe (a primer for Martin Scorsese's *Raging Bull*), and
a wonderful music score by Hugo Friedhofer (with several motifs first
used in his Oscar-winning score for *The Best Years of Our Lives* [1946]
and his variations on the famous Johnny Green song "Body and Soul").
But the real star of the film is Abraham Polonsky, who wrote a very
sophisticated and commercially viable screenplay which put the Enterprise Studio on the map. The best was yet to come for the Garfield-
Polonsky team; in 1948, Polonsky wrote, and Garfield starred in, *Force of
Evil*, a caustic condemnation of American capitalism and corruption
among lawyers. It made the House Un-American Activities Committee
very suspicious, and caused the blacklisting of Polonsky and the demise
of Garfield as a star of independent power. Released by MGM, the film
was poorly distributed and misunderstood by the mass audience. It
probably brought about the downfall of Enterprise, one of the first independent studios in Hollywood. When I met Abraham Polonsky in
New York City on the occasion of the publication of his script of *Force
of Evil*, he had totally accepted his blacklisting but now saw himself as
a champion of the oppressed. Polonsky died in his late eighties; Garfield,
at the age of thirty-nine.

BODY AND SOUL (1981)

The first remake of *Body and Soul* was part of a movement in the
United States for "black cinema." Although Abraham Polonsky is given
screen credit, this version has very little to do with the original. The black
actor/writer Leon Isaac Kennedy deserves the credit (or blame) for reworking the original script to be the story of an amateur boxer who turns
professional to try to earn money for medical treatments needed by his
kid sister. Critic Leslie Haliwell said of it, "Blood in the ring, sentimen-
tality on the sidelines. Despite the credit, this repellent version has virtually no connection with the previous version" (*Halliwell Film Guide*,
1997). Although we watch welterweight boxer Kennedy become a champion who shuns corruption, he is defeated by a poor, sentimental screen-

play. The only saving grace is a short appearance by fighter Muhammad Ali, playing himself.

BODY AND SOUL (1998 [TV])

The latest version of *Body and Soul* (1998) is an HBO special made for cable starring Ray "Boom Boom" Mancini as Charlie "Kid" Davis, Jennifer Beals as Gina (the Lilli Palmer role), Michael Chiklis as Tiny (originally Charlie's friend Shorty), Rod Steiger playing Charlie's ringside manager, and Joe Mantegna playing Alex Dumas, the mob boss. The plot is similar to the original, except this time Charlie is an ambitious small-town fighter with dreams of making it big as a professional boxer in Reno, Nevada. He travels there with his best and unwavering friend, Tiny. On his climb to the top, he loses himself and the people he cares for most.

There are no favorable comments or reviews of this cable film. In fact, one viewer felt John Garfield would probably turn over in his grave if he saw this version. Regarding the script, one wonders if the actors had one. Or did they make up their dialogue as they went along? Polonsky would turn over in his grave, too. Ah, cable television remakes! One wonders why they bother!

FILMOGRAPHY

Body and Soul (1947), d. Robert Rossen, Enterprise Studio (United Artists), 104 min., b&w, sc. Abraham Polonsky, ph. James Wong Howe, m. Hugo Friedhofer, v. Republic.

Body and Soul (1981), d. George Bowers, Cannon Films, 109 min., color, sc. Leon Isaac Kennedy, ph. James Forrest, m. Webster Lewis, v. Cannon.

Body and Soul (1998), d. Peter McAlevey, HBO Cable, 105 min., color, sc. loosely based on the original, ph. Arturo Smith, m. source, v. not available.

10

Dark Passage (1947) and Johnny Handsome (1989)

DARK PASSAGE (1947)

"In Danger as Violent as Their Love!" and "Together Again!" (after *The Big Sleep*): these were the tag lines for the 1947 Warner Bros. production based on David Goodis's crime novel and starring Humphrey Bogart, Lauren Bacall, Bruce Bennett, Tom D'Andrea, and Agnes Moorehead. Bogart plays Vincent Parry, a convict who escapes from San Quentin. He was sentenced to a life term for murdering his wife but breaks out of prison to prove his innocence. We never see his face during the first hour of the film, but director Delmer Daves uses a "subjective camera;" we see all the action through Bogart's eyes. After he undergoes plastic surgery to change his features, our star reemerges, recognizable, as Humphrey Bogart.

Parry is picked up during his escape by Irene Jansen (Lauren Bacall), whose father also was unjustly sent to prison for murder. Irene was at Parry's trial and believed he was innocent. "When I get excited about something, I give it everything I got. I'm funny that way, "she says to Parry, who at first does not understand why Irene is trying to help him. Parry realizes he has to have his facial features changed in order to move in San Francisco society and track down the murderer of his wife.

He meets Sam, a friendly cab driver with underground connections played by Tom D'Andrea. The cabbie recognizes Parry, believes he is innocent, and wants to help him. When Sam asks Parry, "What was she like?"—referring to his wife—Parry answers: "She was all right. Just hated my guts. For a long time, I tried to find out why. Then I didn't care anymore." Sam answers, "I know. Nice, happy, normal home." Sam drives Parry to the shabby office of Dr. Walter Coley (played by old-time character actor Housley Stevenson), and as Bogart goes under the anesthetic, he loses consciousness in a spiraling noir dream about murder with images of Madge Rapf (Agnes Moorehead) knocking at Irene's door, the surgeon laughing repeatedly, and Irene at the center. Seeking refuge when he finds his best friend George Fellsinger (played by Rory Mallinson) murdered, Parry goes to Irene's apartment, and she takes care of him until the bandages are removed.

There are some minor subplots involving a shady private eye (played by Clifton Young) who wants to blackmail Parry but ends up falling off a cliff near San Francisco Bay, and Bob (stalwart Bruce Bennett) an architect and ex-fiancé of Madge Rapf who is now a friend/suitor of Irene. Irene rejects him in favor of Vincent. Parry's friend George had seen Madge's car, an orange convertible, parked near the Parry apartment around the time Vincent's wife was killed. Parry finally visits Madge, sporting his new face and identity (Alan Linnell). But Madge soon uncovers his real identity. Madge tells Vincent that she killed his wife out of jealousy for planning to return to her after a short liason. Ready to call the police, Vincent menaces Madge, who steps back, gets tangled in the drapes near an open French window, stumbles, and falls twelve stories to her death. Realizing the police would think Vincent murdered her, Parry telephones Irene and urges her to meet him at a resort in Piedad, Peru, a few years later. Irene bides her time, and when she arrives at a nightclub by the beach, asks the orchestra to play "Too Marvelous for Words." Vincent hears the music, and greets her at the entrance. They dance closely until "The End" appears on the screen.

Dark Passage is an excellent noir crimer. It has a spiderous femme fatale played by Agnes Moorehead. It has Bogart as Vincent Parry, a doomed man trying to clear his name and getting deeper and deeper into trouble. It has Lauren Bacall as upright Irene Jansen, faithfully supporting her man until the conclusion. The film has a marvelous locale, beautifully photographed by Sid Hickox, and an excellent, thundering score by Franz Waxman that gives a dangerous dimension, especially to the night-time scenes. Director Delmer Davis was particularly faithful to David Goodis's script and did not shoot a single frame that didn't advance the plot. And that finale: Madge Rapf plunging from an apartment window into a parking lot. (I remember an audience applauding her demise because Madge was a thoroughly evil woman. Any man she wanted and could not have, she destroyed. Her greatest pleasure was causing the unhappiness of others.) And that finale: Bogart and Bacall meeting quietly in South America to the strains of that famous Johnny Mercer song!

It was their intimate chemistry that sparked this film, their third collaboration. Just another example of commercial success and film noir magic!

JOHNNY HANDSOME (1989)

Preferring not to opt for the "subjective camera," which originated in MGM's 1946 production of Raymond Chandler's *Lady in the Lake*, in *Johnny Handsome* director Walter Hill introduces Mickey Rourke as John Sedley, a career criminal, deformed at birth, who undergoes plastic surgery and, with a new face and speech lessons, becomes a candidate for rehabilitation and a new life. Sedley is a real film noir character—a loser of 1940s vintage who lives in a cold-water flat and takes his pleasures in local bars. He plans a heist with his childhood best friend, Mickey Chalette (Scott Wilson) and three other losers—Rafe (Lance Henrikson), Sunny (Ellen Barkin), and Larry (J. W. Smith)—all sleazy characters. They rob a rare coin shop, but Johnny and Mickey are double-crossed by the other three. Mickey is killed, and Johnny is shot and left for dead. Arrested by Lt. Drones (Morgan Freeman), he is sent to Angola Prison. Because Rafe learns Johnny is alive and will plot revenge, he hires a convict to knife Johnny to death on a work detail in the fields around Angola. Johnny fights off his attacker but barely survives.

Suddenly, Johnny finds himself in a New Orleans prison hospital, where Dr. Steven Fischer (Forest Whitaker) puts him into a rehabilitation program that depends upon his facial transformation through plastic surgery. A portion of the film deals with Johnny "Handsome's" (ironic) operations and his becoming the "new" Johnny Mitchell. Mitchell receives speech therapy from Sister Luke (Yvonne Bryceland) and is given a job as a welder in a local shipyard. As part of the program, he is paroled (against the wishes of Lt. Drones). He meets a CPA-to-be, Donna McCarty (Elizabeth McGovern in a "good girl" role), and falls in love with her. But Johnny Mitchell still has a problem—can he lead a "straight" life, or should he return to a life of crime and avenge the death of his best friend? He chooses the latter.

Reintroducing himself to Rafe and Sunny as John Mitchell, he masterminds a $5 million heist at the shipyard. Sunny wants Johnny to split the loot two ways because she's bored with Rafe sexually and because (apparently) cheated her out of her share on their last robbery together. Johnny masterminds the new scheme, takes all of the money, and leaves his partners hanging until they meet after the money is laundered by a local lawyer, who is caught and arrested by Lt. Drones.

Donna inadvertently steps into a plot device: she is taken prisoner by Rafe and Sunny and is used as bait to persuade Johnny to give up his gun, and the money at their meeting in a New Orleans cemetery. Rafe suspects Johnny of having hidden a gun in the suitcase containing the money, and fears it will blow up in his face, so he has Johnny open it. Johnny retrieves the gun and shoots everyone dead, but receives a fatal bullet from Sunny's gun. There is no happy ending here! Johnny dies cradled in Donna's arms as Lt. Drones looks on. One plot loophole: it seems inconceivable that Lt. Drones would let Johnny go free to avenge Mickey's death after, in an earlier scene, catching him with the laundered money. Perhaps he wanted all the criminals to kill each other.

New Orleans and San Francisco are both fascinating locales for films with film noir souls. Both Johnny Handsome/Mitchell and Vincent Parry/Alan Linell undergo plastic surgery and seek revenge against people who have plotted against them—Rafe and Sunny in Walter Hill's 1989 film and Madge Rapf in Delmer Daves's 1947 production. But Parry/Linell (Bogart) comes out a winner, and Johnny Handsome/ Mitchell in the remake is a definite loser. Both men indulge their fantasies of revenge, and both are true noir males because they are doomed losers. However, one of them triumphs. When Bogart gets Bacall at the end of *Dark Passage* we cheer for his starting a new life in Peru with a faithful and attractive woman in his corner. When Johnny's new face is beaten almost to a pulp by Rafe, at Sunny's vengeful urging, and Johnny is killed by Sunny, his last words to Donna are about his face, not his love or their future together. Perhaps neo-noir films are more truthful at their denouements.

Johnny Handsome is certainly more downbeat and full of gratuitous violence. We sympathize with Vincent Parry and want him to succeed. When Johnny Mitchell throws out good girl Elizabeth McGovern, the film decidedly goes downhill. We know he is trash, and we don't care whether he lives or dies. True to the film's tag line: "They changed his looks, his life and his future . . . but they couldn't change his past." Some noir heroes can overcome their pasts and the odds. Walter Hill has made a film full of fast car chases, deafening gunfire, screeching brakes, shattering glass, and violent robberies; it is empty of sentiment. We cheer when Rafe and Sunny are gunned down; when Johnny Mitchell dies, we simply do not care. Here is a neo-noir loser who couldn't overcome his past, the seediness of his New Orleans life, or the weaknesses in his character. Perhaps this is what director Walter Hill wanted us to see in his gritty, realistic shots of the not so touristy side of New Orleans, backed by a lowdown bluesy Ry Cooder score. *Johnny Handsome* was filmed in the noir tradition, but as a remake of *Dark Passage*, it has flashy crime scenes and hard-boiled violent action instead of the sterling, deeply felt, and sultry performances that were the core of the 1947 crimer.

The Bogart/Bacall film will endure as a classic; Walter Hill's film is just flash and of little substance—a neo-noir opportunity missed, making little of its New Orleans location and losing the subtleties in the remarkably affecting transformation of John Sedley into Johnny Mitchell. The remake offers promising ideas but is mired down by its lack of faith in subtlety, instead favoring commercial crassness. Give me the quiet black-and-white beauties of San Francisco's location settings and scintillating dialogue from David Goodis's crime novel—real class—rather the over-the-top, commercially viable pyrotechnics of the films of Walter Hill.

FILMOGRAPHY

Dark Passage (1947), d. Delmer Daves, Warner Bros., 106 min., b&w, sc. Delmer Daves, from the David Goodis novel, ph. Sid Hickcox, m. Franz Waxman, v. MGM/UA.

Johnny Handsome (1989), d. Walter Hill, Tri-Star, 94 min., Technicolor, sc. Ken Friedman, based on the book *The Three Worlds of Johnny Handsome* by John Godey, ph. Matthew F. Leonetti, m. Ry Cooder, v. Live Home Video.

11

Kiss of Death (1947, 1995) and *The Fiend Who Walked the West* (1958)

KISS OF DEATH (1947)

"It will mark you for life as it marked him for . . . Betrayal" is the tag line for the 1947 version of *Kiss of Death*. Cashing in on the trend of using actual locations to tell real and/or fictional stories, begun by 20th Century Fox in 1945 with *The House on 92nd Street*, the first version of *Kiss of Death* stars Victor Mature as a small-time criminal, Nick Bianco, who is caught after participating in an unsuccessful Christmastime jewel heist. Sent to Sing Sing for a few years, he learns his wife committed suicide (gassing herself to death because of depression) and his two little daughters were placed in an orphanage. Nettie (beautifully played by Coleen Gray), his former baby-sitter, tells Nick this story on one of her visits to Sing Sing. Because the mob he worked for failed provide for Mrs. Bianco, as it was supposed to, Nick decides to talk to District Attorney D'Angelo (Brian Donlevy) and turn state's evidence so he can be free and be reunited with his children.

Nick is contacted by the mob lawyer, Earl Howser (Taylor Holmes), who wants to maintain the status quo. In a subplot, Nick decides to tell Howser about another heist he pulled, and that he believes a thug named Rizzo (possibly Mrs. Bianco's lover) was the informer who put him in jail. Howser contacts hit man Tommy Udo (Richard Widmark, in his film debut), a sadistic killer with a maniacal laugh, who looks for Rizzo. One of the most famous scenes in the film occurs in Rizzo's dingy apartment. His mother (played by Mildred Dunnock) refuses to give Udo any in-

formation. Udo ties her into her wheelchair, using the cords from ve-
netian blinds, and hurls her down a flight of stairs to her death. This is
probably one of the most brutal and sadistic scenes in American cinema,
especially when Widmark, eyes popping, utters a high-pitched falsetto
laugh as he rolls her over the edge of the top step. Udo is arrested, not
for this murder but for participating in the Christmas jewelry heist gone
awry. When Udo is released because of a legal technicality and finds out
Nick informed on him, Nick, his children, and his new wife (Nettie was
always in love with him), now living in Queens, go into hiding upstate.

There are excellent black-and-white location shots of Queens, suburban train stations, orphanages, and criminal court offices that add to the
realistic, semidocumentary look of the film. Nick decides he cannot run,
but must face Udo. If Udo is caught with a weapon, he will be put in
prison for life. Nick meets Udo in a restaurant, and as he finishes his
meal, Udo (who left a bit earlier) waits for him in a parked car, gun in
hand. Meanwhile, Nick has called the District Attorney, setting Udo up.
As Nick leaves the restaurant, Udo pumps three shots into him just as
the police cars arrive, sirens at full blast. Rather than be caught, Udo
fights it out with the cops and dies in a barrage of bullets. Nettie has
been telling the entire story of this film in flashback, and to the music
of Alfred Newman's "Street Scene," she relates how Nick recovered from
his wounds and how they lived happily ever after.

Kiss of Death (1947) gave Victor Mature, as Nick Bianco, his best dramatic part in many years, and he is probably most remembered for this
role. Whenever interviewed, Mature said that Nick Bianco was the best
role he ever had on the silver screen, and he hoped to be remembered
for it. (He died in 1999, in his mid-eighties.) But Richard Widmark's
portrayal of Tommy Udo is really unforgettable. Widmark recycled this
role several times, especially in William Keighely's *The Street with No
Name* (1948), another semidocumentary film noir, in which Widmark
played gangster kingpin Alex Stiles. He played the role of psychopath
to perfection, intoning such lines as "I wouldn't give ya the skin off a
grape!" in *Kiss of Death*. He modeled Tommy Udo on 1940s gangster
realities and did not invest his interpretation with any notable horror,
nuances, as Robert Evans did in the 1958 western version, *The Fiend Who
Walked the West*. But more of that later.

Kiss of Death is most notable for its dramatic, suspenseful sequences,
played almost in silence in chiaroscuro lighting with an unobtrusive
score by David Buttolph and Alfred Newman. The film is so realistic,
you would think this *was* a documentary based on fact, like *Boomerang*
(1947) and *13 Rue Madeleine* (1946). 20th Century Fox was at its peak in
filming hard-boiled, tough, action dramas, and *Kiss of Death* was one of
the best of this cycle of the late 1940s.

KISS OF DEATH (1995)

The highly touted remake of *Kiss of Death* (1995), in Technicolor and CinemaScope, is an overblown, over-the-top version of the original, which is almost unrecognizable. Starring David Caruso (a television actor from the ABC series *NYPD Blue* in his Hollywood debut) as Jimmy Kilmartin, and giving credit to the writers of the original 1947 screenplay, this new version uses the skeleton plot but changes its setting to the sleazy world of car thieves in Queens.

Kilmartin is tricked by his childhood friend Ronnie (Michael Rapaport) into driving a rig of stolen cars into a chop shop. A former thief who has done jail time, Jimmy is tracked down by the police, wounds a cop (Samuel L. Jackson), and winds up back in jail. While there, he learns his wife, Bev (Helen Hunt in one of her first roles on the big screen), has been killed and that Ronnie had spent the previous night with her. To avenge her death, Jimmy makes a deal with slimy District Attorney Frank Zioli (played to perfection by Stanley Tucci) to nail the head of the mob, Little Junior (played with panache by pumped-up, muscular Nicolas Cage).

It is Nicolas Cage in the role of Tommy Udo that gives this film version all of its verve and intensity. After Kilmartin infiltrates the chop-shop mob run by Little Junior and an FBI infiltrator is killed by Little Junior, Kilmartin informs on the crime kingpin. The rest of the film is just as predictable as the first version. Little Junior is not convicted and goes after Kilmartin (suddenly with a new wife, played by Kathryn Erbe), which leads to his own demise. What director Barbet Schroeder portrays best is the milieu of urban car thieves, their shop, their strip club hangout called Baby Cakes, and the relationship between Little Junior and his father (Big Junior, played by Philip Baker Hall). Big Junior is on his deathbed and Little Junior is trying to win his approval with his tough guy persona and illegal businesses. There are a number of good performances in this 1995 version of *Kiss of Death*: Anthony Heald plays a sleazy lawyer, Jack Gold; Ving Rhames is suitably tough as Little Junior's henchman named Omar; and Michael Rapaport is both venal and misguided as a minor hood working for the car-theft mob. But it is Nicolas Cage's performance as Little Junior, the "loose cannon," that saves this film from mediocrity.

Unfortunately, Davis Caruso's debut film did not strike any sparks for his career in Hollywood. As Jimmy Kilmartin, Nick Bianco's Irish counterpart, he just does not register emotionally or heroically with the audience. Working within a limited emotional range and demonstrating a "capped powder keg" persona, Caruso projects no sense of menace or strength. As the good guy, he seems too uncertain, unfocused, unheroic for the audience to take him seriously as we wind our way through the plot labyrinth. And what a labyrinth it is, Baby Cakes, the meeting place for the mob, is reminiscent of the Bada-Bing Club, somewhere in New Jersey, in David Chase's HBO cable show *The Sopranos*. Whereas Bada-Bing serves only for entertainment, at the conclusion of Schroeder's film, Baby Cakes is the site of a tremendous shoot-out in which the villains perish and the good guys survive. No pushing of little old ladies tied to wheelchairs downstairs in this film—that would be excessive.

THE FIEND WHO WALKED THE WEST (1958)

Between the 1947 and 1995 versions of *Kiss of Death*, 20th Century Fox decided to recycle the plot into a brutal western version photographed in starkly realistic black-and-white and CinemaScope, *The Fiend Who Walked the West* (1958). Robert Evans plays the Tommy Udo role in this version that departs from the 1947 original in several ways.

First, Hardy (Hugh O'Brian) is seen as the cell mate of Felix Griffin (Robert Evans). Hardy tells Griffin where a treasure is stashed. Upon his release, Griffin goes on a bloody rampage to get the hidden loot. Hardy, himself a hardened criminal, is granted a parole to track down and exterminate his former cell mate because Griffin poses a real threat to law and order, and especially to the safety of Hardy's kin.

Second, the writers and director played up the horror scenes: Griffin feeds ground glass to one of his victims, breaks a girl's neck, shoots an arrow through an elderly woman, and scares a pregnant woman into a miscarriage. He mistreats Hardy's wife Ellen (played by Linda Cristal), and his own long-suffering girlfriend, May (Dolores Michaels in one of her tough emotional roles). He finally receives his comeuppance in a fist fight with Hardy.

Finally, the writers attempted to add some minor psychological suggestions to interpret the Griffin/Udo character. For example, Griffin does not like to be touched, but we never discover why. Neither is his sadism explained, but horrible examples of his sadistic acts are exploited on-screen, perhaps to ensure commercial success.

Unfortunately, although the film packs a wallop because of its scenes of sadism, it is decidedly a routine western that barely follows the *Kiss of Death* plot or takes itself seriously. Evans's reprise of the Tommy Udo role of a cold-blooded, sadistic killer is the best reason for seeing the film. This was Evans's third film, and his portrayal of a bloodthirsty, psychopathic killer is thrilling to watch, as is Hugh O'Brian's recycling of his television role of Wyatt Earp. Linda Cristal and Dolores Michaels do the best they can within the limitations of the script, but no serious-minded cinephile can accept this trivialization of the original in western surroundings. Cast the blame on producer Herbert B. Swope for attempting to recycle the original and making it a poor transposition of art.

FILMOGRAPHY

Kiss of Death (1947), d. Henry Hathaway, 20th Century Fox, 98 min., b&w. sc. Ben Hecht and Charles Lederer, from a story by Eleanor Lipsky, ph. Norbert Brodine, m. David Buttolph, v. Fox Video.

Kiss of Death (1995), d. Barbet Schroeder, 20th Century Fox, 101 min., Technicolor, CinemaScope, sc. Richard Price, based on the 1947 collaboration of Hecht and Lederer, ph. Luciano Tovoli, m. Trevor Jones, v. Fox Video.

The Fiend Who Walked the West (1958), d. Gordon Douglas, 20th Century Fox, 101 min., b&w, CinemaScope, sc. Harry Brown and Philip Yordan, based on the 1947 collaboration of Hecht and Lederer, ph. Joe MacDonald, m. Leon Klatzkin, v. unavailable.

12

Out of the Past (1947) and Against All Odds (1984)

OUT OF THE PAST (1947)

"A man—trying to run away from the past . . . a woman—trying to escape her future." Although this is the tag line that went into most of the advertising for Jacques Tourneur's most celebrated film noir, I would have preferred that the advertisers use some of Robert Mitchum's voice-over in the early part of the film, when he tells Virginia Huston, "It was the bottom of the barrel and I scraped it. But I didn't care, I had her." Or "I never saw her in the daytime. We seemed to live by night. What was left of the day went away like a pack of cigarettes you smoked."

Out of the Past was based upon the crime novel *Build My Gallows High*, by Geoffrey Homes, a pseudonym of Daniel Mainwaring. Photographed in beautiful black-and-white by Nicholas Musuraca, with exteriors in and around Lake Tahoe, San Francisco, and Los Angeles, and set to an original moody noir score by RKO's talented composer, Roy Webb, the film tells the story, in multiple flashbacks, of Jeff Markham (Robert Mitchum in his first starring role), a former New York City private detective who is hired by gambler/mobster Whit Sterling (Kirk Douglas) to find his mistress, Kathie Moffat (deliciously played by Jane Greer, the quintessential femme fatale), who apparently shot him and stole $40,000 of his money. Markham's partner, Jack Fischer (played by character actor Steve Brodie), is also hired by Sterling to track her down and bring her back.

After interviewing her former maid, Jeff surmises that Kathie went to Mexico City and then on to Acapulco. He follows her there, and one day she walks into a café, La Mar Azul. Overwhelmed by her beauty and sensuality, Jeff falls deeply in love with her, and they escape Sterling's reach on a freighter bound from Acapulco to San Francisco. Sterling had visited Acapulco, and Jeff blatantly lied to him about Kathie's whereabouts. But "Whit never forgets," as Kathie puts it, so the couple live anonymous lives in San Francisco. One day, Jack Fischer (Jeff's former partner) spies Jeff at a racetrack. Jeff sees Fischer and, thinking he would be followed by Fischer, Jeff carefully reunites with Kathie in a secluded country house outside of San Francisco.

What Jeff does not realize is that Fischer followed Kathie. Once inside the house, Fischer tries to extort them, asking for all of the missing $40,000. A fight ensues between the men, and Kathie shoots Fischer dead. Jeff accidentally finds Kathie's bank book (with a $40,000 balance), buries Fischer offscreen, and leaves her. He opens a gas station in Bridgeport, California, under the name Jeff Bailey. A henchman of Sterling's, Joe Stephanos (played menacingly by stage actor Paul Valentine), discovers Bailey *is* Markham and seeks his whereabouts from a mute gas pump jockey (played by child star Dickie Moore). Jeff finds his past is catching up with him and tells this entire story to Ann (the new love of his life, played winningly by Virginia Huston). She drives with Jeff to Lake Tahoe, where Whit Sterling is waiting for Jeff.

Once in Sterling's mansion, Jeff is surprised to see Kathie there. Whit explains, "She has returned to the fold." Privately Kathie confides to Jeff, "I had to come back. What could I do?" Jeff answers, "You can never help anything, can you? You're like a leaf that blows from one gutter to another." The rest of the film goes downhill in present time, dealing with a subplot in which Jeff must obtain Whit's tax records from a renegade tax account named Leonard Eels (Ken Niles). "You owe me, Jeff," says Whit. Jeff acquiesces because he had not solved the mystery surrounding Kathie and had double-crossed Sterling by loving Kathie. Jeff, knowing he is caught in a frame, tells Eels that his secretary, Meta Carson (played shrewdly by Rhonda Fleming in one of her early noir roles), is duplicitous—he will return to explain. Meanwhile, Meta has taken Sterling's tax records out of Eels's safe and given them to the manager of a nightclub owned by Sterling. She has also placed in the safe an affidavit signed by Kathie attesting to Jeff's "murder" of Fischer, thus giving Jeff a motive for Eels's death.

Jeff discovers Eels's corpse on the floor of Eels's apartment and hides the body in an abandoned apartment, retrieves Sterling's tax records and hides them. Because he left fingerprints at Eels's apartment, Jeff is a prime suspect in his murder. Jeff flees back to the safety of Bridgeport and into the arms of Ann, who still believes in him. But when Sterling finds out about Kathie's maneuvering of Stefanos to murder Jeff and the disappearance of the tax records, he threatens to kill her and reveal that she murdered Fischer. Jeff will be off the hook if he returns the tax records to Sterling. He agrees, but when he returns to the Tahoe mansion, Sterling is lying on the floor, dead. Wearing a snood and a very beautifully tailored coat to match, Kathy says, "You can't make deals with a dead man." Still hunted by the police for Eels's murder, Jeff agrees to go away with Kathie. "We're both no good, but we belong to each other," she says. Jeff agrees, but offscreen he makes a phone call to the police. They drive off. When Kathie spies a roadblock, she shoots Jeff and the car crashes. The police return Kathie's gunfire at them, and both Jeff and Kathie are found dead after the crash.

Back in Bridgeport, the newspapers reveal the entire story. Ann, still faithful to Jeff, asks the gas station attendant (Dickie Moore) if Jeff was going away with Kathie. He signals "yes" with an upward motion of his head, thus freeing Ann from her love for Jeff so she can build a new life with Jim, the local sheriff, (played by Richard Webb).

Out of the Past is quintessential noir—a tremendously stylish, brilliantly scripted, and wonderfully directed classic noir about a man who cannot escape his past. It is one of the first noirs to utilize both city and country locations (Nicholas Ray's *On Dangerous Ground* [1951]) continues this tradition), and contains some of the best narration and dialogue written since Dashiell Hammett's *The Maltese Falcon* (1941). Robert Mitchum is perfect as the ill-fated Jeff Markham. His acting is restrained and his mood, joyless, and there is a look of doom in his mournful gaze.

Jane Greer is also perfect as the lethal Kathie Moffat: erotic, sensual, enigmatic. "I never told you I was anything else than what I was [a murderess]. You just wanted to believe I was someone else [a good woman]," When Kathie shoots Fischer and Jeff turns to look at her, registering the shock of seeing Kathie's true nature revealed, we have one of the most exciting epiphanies ever seen in a noir film. I repeat, *Out of the Past* is the quintessential film noir. All the elements that define noir are here—the character's cynicism, isolation, and a pervading sense of doom. This is one film that keeps you guessing right up to its very last minute. In 1947, film critics noticed the mood and the violence (there are six murders), but they could not evaluate the style of this film. It took French writers like Nino Frank and Raymond Borde and Etienne Chaumenton to label *Out of the Past* as one of the greatest multilayered films noirs of all time, especially because of its perverse and morally ambiguous atmosphere, interwoven with a convoluted, and sometimes confusing, dark plot.

Two final notes. In 1946, Dick Powell was announced to star in *Build My Gallows High* after completing Columbia's *Johnny O'Clock* (1947) with Evelyn Keyes; and in 1976, Jerry Bick and John Ptak announced plans to remake *Out of the Past* as *Build My Gallows High*, to be directed by Jerry

Schatzberg from a screenplay by Marilyn Goldin. Neither of these projects came to fruition.

AGAINST ALL ODDS (1984)

In 1984, *Out of the Past* was loosely remade as the neo-noir *Against All Odds*. Most of the 1980s critics found that this version, directed by Taylor Hackford, works on its own terms, as "glossy, romantic escapism," not adhering at all to the conventions of film noir. Janet Maslin called it "a steamy, sinister, great-looking detective film, even a travelogue" (*New York Times*, Mar. 12, 1984). *Variety* called it "fast-paced, entertaining [but] marred by a murky misanthropic ending . . . simply ending oddly" (Feb 10, 1984).

Jake Wise, a nightclub owner and Hollywood entrepreneur) (James Woods) hires ex-football player Terry Brogan (Jeff Bridges) to find Jessie Wyler (played by Australian actress Rachel Ward), the runaway daughter of Mrs. Wyler (Jane Greer, the original Kathie Moffat), the owner of the football team from which Terry was recently cut. Rachel Ward plays Jessie not as a lethal femme fatale but as a beautiful and emotionally mixed-up heiress. Apparently her mother had driven Jesse into the arms of Jack Wise, but Jessie stabbed him and stole $50,000 to get away from him. Terry tracks Jessie to Cozumel, where they start a torrid affair. Of course Jake wants Jessie back, but Terry does not want to give Jessie up.

The rest of the film suffers from a convoluted plot which has *nothing* to do with the original script by Daniel Mainwaring. Apparently, screenwriter Eric Hughes based his own script on the original skein of *Out of the Past* (no screen credit is given), but there are vast differences. You might call *Against All Odds* a loose remake of *Out of the Past*, but truthfully, it is a film of unfulfilled potential without much excitement (except for the macho car chase at the beginning of the film) or many compelling characters. Despite Jeff Bridges's amiability, the film is clumsy, torpid, and quite forgettable.

The subplot, a land grab in a Los Angeles suburb to build a modern highway and housing complex, is artfully managed by film noir icons Richard Widmark (*Kiss of Death*, 1947) as Ben Caxton, a shrewd lawyer, and Jane Greer (*Out of the Past*, 1947) as Mrs. Wyler, an equally shrewd woman who cares only for herself, her accumulated wealth, and her power (very much like the original Kathie Moffat), but older and smoother.

There are wonderful performances by minor actors such as Alex Karras, a "motherly" football coach to Brogan who is in league with Jake Wise. Dorian Harewood is suitably reptilian as Tommy, a thug in the employ of Jake. Saul Rubinek is equally reptilian as Terry's former lawyer, Steve Kirsch and Swoosie Kurtz, as Rubinek's secretary Edie, tries to extricate Terry from his problems. But however beautiful the location shots (in Metrocolor and CinemaScope) of Cozumel and Tulum are, however exciting the car chase scenes are, however obsessive the love affair in the star-studded Terry–Jessie–Jake triangle is, however upbeat the score by Michel Colombier and the musical performances of Kid Creole and the Coconuts are, *Against All Odds* fails miserably as a remake, even as a neo-noir, because we simply do not care about the characters or their destinies.

Although the director, Taylor Hackford, has certainly made some fine films, especially the 1982 *An Officer and a Gentleman*, *Against All Odds*— although it has all the elements of an obsessive love affair, a tropical idyll, treachery, political corruption, blackmail, and murder, as well as fashionable Los Angeles nightclub entertainments—is curiously antiseptic, and at the same time, glossy, with a denouement that just does not work. Richard Widmark as Ben Caxton is the supervillain of the film. It is he who sends football coach Hank Sully (Alex Karras) after Terry to retrieve Jessie for Jake. It is he who covers up Hank's death at Jessie's hands in Cozumel, and frames Terry so he will retrieve lawyer Steve Kirsch's records of illegal football gambling and so, murders the latter. (Kirsch is played by Saul Rubinck.) Caxton is also Jake's behind-the-scenes partner at his nightclub, The Palace, his "bank," and the mastermind behind the creation of Wyler Canyon, housing for the very wealthy that masks a landgrab and corruption that benefit Caxton, Mrs. Wyler, and their entourage. Jake is killed in a mountaintop shoot-out, and Jessie agrees to follow orders from Caxton (because she murdered Hank and now Jake). A year later Terry attends the opening of the Wyler Canyon Project, while he and Jessie gaze at one another during the party.

Whereas six murders were essential to the plot of *Out of the Past*, the murders in *Against All Odds* are barely memorable. All of the leading actors survive the exigencies of the script. Perhaps the title *Against All Odds* should be stripped of its emotionally wrenching urgency and be *The Games People Play*.

FILMOGRAPHY

Out of the Past (1947), d. Jacques Tourneur, RKO, 97 min., b&w, sc. Daniel Mainwaring, ph. Nicholas Musuraca, m. Roy Webb, v. Nostalgia Merchant.

Against All Odds (1984), d. Taylor Hackford, Columbia, 128 min., Metrocolor, CinemaScope, sc. Eric Hughes, ph. Donald Thorin, m. Michel Colombier and Larry Carleton, v. Columbia.

13

Ride the Pink Horse (1947) and
The Hanged Man (1964 [TV])

RIDE THE PINK HORSE (1947)

Based upon a mystery novel by Dorothy B. Hughes, *Ride the Pink Horse* was the second of three of her books that were successfully filmed—the others were Richard Wallace's *The Fallen Sparrow* (1943), with John Garfield, and Nicholas Ray's *In a Lonely Place* (1950), starring Humphrey Bogart. Robert Montgomery—not the tough-guy actor we would expect to play Lucky Gagin, the protagonist of *Ride . . .*,—also directed the film and gave special emphasis to developing the roles of his costars, especially youthful Wanda Hendrix as the Mexican teenager Pila, Thomas Gomez as the carny man Pancho who runs the carousel referred to in the title, Fred Clark as the cigar-smoking gangster Frank Hugo, and Andrea King as Marjorie, possibly Hugo's mistress and the only rotten femme fatale in the film.

Ride the Pink Horse is a fair film noir set in the border town of San Pablo, New Mexico, during a fiesta. Lucky Gagin arrives in the town with a canceled check which he places in a rental locker at the bus station. He is a veteran of World War II and a petty blackmailer whose best friend, Shorty, was cheated by Frank Hugo and ultimately killed by him. Gagin seeks revenge and cash by selling the check to Hugo for $30,000 so that an FBI Investigator, Rets (played by Art Smith), will not be able to prosecute Hugo for graft and black-market profiteering. Gagin's biggest problem is that he cannot find a hotel room. When he meets Pila and Pancho, he finds both friendship and lodging.

Unfortunately, Pila has powers which tell her Gagin is marked for death. In fact, Hugo sets two henchmen upon Gagin, and they almost stab him to death. The rest of the film deals with Gagin staying out of harm's way, protected by Pila and Pancho. Ultimately, he hands over the incriminating check, proof of Hugo's guilt, to Rets, who arrests Hugo's whole mob. *Ride the Pink Horse* ends with Gagin saying good-bye and thank you to Pila and Pancho, then walking off with Rets to the bus station, a denouement not unlike that in Michael Curtiz's *Casablanca* (1942).

Russell Metty's fluid camera work and black-and-white photography are ably complemented by Frank Skinner's wall-to-wall score. Robert Montgomery as Gagin was conceived in the spirit of Dick Powell's Philip Marlowe or of Montgomery's own performance as Marlowe in *Lady in the Lake* (1946), in which he also directed—tough, laconic, unshaven, and ultimately on the side of justice (although it takes a near-fatal stabbing for Gagin to decide to go with the good guys). Filmed mostly on studio sets, *Ride* . . . excels only in its writing—the script is by Ben Hecht and Charles Lederer.

Ride . . . is one of the most uninvolving films noirs this writer has ever seen, mostly because Robert Montgomery is a "cold" actor and seems out of place playing a tough guy or a detective. The only convincing actors in the film are Fred Clark, a comedian, as an average American gangster (casting against type) and Andrea King as his mistress, who watches Gagin being stabbed, tries to prevent the FBI agent Rets from stopping the crime, and returns to the bar with hardly a hair out of place. Wanda Hendrix seemed miscast as Pila, a young Mexican girl with mystical powers, dark makeup, and a poor Spanish accent. Only Thomas Gomez is exactly right in the role of Pancho, with his porcine body and excellent Spanish accent, but he, too, suffers from a believability problem because he does not seem seedy enough to own a carousel in a border town. And I have always wondered about the title—when Gagin tells Pila to "ride the pink one," is there any significance to the color? Although I think not, you watch the film and decide.

THE HANGED MAN (1964 [TV])

The remake for TV of *Ride the Pink Horse*, titled *The Hanged Man* (1964), is loosely based on the original novel. In fact, it was filmed by Universal-TV to be shown only on American television and then released to foreign markets. Despite excellent direction by Don Siegel, *The Hanged Man*— despite color, a cast loaded with cameo performances, and wide American exposure on NBC Television—fails miserably as prime time fare and should have been relegated to the second half of a double bill. It's a true "B" feature.

Harry Pace (Robert Culp) comes to the New Orleans Mardi Gras seeking revenge for a friend he believes was murdered. He becomes enmeshed with Arnie and Lois Seegers (Edmond O'Brien and Vera Miles), corrupt labor leaders involved in shakedowns and cross upon double cross which ultimately lead to murder and result in their convictions for these crimes. Gene Raymond, Norman Fell, J. Carrol Naish, Edgar Bergen, and Seymour Cassel play an assortment of Southerners who weave in and out of this complicated story of crime and shady union politics. Stan Getz and Astrud Gilberto play themselves and add some music to the proceedings. *The Hanged Man* is a TV film that lacks the clear-cut characterization and toughness of the original that would make it a satisfying remake. If only this new version of *Ride the Pink Horse* were moderately interesting. Despite Culp's fiery performance, *The Hanged Man* deserves its European exile. It is weakly motivated, poorly written, and not deserving of our attention.

FILMOGRAPHY

Ride the Pink Horse (1947), d. Robert Montgomery, Universal International, 101 min., b&w, sc. Ben Hecht and Charles B. Lederer, based on the Dorothy B. Hughes novel, ph. Russell Metty, m. Frank Skinner, v. not available.

The Hanged Man (1964 [TV]), d. Don Siegel, Universal TV, 87 min., color, sc. Jack Laird and Stanford Whitmore, based on Dorothy B. Hughes's novel *Ride a Pink Horse*, ph. Bud Thackery, m. Stan Getz and Astrud Gilberto songs, v. not available.

14

The Big Clock (1948) and *No Way Out* (1987)

THE BIG CLOCK (1948)

"The strangest and most savage manhunt in history!" is the tag line from *The Big Clock*. The Paramount Pictures logo appears onscreen backed with an ominous Victor Young thriller score. The camera observes New York skyscrapers late at night and travels to the Janoth Publications Building, swoops to the top of a multisided clock, and inside to a dark corridor where a man gets off an elevator and runs inside a room that houses the guts of this enormous timepiece. The man is George Stroud (Ray Milland), reporter for *Crimeways* magazine, a Janoth publication. Once inside the room, he tells us in a voice-over that he is now a hunted man, but thirty-six hours earlier, his life was quite fine indeed.

Stroud is the editor of a magazine whose very essence depends upon the entrapment of criminals and getting the scoop on their crimes before the law steps in. He is wrapping up a sensational manhunt when he announces to Steve Hagan (George Macready), Janoth's right-hand man, that he is quitting his job and going on his long-overdue honeymoon with his wife, Georgette (Maureen O'Sullivan), and their five-year-old son. Georgette visits George in his office to confirm their meeting at the railroad station, and George says nothing will stop him.

After finishing his day at Janoth Publications, George has a few drinks at a local reporters' hangout; meets Pauline York (beautifully played by petite, blonde Rita Johnson), who is Earl Janoth's mistress; misses his train; and goes out on the town with Pauline. She had overheard

George's conversation with Steve Hagan over the intercom in Janoth's office. It's unclear why Pauline hooks up with George and goes barhopping with him. They wind up at a Third Avenue antiques store (where George buys a nondescript painting) and a bar where George buys a sundial with a pointed arrow. Pauline takes George home to her apartment, planning to seduce him to spite Earl Janoth (juicily played to the hilt by Charles Laughton), knowing Janoth will arrive at 10:57 P.M. for his rendezvous with her.

George is too drunk to play, so Pauline ushers him out the door and, as the elevator with Janoth in it ascends, George runs down the stairs. When Janoth gets off the elevator, he spies someone on the stairs looking at him, and George sees Janoth through the leaves of a potted palm. When Janoth enters Pauline's apartment, he is aware someone had been there before him. Pauline has been blackmailing Janoth for "acting lessons" and demands more money. She calls him fat and ugly, and says no woman would have anything to do with him if he were not wealthy. Janoth picks up the sundial and strikes Pauline with it, killing her with one blow. Laughton's playing of this scene, especially his contorted face and nostrils flaring in anger, is one of the acting marvels of the film.

Janoth goes to the home of Steve Hagan and tells him what happened. Steve goes to Pauline's apartment; takes the sundial, Pauline's address book, and a man's handkerchief (George Stroud's, which Pauline used and mistakenly pocketed); and removes all traces of Janoth's presence there, even wiping away fingerprints.

Meanwhile, George has flown to Virginia and goes to the house they rented; he tells Georgette he has quit his job. Their phone rings in the middle of the night. Steve Hagan tells George of Pauline's death and urges him to return to solve the crime. Realizing he will be the chief suspect, George leaves, and the next morning he is placed in charge of the investigation of Pauline's murder.

The rest of the film is really a cat-and-mouse game for George, avoiding potential witnesses who saw him in the antiques store and various bars with Pauline the night before. His one hope is to find witnesses or proof of Janoth's guilt before he is arrested as the suspected murderer. After nearly thirty-six hours of dodging security guards, he enters Steve Hagan's office, finds his handkerchief and other items in Pauline's handbag in Steve's desk drawer, and realizes Steve is protecting Janoth. In a brilliant scene, when Janoth discovers George knows the entire truth, he asks Steve to take the blame for him. Steve is unwilling to do so. Janoth shoots Steve and runs toward the partially open door of his penthouse office elevator, then topples to his death in the empty shaft.

Very Hitchcockian in tone, *The Big Clock* has many messages for its viewers. One is of the innocent man, caught in circumstances beyond his control, finding his way out of the labyrinth. Another is how corporate life is corrupting American family values—Georgette says, "Sometimes I think you are married to the magazine and not to me!" Another is our national obsession with time—the "big clock" of the title: its setting atop the Janoth Building, Janoth's unwillingness to let George have a vacation for *seven* years! "What does Janoth think I am—a clock with springs and gears instead of flesh and blood?" George asks. The publishing house boasts that it has the most accurate, the most unique, privately owned clock in the world. The big clock is the essential metaphor behind this film noir. And time is running out, until George finally proves his innocence.

Some of the character actors in the film inhabit their roles realistically and beautifully. Steve Hagan as played by George Macready is more than just a guy Friday, he is possibly also Janoth's homosexual lover. Harry Morgan as Janoth's masseur/bodyguard/thug sends chills up our spines when he hunts George Stroud in the clock room among the gears. He also gives us a homosexual frisson as the man who would do anything for his boss. Elsa Lanchester (Laughton's real-life wife) appears as Louise Patterson, a somewhat dotty artist hired to do a painting of the killer; turns out to be a surrealist portrait of an unrecognizable man, the only real joke in the entire film. Ray Milland turns in a competent, totally believable performance as the man hunting himself, and Charles Laughton is truly scary and demonic as the manipulative executive who is both admirable and hateful, with a great deal to hide—his entire publishing empire is at stake. *The Big Clock* is more than melodrama—it is film noir that moves at lightening speed until its unpredictable conclusion.

NO WAY OUT (1987)

"Is it a crime of passion or an act of treason?" is the tag line for the remake of *The Big Clock*, also based on Kenneth Fearing's novel, now called *No Way Out*. Directed by Roger Donaldson and filmed in color and CinemaScope with an excellent cast that includes Kevin Costner in the Ray Milland role, Gene Hackman in the Charles Laughton role, Sean Young in the Rita Johnson role, and Will Patton in the George Macready role, Fearing's novel has been completely reworked by Robert Garland—without the metaphor of a "big clock." The setting is now Washington, D.C., during the Cold War, and a supposed Russian "mole" is being hunted. It is a true neo-noir that, in its own fashion, is an improvement on the original.

Gene Hackman plays Senator David Brice, a married man who is obsessively attracted to Susan Atwill (played with sexual ferocity by beautiful Sean Young), and, as in the earlier version, commits murder in a jealous rage. Knowing she has been with a man she picked up earlier (Kevin Costner, as Navy Captain Tom Farrell) and spent a weekend with in a Maryland resort, Brice pushes Susan over a banister to her death. Not knowing what to do next, he calls his aide-de-camp, Scott Pritchard (winningly played by Will Patton), to clean up the mess. Pritchard, like Steve Hagan, takes the incriminating evidence and plants a story that there is a "mole" in the U.S. Department of Defense. Farrell, having seen Brice entering the apartment of his new girlfriend, knows that he is the real murderer. He is assigned to investigate the case and find the murderer. But all of the evidence points to Farrell.

As in the original, Farrell participates in a cat-and-mouse chase in the Pentagon with witnesses who have seen him with Susan. Costner inhabits his role well as the CIA's liaison who sets out to find the notorious Russian mole Yuri, who works within the Pentagon but has never been seen. But Costner knows he is the man they are looking for—and the true identity of the murderer. And so the movie winds its way to a mind-blowing conclusion as a political thriller. Whether Brice is caught or not is no longer important. Political exposure of the Soviet mole is . . . and it turns out to be Farrell!

Hackman's Brice is more of a weakling than the monster/murderer Charles Laughton was. Will Patton's Pritchett is the real villain of the piece—openly gay, fiercely jealous of Brice and equally loyal, he is Iago to Hackman's Othello. He is the ideal cleanup man: smooth, efficient, and amoral. And there are political subplots involving Senator Duvall, played by Howard Duff, and the head of the CIA, Marshall (played by Fred D. Thompson), whom Brice opposes on the question of building an unnecessarily costly atomic submarine. So although the characters in the updated version of *The Big Clock* have much more to do in Washington, D.C., this thriller runs the risk of foolishness when a Polaroid negative of Farrell, found in Susan's apartment, is regenerated by a gigantic computer at the Pentagon, revealing Farrell/Yuri at the same time . . . which makes Farrell's hunt for Brice quite pointless.

Nevertheless, *No Way Out* is a riveting thriller, more melodrama than noir, but it is still one of the most competent thrillers ever made—it's on a par with John Frankenheimer's 1964 *Seven Days in May*. It has brilliant plotting devices, crisp performances, a lean tautness that adds to its drama, and constant surprises right up to the conclusion, when we hear Farrell speaking in Russian to his Soviet chief in Washington, D.C. Chicago-based critic Roger Ebert said, "The test of a good thriller [is] when you stop thinking about the plot and start caring about the people" (*Chicago Tribune*, Aug. 14, 1987). I totally agree. *No Way Out* is a twisty thriller, truly labyrinthine and very ingenious. It is not a real remake of *The Big Clock* but, in the words of that New Orleans chef Emeril Lagasse, "Bam! Let's kick it up a notch or two!" Garland's reworking of Fearing's original screenplay does exactly that, and provides us with wonderful entertainment along the way.

FILMOGRAPHY

The Big Clock (1948), d. John Farrow, Paramount, 95 min., b&w, sc. Jonathan Latimer, from the novel by Kenneth Fearing, ph. John Seitz, m. Victor Young, v. Universal Noir Series.

No Way Out (1987), d. Roger Donaldson, Orion Pictures, 116 min., Metrocolor, CinemaScope, sc. Robert Garland, based on the novel *The Big Clock*, by Kenneth Fearing, ph. John Alcott, m. Maurice Jarre, v. Columbia.

15

They Live by Night (1948) and Thieves Like Us (1974)

THEY LIVE BY NIGHT (1948)

Although the tag line for *They Live by Night* reads rather dramatically— "Cops or no cops, I'm going through!"—making the film sound like some Okie-gangster opera, the opening narration is far more appropriate: "This boy and this girl were never properly introduced to the world we live in." And so unfolds the love story of Bowie (Farley Granger) and Keechie (Cathy O'Donnell, fresh from her triumph as Wilma in William Wyler's *The Best Years of Our Lives* [1946]), set in the backcountry of Mississippi in the early 1930s.

This black-and-white film, based upon Edward Anderson's novel *Thieves Like Us*, is a noir-realistic study of three prisoners who escape from a state prison farm—Bowie, T-Dub (Jay C. Flippen), and Chicamaw (Howard DaSilva); Bowie spent seven years of his life there, and wants to prove his innocence. T-Dub and Chicamaw are confirmed criminals, older men who use Bowie to rob banks and manipulate the press into thinking that "Bowie the Kid" is their leader. Along the way, Bowie meets Keechie at a country hideout. They fall in love and marry, and Keechie becomes pregnant. Bowie wants to leave with Keechie and rid himself of his crime pals. But he is inveigled into another bank robbery, and is wounded. At the end of the film, T-Dub's wife (robustly played by Helen Craig) makes a deal with the cops for reward money and her husband's freedom when she reveals Bowie's whereabouts. The police shoot Bowie dead, and Keechie is left forlorn with her unborn child.

What distinguishes this film from many others of its type is the excellent acting of the fugitive couple. Farley Granger brings the right amount of innocence and nervousness to his role as Bowie, and Keechie is delicately played with softness and integrity by Cathy O'Donnell. Their romance is entirely believable, especially the wedding ceremony scene, in which the preacher (Ian Wolfe) is trying to get every nickel and dime they can give him. Their trepidation during the ceremony is captured exactly right by director Nicholas Ray, who later filmed the great James Dean flick, *Rebel Without a Cause* (1955), another sensitive portrayal of teens in love. Ray was particularly innovative in his early use of helicopter shots, cameras following the fugitives' car after bank robberies and other assorted crimes. Ray also photographed his principal actors against realistic backgrounds—diners, old country houses, tourist camps, bleak motels, small-town stores, and the like, and used natives of the area, which also helped to capture the realism (or is it neorealism?) of his story. *They Live by Night* was not the successful film RKO Radio Pictures had hoped for; in fact, it was retitled several times (once called *The Twisted Road*) before it was released under its present title. Perhaps in 1949 the theme of fugitive couples, despite noir stylistics, had run its course.

THIEVES LIKE US (1974)

It was director Robert Altman who decided to remake the original Edward Anderson novel in color and CinemaScope. Owing to the success of other films of couples on the lam, like *Bonnie and Clyde* (1967) with Faye Dunaway and Warren Beatty; of its predecessors, beginning with Fritz Lang's saga *You Only Live Once* (1937) with Sylvia Sidney and Henry Fonda, Nicholas Ray's *They Live by Night* (1949), and Joseph L. Lewis's *Gun Crazy* (1949) with Peggy Cummins and John Dall; and its later imitators, like Oliver Stone's *Natural Born Killers* (1994) with Juliette Lewis and Woody Harrelson, *Thieves Like Us* built upon the popularity of past fugitive couples and helped continue its spiral to its apogee in the mid 1990s.

Thieves Like Us tells exactly the same story as Nicholas Ray's *They Live by Night*, but is a much better film. Whereas Ray's film is steeped in realistic noirish romanticism, Altman's film has a much better script, which he worked on with Calder Willingham and Joan Tewkesbury. The casting is perfect. Keith Carradine plays Bowie, Shelley Duvall is Keechie, John Schuck is Chicamaw, Bert Remsen is T-Dub, and Louise Fletcher plays Mattie Remsen. Altman makes the Depression era come alive in CinemaScope and Deluxe color. The script is lean, and although the film runs a bit long (123 minutes), it feels like Altman has transported us visually and aurally back to 1934. Besides the excellent re-creation of the period atmosphere and strong characterizations, Altman uses the radio programs of the era to reinforce the action on the screen, sometimes inappropriately. For example, when Bowie and Keechie are falling in love, we hear a radio version of Shakespeare's *Romeo and Juliet*, appropriate but corny. When banks are robbed and car chases ensue, we hear heavy music and narration from *Gangbusters*, a popular 1930s airwaves favorite, but inappropriate. And all that country music on the soundtrack—contrived, down-home music overloading our ears!

Nevertheless, Altman's re-creation of Anderson's novel is better than its original. Whereas Ray's film was preachy and nostalgic, Altman's avoids the heavy sociological statements—he lets the audience judge the story and characters for themselves. The only scene that rankles is the one where Mattie has informed on Bowie, Bowie is killed, and Mattie holds Keechie back from being riddled by police bullets. The scriptwriters have added a scene in which Keechie lies about her husband's death, evidencing great psychological trauma and an uncertain future for her and her unborn child. *Thieves Like Us* is the definitive version of the Anderson novel and one of the great "couples on the run" additions to the genre.

FILMOGRAPHY

They Live by Night (1948), d. Nicholas Ray, RKO Radio, 95 min., b&w, sc. Nicholas Ray and Charles Schnee, adapted from the novel *Thieves Like Us* by Edward Anderson, ph. George E. Diskant, m. Leigh Harline (Woody Guthrie uncredited), v. not available.

Thieves Like Us (1974), d. Robert Altman, United Artists, 123 min., Deluxe Color, CinemaScope, sc. Calder Willingham, Joan Tewkesbury, and Altman, based on Edward Anderson's novel, ph. Jean Boffety, m. source, v. not available.

16

Criss Cross (1949) and
The Underneath (1995)

CRISS CROSS (1949)

"Love . . . love . . . you have to watch out for yourself . . . that's the trouble with you. . . . You just don't know what kind of world this is." Anna (Yvonne De Carlo) confides this philosophy of life to her former lover, Steve Thompson (Burt Lancaster), as she walks out on him with the heist money. She is shot by Slim Dundee (Dan Duryea), her present husband, as we hear the wail of police sirens and "The End" comes up on the screen with stark Miklos Rozsa chords emphasizing the gruesome scene of two bodies entwined in death.

This is *Criss Cross*, Robert Siodmak's 1949 tale of love, murder, robbery, and vengeance shot in glorious black-and-white, a solid film noir made on location in Los Angeles. Steve Thompson has returned to his hometown a year after his divorce from Anna and finds himself in a nightclub, The Roundup, where he courted his ex-wife. Anna is there, dancing a rumba with wild abandon (with a very young, "Anthony" Curtis); Steve cuts in and is overwhelmed by her sensuality. He is still in love with her, even though she is going to marry the club's shady owner, Slim Dundee. Anna is after wealth, which Dundee can provide, but in no way is it a substitute for the physical relationship she shared with Steve. The two become lovers again after Steve runs into Anna at Union Station, where she is seeing Dundee off on a business trip. Anna shows Steve some bruises, proving to him that marriage to Dundee is no bargain. Steve's good friend Pete Ramirez (Stephen McNally), a cop, warns him about Anna: "I shoulda been a better friend . . . I shoulda grabbed you by the neck and kicked your teeth in." But Steve continues seeing Anna, sleeping with her until, one day, Dundee catches them in bed. Thinking fast, Steve, who is now working for an armored car concern, tells Dundee about a heist that could make them all rich. Once he has obtained the money, Steve believes Anna will go away with him—but Dundee is preparing a double cross to obtain both Anna and the money. "When you double-cross a double-crosser, it's a crisscross!"

All the above is seen in one elaborate flashback as Steve rides in an armored car, preparing for the heist, which goes completely awry. During the robbery, Dundee's men kill Steve's partner and Steve is critically wounded in a shoot-out. Everyone considers Steve a hero, but Ramirez suspects him of involvement in the robbery.

Steve is abducted from the hospital by a henchman of Dundee's, but Steve pays the man to take him to an isolated cottage on the outskirts of Los Angeles. Anna has a rendezvous there with Steve, who is unable to travel. Dundee's henchman (played by Robert Osterloh) betrays the location of Steve's hideout to Dundee for a price. Dundee kills Anna and Steve in one of the most thrilling conclusions to a film noir ever filmed.

What makes *Criss Cross* so thrilling is that Burt Lancaster's performance as Steve is so real. He has been through the life-and-death struggles of World War II, and as a small-time hoodlum, he is willing to risk his life for love and money. Yvonne De Carlo makes a wonderful femme fatale as Anna because she, too, is willing to commit adultery for big bucks, risking discovery—even death! Like Steve, she is a child of the Depression and hard times, so money and security are paramount in her mind.

Criss Cross is such a fabulous film noir because the director, Robert Siodmak, has transformed Don Tracy's original novel into an exercise in how the protagonists cannot avoid their destinies, no matter how hard they try. Siodmak uses helicopter shots at the very beginning of the film to sweep into the parking lot of the nightclub where Steve and Anna are meeting clandestinely. They are the little people caught in a web of circumstances of their own making.

Another fabulous scene is the armored car robbery. The crooks, headed by Slim Dundee, set off tear gas canisters and, wearing masks, enter the truck, kill the guards, and take the cash. The scene is filmed from above, with occasional street shots—everything in a kind of dense white fog. There are occasional street-level shots where Steve sees Pop (Griff Barnett) get shot and realizes he, too, is in a crisscross situation. And he himself is almost killed by Dundee.

There are some excellent character actors in *Criss Cross*. Alan Napier is Finchley, the brains behind the robbery, planning it down to the last detail. Griff Barnett (Pop) is also terrific as Steve's partner, who is a victim of the double cross. Meg Randall and Richard Long are wasted in tiny roles as a B-girl and a relative of Steve's, respectively. But the real surprise is Esy Morales's rumba band, whose dynamic, sensual music permeates the nightclub atmosphere. It helps to turn us into spectators who become involved with the lovers, the robbery, and their fate. *Criss Cross* is film noir at its most brilliant.

THE UNDERNEATH (1995)

"For passion, betrayal and murder . . . there is still no place like home" is the tag line for Steven Soderbergh's adaption of Don Tracy's original novel, *Criss Cross* (Daniel Fuchs, the screenwriter of the original 1949 film, is also credited). Filmed in color and Panavision, the remake opens out the original plot. In the mid 1990s, Michael Chambers (played by bushy-browed Peter Gallagher) returns home to Austin Texas, having left under a cloud, in debt to gamblers. He also walked out on his wife, Rachel (played by newcomer Alison Elliott). Michael has returned home for the wedding of his fifty-six-year-old mother (played by the former film ingenue Annjanette Comer) to Ed Dutton (Paul Dooley, in a sympathetic role), who works as an armed guard for the Perennial Armored Truck Company, run by Clay Hinkle (Joe Don Baker). Michael's brother David (played by Adam Trese) is a cop who despises him for walking out on his wife and bringing grief to their mother: "I can't believe you'd wear our father's suit to our mother's [second] wedding!" Michael meets Rachel at The Ember, a new Austin club run by Tommy Dundee (played with a tough sneer à la Dan Duryea by William Fichtner). She quickly spurns him, but later resumes her sexual conquest of him. Michael is unaware that she is engaged to Dundee. When Dundee discovers Michael and Rachel in bed, Michael quickly tells Dundee that he lured Rachel to his apartment to draw Dundee away from his club so he could bring him into a plan—an armored car heist, with Michael as the inside man.

One evening, Rachel goes to Las Vegas with Dundee, and returns married to him! This is another reason for Michael to involve Dundee in the heist. If they are successful, Michael intends to pay off his gambling debts and then go off with Rachel. But Rachel has her own game plan—she wants to use her share of the money to become an actress and leave Dundee. There are flashbacks and flashforwards as Michael thinks about past, present, and future relationships while riding in the armored van. In the past, Michael wears a beard and is slovenly, lazy, and a spendthrift. In present time, he is clean shaven. Flashforwards show him wearing his uniform as he is ready to participate in the armored car heist, which is perfunctory and has little dramatic value.

The robbery takes place, and Michael's new stepfather is killed. Michael is seriously wounded and is hospitalized. His brother visits him there, knowing that Michael is implicated in the robbery. Rachel also visits Michael. Realizing that Michael is an itinerant loser, she takes off with the money. What she does not know is that the big shot who has manipulated everyone from behind the scenes (he is the "money man" behind Dundee's club who has just killed Dundee) is after her. He is also the owner of the armored car company!! While Michael, Rachel, and Dundee spend time betraying each other, it is Clay Hinkle who walks off with the loot—perhaps one twist too many from the original *Criss Cross*. The original noir conclusion has been reworked, but not to the film's benefit. Yes, like Steve Thompson in the original 1949 film, Michael is abducted from the hospital by Dundee's henchman. When Michael regains consciousness, Dundee kills Michael's abductor with the aid of Rachel. When he is alone with Rachel, Michael begs her to spare his life. When Dundee returns after dropping the body of the abductor in his car trunk, Michael shoots Dundee, after the latter dares him to. Rachel leaves Michael lying on the floor, alive, having been shot by Dundee, and goes off in her car with the money, followed by a white van. Hinkle watches the entire proceedings.

Another interesting plot element partially retained from the original is the threat by Michael's brother to frame Rachel for and make sure she goes to Tehachapi Women's Prison. He has seen Michael and Rachel together, and wants her for himself. (Peter Ramirez threatens Anna in the same way in *Criss Cross*.)

Although *The Underneath* is certainly not faithful to the original story, it is nevertheless a very pleasant remake of the original. Whereas Burt Lancaster projected a saturnine physicality and sexuality, Peter Gallagher comes off unmuscular, indolent, and self-absorbed. Alison Eliott is right to run off with the money; in the earlier version, Yvonne De Carlo projected such lust and sensuality that Lancaster was right in wanting her above all. The biggest problem with *The Underneath* is that you never really get "under" anybody's skin. There is an emotional flatness that permeates the script and affects the actors throughout. Only Elisabeth Shue as Susan, a bank clerk who is Michael's short-term lover, makes her short role on the big screen really count. You feel sympathetic to her when Michael dumps her for Rachel. And William Fichtner is the only real villain of the piece—a psychopathic, possessive lover whose rage overpowers us, much as Dan Duryea did in the original film. Fichtner could easily fit into Richard Widmark's psychotic killers of the 1940s film noir classics like *Kiss of Death* and *The Street with No Name*. It is unfortunate that the principal actors, Gallagher and Eliott, have no real charisma or sexual chemistry to keep us interested in this very updated remake. Perhaps the director was betrayed by the "modernizing" of the script and adding just a few twists too many. And the film's title—what does it mean, exactly?

FILMOGRAPHY

Criss Cross (1949), d. Robert Siodmak, Universal International, 87 min., b&w, sc. Daniel Fuchs, from the Don Tracy novel, ph. Franz Planer, m. Miklos Rozsa, v. Universal/MCA.

The Underneath (1995), d. Steven Soderbergh, UIP/Gramercy, 99 min., color, Panavision, sc. Sam Lowry (Steven Soderbergh) and Daniel Fuchs, based on the Daniel Fuchs original screenplay and the Don Tracy novel, ph. Elliot Davis, m. Cliff Martinez, v. Gramercy.

17

Gun Crazy (1949) and Guncrazy (1992)

GUN CRAZY (1949)

There were so many tag lines for the 1949 Joseph H. Lewis film originally titled *Deadly Is the Female* (sometimes reviewed under this title) that one wonders why the King Brothers (producers) did not stick with this title. But it is easily seen why they chose to rename the John Dall/Peggy Cummins starrer *Gun Crazy*—because Bart (John Dall) says to Laurie Starr (Peggy Cummins) at one point, "We go together, Laurie . . . like guns and ammunition go together!" Yes, Bart and Laurie are "Thrill crazy . . . Kill crazy." Advertising refers to English actress Peggy Cummins as "Notorious Laurie Starr . . . wanted in a dozen states . . . hunted by the F.B.I." and "She was more than any man can handle!" and claims to present "The Flaming Life of Laurie Starr (The Lethal Blonde)" and "Her Violent Loves! Her Vicious Crimes! Her Wild Escapes . . ." "Nothing Deadlier Is Known to Man." An obvious forerunner of the *Bonnie and Clyde* type of action crime movie about the flight of a fugitive pair of mad lovers and robbers, *Gun Crazy* thrills its audience like no other film noir of the late 1940s. It is the last word in B-noir commercial movies.

Written by MacKinlay Kantor (previously known for his Academy Award-winning screenplay of *The Best Years of Our Lives* [1946]) in collaboration with blacklisted Dalton Trumbo ("Millard Kaufman"), *Gun Crazy* has become a cult film, a midnight movie, because of its dazzling sexual story with love for guns as its subtext, its vicious femme fatale who entices an ex-soldier into a life of robbery and murder, its wonderfully staged one-take robbery scenes filmed from the backseat of a getaway car, its tight dialogue and original direction by Joseph H. Lewis, its splendid black-and-white photography by Russell Harlan, and its haunting music score by Victor Young, especially his song "Mad About You," which frames the romantic moments of the lovers and emphasizes their lust for sex and guns.

For all of its eighty-six minutes, *Gun Crazy* seems to run much longer because it begins with fourteen-year-old Bart Tare (played by a young Rusty [later Russ] Tamblyn), and his obsession with guns. Caught stealing an ivory-handled six-shooter from a store in an unnamed midwestern town, Bart is brought before Judge Willoughby (adeptly played by Morris Carnovsky), who sends the orphaned boy to reform school. Bart (now played by John Dall) returns home after he has served a stint in the Army. He meets up with his childhood friends, Clyde (Harry Lewis) and Dave (Nedrick Young). Bart was a shooting instructor in the army and is now considering a job demonstrating guns for Remington. The three young men decide to go to a local carnival, where they come upon a "star act" featuring Miss Annie Laurie Starr, "The darling of London, England!" Bart is clearly electrified by her show of sportsmanlike prowess with guns and her obvious sexuality. Participating in a contest arranged by the carnival owner, Packet (leeringly played by veteran actor Berry Kroeger), for a $500 cash prize, Bart puts up his $50 and succeeds in igniting by gunfire all the matches in a crown worn by Laurie. When Laurie's turn comes, she fails to ignite the last match in a crown worn by Bart. The gentlemanly Bart returns Laurie's diamond ring, given in lieu of the cash, and accepts a job with the carnival. He wants Laurie and will do anything to be near her. When Laurie tells Bart of Packet's blackmailing her for "killing a man in St. Louis," the two decide to leave the carnival and set out on their own.

Bart wants to get a $40-a-week job at Remington, but Laurie wants big money—she wants "a guy with spirit and guts," who can deliver. Bart says, "I don't want to look in that mirror and see nothing but a stickup man staring back at me." Laurie answers, "You'd better kiss me goodbye, Bart, because I won't be here when you get back." But their attraction is too powerful to deny. And so the lovers passionately embrace and begin a crime rampage.

The rest of the film deals with their deftness as robbers of small hotels, liquor stores, cars, and finally three superb scores—the first at a bank in the town of Hampton (that famous long take from the backseat of the car); the second at the Rangers' and Growers' Exchange, in which they are almost captured by the police until Bart shoots out a front tire of the police car; and third, an Armour meatpacking plant in Albuquerque, where they become employees, stage a robbery, and agree to take separate cars in opposite directions. However, they flee in one car, and finally reach California, Bart's home state. Living off the cash proceeds of the Armour heist, they do not realize the cash was marked and the serial numbers are known by local police. While dancing one night, they realize the local police are on to them, and they flee hurriedly, leaving behind all their possessions and the cash.

The denouement of the film comes in Bart's hometown. He returns to his sister Ruby (Anabel Shaw), with whom he lived as a boy, and she hides them. Bart's friends ask the couple to give themselves up. Laurie threatens to take Ruby's baby as a hostage, but Bart dissuades her. They drive to the San Lorenzo Mountains, and after crashing their car, they wind up, breathless and tired, in a misty swamp covered with snow. Laurie wants to kill their pursuers, but Bart dissuades her. As his boyhood friends Dave and Clyde come closer, Laurie fires her gun into the fog. Bart shoots her, the only murder he commits in the film, and is killed by a barrage of police bullets. The camera pulls back from the bodies on high, and we watch the police enter the area where Bart and Laurie are lying dead next to one another. The music swells to the melody of "Mad About You," and "The End" zooms out at us.

Produced by the King Brothers, who were known mostly for their cheapie B-noirs made for Monogram—*Dillinger* (1945) with Lawrence Tierney and *The Gangster* (1947) with Barry Sullivan, *Gun Crazy* was released by United Artists and really deserved to be in the A category. I have always seen it in theaters as the top half of a double feature, because it certainly was an extraordinary film as a result of its frank sexuality, its expressionistic photography, its sexual symbolism, and its noir ambience and psychological underpinnings. French director Jean Luc Godard said of the film, "If you have never seen *Gun Crazy*, you don't know what a truly great noir film is!"

GUNCRAZY (1992)

Guncrazy (1992) is the story of a pair of fugitive lovers, crazy for guns as a substitute for sex, but it is not exactly a remake of the Joseph H. Lewis film noir of 1949. Rather, it contains echoes of the original screenplay—but it has been updated, modernized, and bowdlerized. Touted as a film for teenager Drew Barrymore, *Guncrazy* is the story of Anita Minteer, a sexy high schooler of sixteen who looks for sex in all the wrong places in order to gain social acceptance. When her surrogate father, Rooney (played by an aging Joe Dallesandro), begins to sleep with her in a trailer they share (Anita's mother has walked out on the family),

Anita realizes she has to remove herself from this situation. As part of a high school English project, she has been corresponding with Howard Hickock (played by James LeGros), a prison inmate who so profoundly affects Anita that their letters become an enveloping love affair. When Howard writes to Anita that he always loved girls who could shoot guns, she begins to take lessons and kills Rooney when he tries to seduce her one more time. (The lovers later take Rooney's decaying body from a storage dump and throw it into a furnace.)

Anita obtains a job for Howard before he gets out of prison, then arranges for his release. The two are smitten with one another—their bond goes deeper than their mutal love for guns. Howard is impotent, but Anita doesn't care. She has had enough casual sex to last her a lifetime. When Howard comes along, Anita is ready for love, and she would rather shoot guns with him than sleep with him.

Obviously, this story is not the real remake of the original, but it does have its own charms. The director, Tamra Davis, shows us a part of rural California of the early 1990s that we find almost unrecognizable. Religion seems to be important in this part of the state; Howard becomes a born-again Christian, and the couple try to live a straight life. Hank Fulton, the preacher of their church, who has a fondness for snakes, is beautifully played by Billy Drago. All around them are dumb locals, Jesus freaks, horny rednecks. In this milieu their gun lust takes over, and they are off on a crime spree. Anita cannot help her criminal impulses, and shoots her mother's ex-boyfriend. Howard has returned to a life of crime, a life he tried to avoid but to which he has succumbed. Accepting their destiny, the couple spend the rest of the film on the run, robbing storekeepers in order to survive on a day-to-day basis. Howard tells Anita, "Our lives are over now," and they meet a fairly predictable end, like their predecessors of the 1949 version.

The film turns murderous when Howard is forced to kill two teenagers who previously slept with Anita and refused to apologize to her for their bad manners (wanting her to go to the "dump" with them again). Another subplot deals with Howard's parole officer, Kincaid (deftly played by Michael Ironside), who considers Howard and Anita "trash" and wants to revoke Howard's parole. Howard runs away, and Anita shoots a cop pursuing them. They decide to look for Anita's mother in Fresno, but when they arrive, they find out her mother is a prostitute and has run out on a $1500 bond provided by her pimp. So the couple decides to go to an empty house; they are discovered there the next morning by the police. Howard tells Anita he will get her out of all of this and goes down the stairs, two guns blazing, only to be riddled with police bullets. Kincaid arrives on the scene and hustles Anita out of the house as she tells him, "He made me do it." At one point, Howard had taken Kincaid hostage, and Anita saved the parole officer's life. Besides, Kincaid's daughter Joy (a small role played by Ione Skye) has been Anita's best friend since childhood. This is certainly a different ending from the original *Gun Crazy* (1949).

Guncrazy (1992) has some credible performances, especially from stars Drew Barrymore as Anita and James LeGros as Howard. Barrymore sounds very Californian and LeGros affects a kind of midwestern accent with a slight twang. The only physical problem I had with LeGros was watching his face; his kind of Fu Manchu mustache seemed unreal for his character. Also, the mood of the 1992 film is less of action and more emotionally somber than the original. Matthew Bright's screenplay contains little from the original MacKinley Kantor story. He lets his audience draw its own conclusions regarding the mores of rural California life, its gun culture, its revivalist religious passions, the lack of sustenance in the lives of its youth. This film is more of a reinterpretation than a remake of the original. This version is much closer to a 1997 film starring Martha Plimpton and Kevin Anderson, directed and written by Tim Blake Nelson. Titled *Eye of God*, it is about a pen pal relationship that turns murderous when Anderson, an ex-con, wants to keep Plimpton, a midwestern waitress, sequestered after their marriage. But after learning she has aborted their child, he kills and mutilates her. No fascination with guns here, but the emptiness of rural societies seems to lead young people into criminal acts.

The one salient feature lacking in the 1992 remake of *Gun Crazy* is that Drew Barrymore is no "femme fatale" and we have no real story of lovers driven by their sexual passions to commit crimes until death does them part. Peggy Cummins and John Dall were like wild animals, circling each other as if they were both ready for the kill. When Dall hungered for Cummins, there were sexual sparks that lit up the silver screen. Aided by that wonderful Victor Young song, "Mad About You," *Gun Crazy* (1949) is perfectly conceived as a terrific example of film noir. The 1992 version is more of a "new" noir; it has a fairly annoying musical score, not such wonderful color photography (very grainy in interior scenes), and a kind of high-minded artlessness that may please a generation of videomakers who use music to back up their visuals. It is more concerned with sociology and impotence than with real noir themes. Warren Beatty and Faye Dunaway, the stars of *Bonnie and Clyde*, in which the criminal also was impotent, could act the pants off Drew Barrymore and James LeGros. And *Gun Crazy* (1949), compared to the 1992 version—especially in action, dialogue, writing, themes, photography, music, and direction—is a totally, uniquely conceived work of art! It is incomparable, and represents the best kind of filmmaking of its generation.

FILMOGRAPHY

Gun Crazy (1949), d. Joseph H. Lewis, United Artists, 86 min., b&w, sc. Mac-Kinlay Kantor and Dalton Trumbo, from a story by Kantor, ph. Russell Harlan, m. Victor Young, v. Fox.

Guncrazy (1992), d. Tamra Davis, First Look Pictures for Showtime Cable, 96 min., Foto-Kern Color, CinemaScope, sc. Matthew Bright, ph. Lisa Rinzler, m. Ed Tomney, v. New Look.

18

House of Strangers (1949) and Broken Lance (1954)

HOUSE OF STRANGERS (1949)

Toward the end of *House of Strangers*, Theresa Monetti (played by Esther Minciotti), wife of Gino Monetti (broadly played by Edward G. Robinson), states that her family is "a house of strangers," brother pitted against brother. In 1932 Gino left barbering on New York's Lower East Side to open his own savings and loan association, charging exorbitant interest to his customers, especially when they can't provide collateral. The film begins with Gino's youngest son, Max (strongly played by Richard Conte), staring up at Papa Monetti's portrait. Max has just served seven years in prison for attempted jury tampering (his eldest brother, Joe, played by Luther Adler, informed on him because he was Papa's favorite).

Max has already visited his brothers Joe, Tony (Efrem Zimbalist, Jr., in an early role), and Pietro (played by Paul Valentine), called "Dumbhead" throughout the film because of his penchant for boxing, (he usually loses the bout). Papa Monetti died during Max's prison term, and the brothers, especially Joe (who now runs the bank), offer Max $1000 to leave in peace. Max throws the packet of money on the floor in defiance, then visits the apartment of Irene Bennett (his former society-girl lover, dazzlingly played by Susan Hayward). After an evening of lovemaking, he revisits the family home, where a flashback to the early 1930s begins.

There is much stereotyping of the Italian-American family in this film—Papa prefers to hear Italian grand opera records while having dinner; every Wednesday night, the entire extended family gathers for Mama's homemade spaghetti dinner as Papa serves everybody and rules the roost. He is vulgar, loud, cigar-chomping, but not quite as assertive as "Little Caesar" (a role Edward G. Robinson made famous almost twenty years earlier). Joe, Tony, and Pietro are virtual slaves of their father—they all work in the bank for $65 each per week. Max is a lawyer and is the spokesman for the brothers, the only one who is able to stand up to Papa. Joe's Philadelphia Main Line wife is fed up with living in two rooms and her husband's small salary. Tony seems comfortable and is eyeing Max's fiancée, Maria (played by a very young and beautiful Debra Paget). Pietro works as a bank guard with no eye to the future except occasional amateur boxing matches.

Most of the film's drama centers on Max, his love for Irene despite his engagement to Maria, and his family obligations. When bank examiners come to inspect the books of Monetti Savings & Loan and the government brings a suit against Gino, his sons refuse to take part of the responsibility. When Gino's put on trial, Max bribes a juror. He also takes the blame for "banking irregularities" and spends seven years in jail. To punish Max for ending their affair, Irene appeals to Gino not to write to Max in prison, thus poisoning Max's mind against his brothers. Gino dies and Max vows vengeance, but at the end of the film, when the brothers are united in their family home, he renounces his vendetta. Joe, however, believes it is better to kill Max than let him go. After beating Max unconscious, Joe orders Pietro to throw Max from a high balcony onto the street. Tony objects, and Joe cries, "Dumbhead, what are you waiting for?" Max awakens in Pietro's arms and tells him to put him down, because it is their father who will win if brother is pitted against brother. Max then goes off with Irene and "The End" comes up on the screen.

Photographed in glorious black-and-white with some New York City location shots, from the Jerome Weidman novel *I'll Never Go There Again, House of Strangers* is a "den of vipers" story with brisk, crackling dialogue and some top drawer performances, especially from Edward G. Robinson, Richard Conte, Susan Hayward, and Luther Adler. Filmed in noir style, most of the real action of the film takes place at night: on the streets, in hotel restaurants, nightclubs, bars, and the old Monetti home. Realistically photographed by Milton Krasner, and with a particularly good urban-sounding score by Daniele Amfitheatrof, *House of Strangers* ends on a positive note—we hear the last bars of Newman's score for *The Razor's Edge* (1946), promising hope to both Max and Irene as they drive away.

When I first saw *House of Strangers* at age twelve, I was overpowered by the strong emotionalism of this immigrant family, and had no idea it was a financial flop for the filmmakers. Many years later, Edward Dmytryk remembered the excellent story and the wonderful acting of Edward G. Robinson; he believed the film flopped at the box office because audiences were not interested in bankers in 1949–1950. They were more interested in westerns. And so five years later, one year after the arrival of CinemaScope at 20th Century Fox, Dmytryk was hired by Darryl F. Zanuck to remake *House of Strangers* as *Broken Lance*. He needed the film to relaunch his broken career, having served six months in prison as one of the famous "Hollywood Ten" who refused to inform on Communists during the McCarthy hearings.

BROKEN LANCE (1954)

Taking the original Philip Yordan screenplay of 1949, and without giving credit to the Jerome Weidman novel, screenwriter Richard Murphy followed the plot of *House of Strangers* almost exactly, with a few minor twists. Opening out the original from New York City to Arizona in Color by Deluxe and glorious CinemaScope, this new version is certainly one of the best remakes ever done by the Fox studio, and brings to the fore all of the studio's technology and casting skills. Spencer Tracy as Matt Deveraux is exactly perfect as the controlling Irish immigrant father of four sons, three by his first wife and one by an Indian princess (called Señora Deveraux, (winningly played by Mexican actress Katy Jurado), who received a Best Supporting Actress nomination for her role). Robert Wagner does his best acting to date as the half-breed son, Joe (the Max Monetti role), who goes to jail for his father's for tearing down a copper smelter on his land that is polluting the river and killing his cattle. The weak-willed sons are Ben, the eldest (icily played by Richard Widmark, Mike (played by Hugh O'Brian, of TV's *Wyatt Earp* fame), and Denny (the "Dumbhead" role, played by Earl Holliman in the early stages of his film career).

Joe returns home after a three-year stint in prison and stands in front of the portrait of his father. Most of the film is a flashback from then on. We see Matt Deveraux riding on horseback, using his bullwhip to keep both cattle and people in line. His favorite son is Joe, who meets Barbara (lustily played by Jean Peters), the daughter of the governor (E. G. Marshall as a racist father), who tries to discourage the romance because of his racial prejudice. Dmytryk wanted to make this film because racial hatred was a timely theme, and he felt the film would have much social significance. However the fictional elements won out over the social ones, and *Broken Lance* is still a strong story, though more of an entertainment than a film of social commentary.

Besides the half-breed character, a basic change occurred in the role of Ben Deveraux (Joe Monetti in the 1949 version). As played by Richard Widmark, he is totally responsible for selling off the Deveraux land against his father's wishes, then taunts him about it. His father never had time to listen to Ben's youthful desires, and Ben holds him account-able. It is the land deal that causes the father to saddle up and ride to stop the brothers, pistol in hand, from taking over his land and fortune and possibly killing his half-breed son. He dies in the saddle, having suffered a heart attack. Ben's resentment of Joe grows when the latter wants to leave peaceably, and he decides to kill his half brother. In a wild gun battle among boulders, Ben almost kills Joe but is brought down by a rifle bullet shot by Two Moon (Señora Deveraux's faithful Comanche retainer, played by Eduard Franz). Joe and Barbara go off in a buckboard after laying her wedding bouquet on his father's grave as his mother watches from behind a clump of trees. Just before they leave on their honeymoon, Joe takes the Indian lance with which he defied his brothers and breaks it in two over his left leg. Hence the title *Broken Lance* (representing peace from family strife).

Broken Lance is a far more complex film than the original. It comments upon land barons losing their grip with the coming of civilization (cop-per smelters and the like), discrimination against Indian tribes, and the psychological interactions of brothers dominated by a patriarch. It also makes ample use of Hollywood's newest technology—DeLuxe Color, the 55mm anamorphic lens for the CinemaScope process, and six-channel stereophonic sound. The photographer, Joe MacDonald, worked very hard to include in his exterior shots all the widescreen beauties of the Arizona landscape, which show up breathtakingly in the film. And Leigh Harline's score is supportive, never overwhelming the action or the vis-uals. *Broken Lance* is probably one of the best remakes of an earlier noir-style film because it is simply made with a great amount of artistic ex-pertise; has extremely fine performances from Spencer Tracy, Robert Wagner, Richard Widmark, and Katy Jurado; delineates the psycholog-ical problems of several of the characters; and is played with great re-straint and dignity by all concerned. This is one of the best films I have ever seen from 20th Century Fox in its wide-screen era, when story con-tent, acting, and direction were complements to the technical expertise of the early 1950s. Philip Yordan certainly deserved the Oscar for Best Screenplay, even if it was recycled into the fascinating *Broken Lance*.

FILMOGRAPHY

House of Strangers (1949), d. Joseph L. Mankiewicz, 20th Century Fox, 101 min., b&w, sc. Philip Yordan, based on the Jerome Weidman novel *I'll Never Go There Again*, ph. Milton Krasner, m. Daniele Amfitheatrof, v. Fox.

Broken Lance (1954), d. Edward Dmytryk, 20th Century Fox, 96 min., Color by Deluxe, CinemaScope, sc. Richard Murphy, based on Philip Yordan's earlier work, ph. Joe MacDonald, m. Leigh Harline, v. Fox.

19

The Asphalt Jungle (1950),
The Badlanders (1958),
Cairo (1963), and Cool Breeze (1972)

THE ASPHALT JUNGLE (1950)

"The City Under the City" is the tag line for John Huston's caper film noir, *The Asphalt Jungle*, probably the best crime film of the 1950s, and one of the most influential. Without Huston's film, Stanley Kubrick's *The Killing* (1956) and three remakes would never have appeared, because *Asphalt Jungle* is one of the best caper melodramas ever produced. It served as a model of its kind for directors like Jules Dassin, whose fabulous heist film *Rififi* (1954) is considered the "granddaddy of all heist films" (said Leonard Maltin) because its jewel robbery scene is executed in complete silence. Not so in Huston's film.

The Asphalt Jungle is based on W. R. Burnett's famous crime thriller and contains excellent dialogue by screenwriters Ben Maddow and John Huston, the director. The dialogue is literally shaped for each character. There is a comfortable use of slang—for example when Dix (Sterling Hayden) says of Cobby (Marc Lawrence), "He tried to 'bone' [embarrass] me in front of other people. I don't like being 'boned' like that." It's slang that may be dated now, but it sounds just right. And when Doll (Jean Hagen) calls Dix "Honey"—she has been locked out of her room and wants to spend a few days in Dix's apartment—there is a world of sexual experience behind her use of the word. It is little moments like these that make *Asphalt Jungle* an atmospheric film, stark in its details, natural and intelligent in its execution of character and plot, brilliant in its black-and-white cinematography, and totally engrossing.

The best review I have ever read of *The Asphalt Jungle* comes from Lawrence Russell's Internet site *Fcourt reviews*, written in May 1999, from which I will quote liberally. Mr. Russell is an excellent film critic with a modern perspective that deserves commendation, and his thoughts (similar to mine) deserve to be fully reproduced here. I have taken the liberty of reversing the first two paragraphs of his review of *The Asphalt Jungle*, and have interpolated some of my own comments (and corrections, where necessary) in brackets.

In *The Asphalt Jungle*, the streets are empty corridors of stone and concrete, a cage of trolley wires and power poles, where the characters move in a lonely passage between dusk and dawn. Unlike the movie criminals of the nineties, there are people behind them—families, lovers—so their actions have consequences. And unlike most contemporary crime dramas, the story doesn't end with the last bullet, although the last bullet is carried to the end.

The modernism in this drama is in the documentary feel of the settings and the real-time sequences that depend on characterization for emotion rather than music. [However, Miklos Rozsa's noirish score is simply brilliant.] The style is not unlike the "neorealist" drama of [Vittorio De] Sica, where humans are isolated within an indifferent urban architecture, moving through a semi-tone universe in a gray anticipation of Fate.

Doc Reidenschneider [marvelously played by Sam Jaffe of *Gunga Din* fame], a Jewish criminal of German origin, is released from prison and immediately heads to see Cobby [brilliantly played by long-time character actor Marc Lawrence], an illegal bookie, with a plan to steal some diamonds from an upscale jewelry store called Belleteers. Cobby is the eye of the needle, as it's through him that the essential characters pass who come to make up the gang that performs the heist: Dix Hanley [a blonde and tough Sterling Hayden]; the big [Southern] American 'hooligan' with an obsession for horses and gambling [a mean and bitter hood who dreams of restoring an old Kentucky horse farm]; Gus Minissi [strongly played by James Whitmore], the hunched-back greasy-spoon operator with a heart of gold; Louis Ciavelli [played by Anthony Caruso, who later appeared in *Badlanders*]; the "soup" (nitro) man who can "crack any safe in under four minutes"; and Alonzo D. Emmerich [artfully played by Louis Calhern], the crooked lawyer with an anxiety-invalid for a wife [Dorothy Tree] and a niece [Angela] for a mistress [played by a very young Marilyn Monroe before her rise to fame].

The robbery is a simple "hole-in-the-wall" forced entry into the store Belleteers from the furnace room. The safe is blown with some nitro. The blast disturbs the alarms, which attract the police . . . and the night watchman, who is easily overpowered as the trio of Doc, Dix, and Louis coolly make their exit. [There is also some tricky maneuvering to avoid the beam of an electronic alarm.] As the watchman's gun hits the floor, it discharges and [mortally] wounds Louis, the safecracker, in the stomach. . . . Nonetheless, they slip into the night, [and] return

Louis to his wife [grimly played by Teresa Celli] . . . he dies later, in the company of a priest.

The next consequence has been foreseen by the canny Doc—a double cross by . . . Emmerich . . . who is supposed to buy the diamonds before reselling them to a fence. Emmerich is waiting for Doc and Dix with his shakedown man, the volatile [private eye] Bob Brannon [icily played by suave Brad Dexter], who has had one whiskey too many . . . and is shot dead by Dix, although Dix takes a bullet, too. Emmerich confesses that he did the double cross because he's broke, and invites Dix to shoot him. But Doc suggests he approach the insurance company, [and] negotiate a 25% buyback of the jewels. Emmerich is forced to dispose of Brannon's body in the river and use his mistress Angela as a false alibi.

The police visit Emmerich as he plays casino with his wife, [and] interrogate him about his associate Brannon, whose body has just been pulled from the river. When they leave, his wife expresses dismay when Emmerich tells her Brannon may have been connected to the Belleteer robbery.

Wife: Oh, Lon, . . . when I think of those awful people . . . some of them downright criminals!

Emmerich: Oh, there's nothing so different about them. After all, crime is only a left-handed form of human endeavor [probably the most famous line in this film].

Later, when Emmerich's alibi collapses [under the careful questioning of Police Commissioner Hardy, capably played by long-time character actor John McIntire] and the police prepare to arrest him, his . . . mistress frets about Cuba.

Angela: What about my trip to Cuba, Uncle Lon?

Emmerich: Don't worry, baby—you'll have lots of trips.

Emmerich withdraws to another room, on the pretext of phoning his wife, and shoots himself.

Meanwhile, Cobby the bookie is slapped around by the corrupt cop Lt. Ditrich [Barry Kelley in one of his fat-nasty roles] and confesses, betraying the gang for a better deal with the judge. The police descend on Louis as he receives the last rites. Gus and Cobby are already behind bars [Gus tries to choke Cobby to death because he is a stool pigeon] as Dix and Doc read the papers and realize they have to get out of town. Doc has bonded with Dix, both men recognizing the other's innate integrity. Doc offers Dix half of the jewelry, but Dix declines, and gives Doc a thousand dollars to help him get to Cleveland.

Dix pulls back the curtain, watches as Doc crosses the street, disappears into the night. Doc is picked up [by police] on the outskirts of town when he lingers in a cafe to watch a young girl dance at the jukebox. [Meanwhile, Doll, appealingly played by Jean Hagen, buys Dix a used car and forces him to take her with him to his Southern home. She knows Dix is bleeding badly from his gunshot wound. At one point, he passes out while driving, and Doll takes him to a doctor. Dix realizes the doctor is calling the police, removes the IV needle from his arm, and they head out—fast.] Dix dies from his bullet wound in a meadow near the farm where he grew up, he staggers to meet some horses in a hallucinatory quest to complete his unfulfilled dream. Yes, crime doesn't pay. As the Commissioner tells the press when they question him about the corruption in Lt. Ditrich's ward: "Suppose we had no police force? The jungle wins."

The approach [of this film comes] out of the tradition of American naturalism as seen in the novels of Norris, Dreiser, Lewis and others, where character is determined by environment, the architect of fate. The characterizations are driven by the human need for freedom rather than the psychopathic need to kill. Each man has a weakness, but none have the pathology, which marks *The Asphalt Jungle* as quite different from the gangster films of the time, where greed and nihilism presage the future we understand today.

A bit slow for contemporary tastes [I don't know if I agree with this], it nevertheless has that moody "noir" feel and raw dialogue that represent the period. Most of the scenes are interiors, so the ambience is controlled by shadow and artificial light, a sunless world where gray is reality. The opening sequence shows Dix walking through empty business arcades and alleys of a silent, anonymous American city as a black police cruiser trolls the streets, looking for a robbery suspect . . . a tall man, Caucasian." "The loneliness is pervasive, so crime is an attitude, the only road to freedom when you live in a concrete [jungle]." [Russell uses the word "crypt" instead of "jungle," but I feel there is always a way out of the city—we are not entombed.]

Reinvented as a Western, *The Badlanders*—in 1958, again from a [the] novel by W. R. Burnett. *Cairo* is a 1962 remake set in Egypt, while Barry Pollack's 1972 version *Cool Breeze* is a response to the black crime vogue started by *Shaft*. Influential, as a film by John Huston often is. [I would have said "always" is!]

Variety said of *The Asphalt Jungle*, "[it is] . . . a study in crime, hard-hitting in its expose of the underworld . . . ironic realism is striven for and achieved in the writing, production and direction." Bosley Crowther of the *New York Times* called the film "brilliantly naturalistic, . . . electrifying, . . . ruthless, . . . tough, . . . intriguing, . . . suspenseful. . . . Everyone . . . gives an unimpeachable performance. If only it all weren't so corrupt!" Burnett and Huston have long departed from the days of *Little Caesar* (1930) and the rise of the gangster film and have made, with *The Asphalt Jungle*, one of the greatest heist noirs ever . . . !

THE BADLANDERS (1958)

Shot in CinemaScope and Metrocolor by MGM and starring Alan Ladd (the Doc Reidenschneider role), Ernest Borgnine (the Dix Handley role), Katy Jurado (the role of Doll), Kent Smith (the Emmerich role), and Claire Kelly (the Angela role immortalized by Marilyn Monroe), *Badlanders* tells a story similar to that of *Asphalt Jungle*; however, as a remake it is definitely *not* a film noir: it has no dramatic edge, it substitutes a gold ore robbery from a mine for priceless jewels, and has a happy ending. There are no immortal lines from the original film, although some of the original dialogue is used sparingly. There is no desperation among the criminals, and nobody meets a bad end. Anthony Caruso, the only actor from the original film (he originally played Louie, the safecracker), is reduced to playing a desperado who works for Kent Smith. The plan of the heist is to set dynamite charges to go off at the very same time, so the robbers will not be found out by the miners working not more than 100 feet from them. There is some interesting mine shaft photography, but *Badlanders* is no *Asphalt Jungle*. The only saving grace is watching the beautiful Mexican actress Katy Jurado playing a "woman of the town," who is led away from a life of prostitution by Borgnine, who wants to marry her. The heist is successful, and even Ladd goes off with Smith's mistress. Perfect symmetry for a genuinely poor remake. How did director Delmer Daves, who made such wonderful films noirs as *Dark Passage* (1947), ever get into this wild potboiler?

CAIRO (1963)

If *The Badlanders* was an "A" remake of *The Asphalt Jungle,* then *Cairo* definitely belongs in the "B" category. It's an MGM British Studio production, this time starring George Sanders as Major (the Doc Reidenschneider role), just out of a German jail, who organizes a group of thieves to steal the gold treasures of King Tut's tomb. They are a group of stock actors, among them the young Richard Johnson as Ali (an early role in a fairly distinguished career). The film is closer to *Asphalt Jungle* than *Badlanders* because the heist is successful but Major, like Reidenschneider, is caught by his own vacillation (he delays his escape from Cairo, tantalized by the gyrations of a belly dancer). Lechery still serves, thirteen years later, as the undoing of the major criminal. George Sanders gives the only credible performance in the film. As for location values, the city of Cairo is hardly seen except in stock shots. And if it so easy to break into the Cairo Museum, the Egyptian police should guard their treasures more assiduously. Whatever . . . this film concoction is nothing more than a "cross of the two staples of the cinema: the hashish opera and the safe-cracking escapade" (*Variety*, June 30, 1963). Except for Wolf Rilla's excellent direction, literally making something out of nothing, *Cairo* deserves its fate—never to be reissued on video.

COOL BREEZE (1972)

"He hit the man for $3 million. Right where it hurts. In the diamonds. And baby, that's cold!" This is the tag line for another routine remake of *The Asphalt Jungle*, except, this time, the proceeds from the diamond heist will go to fund a black people's bank! *Variety* called the film, produced again by MGM, "an excellent black-oriented update . . . with a hot outlook in urban keys among all younger audiences."

Cashing in on the "blaxploitation" of MGM's big hit of the summer of 1971, *Shaft* (starring Richard Roundtree), *Cool Breeze* stars Thalmus Rasulala as Sidney Lord Jones, a "cool" professional criminal on parole whose plan is to steal $3 million in jewelry and cash it in to start a bank for black businessmen. Playing the Doc Reidenschneider role, Rasulala engages the help of Bill Mercer (Raymond St. Jacques, in the Emmerich role), who plans to double-cross the robbers. Margaret Avery plays St. Jacques's explosive mistress, Lark (the role originated by Marilyn Monroe) to fine effect. There is corruption among the black police officers in the local precinct, and it is a white detective (John Lupton) who uncovers the plot. As in the original film, the denouement ends in defeat for the robbers, and despair, painful death, and frustration for most of the principal characters. Produced by Gene Corman, tightly directed by Barry Pollack, and with some location shooting in San Francisco and Los Angeles, *Cool Breeze* has its own charms, but is still a substandard heist drama like so many of the remakes of *Asphalt Jungle*. MGM should stop recycling this property and finally put it to rest, then dust off and rerelease the great 1950 original.

FILMOGRAPHY

The Asphalt Jungle (1950), d. John Huston, MGM, 112 min., b&w, sc. Ben Maddow and John Huston from the W. R. Burnett novel, ph. Harold Rosson, m. Miklos Rozsa, v. MGM.

The Badlanders (1958), d. Delmer Daves, MGM, 83 min., Metrocolor, Cinema-Scope, sc. Richard Collins, based on *The Asphalt Jungle* by W. R. Burnett, ph. John F. Seitz, m. no credit, v. MGM.

Cairo (1963), d. Wolf Rilla, MGM British Studios, 91 min., b&w, sc. John Scott, from the W. R. Burnett novel *The Asphalt Jungle*, ph. Desmond Dickinson, m. Kenneth V. Jones, v. not available.

Cool Breeze (1972), d. Barry Pollack, MGM, 101 min., Metrocolor, CinemaScope, sc. Barry Pollack, based on the W. R. Burnett novel *The Asphalt Jungle*, ph. Andrew Davis, m. Solomon Burke, v. MGM.

20

D.O.A. (1950, 1988) and
Color Me Dead (1969)

D.O.A. (1950)

"A picture as excitingly different as its title" is the tag line for United Artists' *D.O.A.*, short for "dead on arrival." Shot on location in San Francisco and Los Angeles, *D.O.A.* tells the story of an insurance salesman, Frank Bigelow (Edmond O'Brien in one of his best roles ever), who goes to a sales convention in San Francisco, before settling down with his secretary, Paula Gibson (played by Pamela Britton).

Frank is on the make for women in San Francisco's jazz clubs, and at one of them, he is slipped a deadly drink containing a luminous poison because, we later find out, he notarized a document for an illegal uranium sale, and if the nature of the sale is exposed, it will have dire consequences for the killer.

The film begins with Bigelow walking into a Los Angeles police station to report a murder—his own—and tell how he gunned down Halliday, the man who slipped him the poison (William Ching). The rest of the film is told in flashback, and at the end we see Bigelow Falls dead and is tagged D.O.A. by the police.

O'Brien gives on of his best performances as the everyman, the anti-hero who finds the man who murdered him before time runs out. *D.O.A* was made by German expatriate Rudolph Maté in the Expressionist noir tradition of starting a film with its protagonist already dead (or nearly so)—like two of Billy Wilder's films, *Sunset Boulevard* (1950) and *Double Indemnity* (1944)—and narrating past events. However, Bigelow is not trapped by a femme fatale, the true noir tradition. Rather, he was just in the wrong place at the wrong time—a victim of a simple twist of fate.

Photographed by Ernest Lazlo and with a wonderful score by Dmitri Tiomkin that underlines Bigelow's frantic odyssey to find his murderer, *D.O.A.* has some marvelous supporting players who captivate the audience. Luther Adler is Majak, a highly suspicious importer/exporter in league with Marla Rakubian (starlet Laurette Luez) to halt Bigelow's quest for his murderer. To do that, Majak sends his henchman Chester (loonily played by a young Neville Brand), whose sadistic tendencies are easily satisfied by repeatedly punching Bigelow in the belly.

At one point in the film, Halliday has given the luminous poison to his partner, Stanley Phillips (played by Henry Hart), because Phillips knew Halliday was responsible for the illegal uranium transaction that Bigelow notorized. Bigelow advises Phillips's wife (Lynn Baggett) to have his stomach pumped.

There are two wonderful chase scenes: one in San Francisco, where Bigelow eludes Chester, who is shot dead by police in a local drugstore and another that takes place in the Chanin Building in Los Angeles, when Halliday tries to escape Bigelow's revenge and is gunned down by him, wearing the hat and raincoat with a striped collar, the identical outfit he wore on the night he poisoned Bigelow. Bigelow saw the rain gear then, but now he see his face as he guns his murderer down. Perhaps Paula Gibson is better off without Bigelow. Her portrayal of a 1950s woman who regards marriage as a lifetime trap—not exactly a commitment of love—is probably accurate for the period, but totally unsavory. Bigelow would have been better off free of her—and alive!

COLOR ME DEAD (1969)

The Australian film *Color Me Dead* (1969), first shown on U.S. television in 1970, hardly received a nationwide release despite its status as a motion picture intended for theaters. Directed by Eddie Davis, it stars Tom Tryon (author and American leading man, most famous for his role in Otto Preminger's *The Cardinal* [1963]) in the Frank Bigelow role, Carolyn Jones as Paula Gibson, Tony Ward as Halliday, and Rick Jason as Bradley Taylor (the Majak role originated by Luther Adler). The original Russell Rouse and Clarence Greene screenplay is credited, but the screenwriter of the new version is not. The remake, in EastmanColor, follows the dialogue and the plot of the 1950 film noir with exactitude. *Color Me Dead* was also known as *D.O.A. II* and tells the same story: a poisoned man spending his last days tracking down his murderer. Except for the Australian locale, color, and capable performances by Tryon, Jones, and Jason in the updated screenplay, *Color Me Dead* has little to offer other than being the first remake of the original.

Variety says this version "lacks the punch and tautness" of the original. Tom Tryon's performance is mellow. Even the sadistic Chester (Sandy Harbott) has become somewhat of an Australian Milquetoast in the remake. Bigelow tracks down the murderer who slipped him the luminous poison in a topless bar. In the 1950 version he is identified by a raincoat with a striped collar and matching hat, whereas in the Australian version, Halliday wears a pinky ring that is nowhere to be seen in the denouement. Bigelow's killer is revealed by name only in a conversation, and Halliday meets his fate as in the original film. Because of the strippers who bare their bosoms in the topless bar, the film was given an "R" rating. With the addition of some calypso music, grainy EastmanColor, and fifteen additional minutes which seem to slow the action on the screen, this remake is not much of a contribution to noir, neo-noir, or the art of film remakes.

D.O.A. (1988)

"Someone poisoned Dexter Cornell. He's got to find out why. He's got to find out now. In twenty-four hours, he'll be Dead On Arrival" is the tag line from the totally new remake of the 1950 original film starring Dennis Quaid as Dexter, a college professor of English who has ingested a luminous poison and has twenty-four hours in which to find his killer. Dexter is also a successful writer who suffers from writer's block and has not had a successful novel published in the last four years. Teaching at an unnamed university in California, he refuses to read a first novel by one of his best students, Nicholas Lang (played by Rob Knepper). The latter apparently commits suicide (falling past Dex's window from the roof), not because of the professor's disdain for his work but because he's distraught over his love affair with Dex's wife, Gail (beautifully played by Jane Kaczmarek).

We find out later in the film that Nick was really murdered, pushed off the roof of Dex's office building. Dex's wife also was murdered because she read Nick's first novel, which Hal Petersham (played by comic actor Daniel Stern in a serious role), a colleague of Dex's, wanted to steal and publish it as his own work in order to gain tenure in the English Department.

There is another subplot, involving the murder of Mrs. Fitzwaring's husband by Nicholas Lang's father. Mrs. Fitzwaring (Charlotte Rampling) is sending Nicholas (her son) through college, and he is having an affair with her daughter Cookie (played by Robin Johnson). It is revealed in a flashback at the very end that Mrs. Fitzwaring murdered her husband and her former lover (Nick Lang's father)—so there has been an incestuous relationship going on, unknown to Nick and Cookie. The subplots only obfuscate the film's central theme—who poisoned Cornell, and will he catch the murderer before he expires?

Meg Ryan costars with Dennis Quaid (they later married in real life) as Sydney Fuller, a student who has a crush on Dexter. There is a ridiculous bonding scene (literally) in which they are stuck together with Crazy Glue (like the handcuffed couple in Hitchcock's *The 39 Steps*) practically until the film ends. Dexter finally hears Mrs. Fitzwaring's story in her mansion. Because both her children are dead—Cookie was accidentally shot by her chauffeur—as are her husband and her lover, she has nothing to live for. Clad in a designer gown, she commits suicide with a handy revolver, falling onto a billiard table. Dexter leaves the mansion in disgust, in quest of his own murderer.

D.O.A. (1988) is not a remake of the 1949 film, but rather a refurbishing of the original plot with lots of new details added, especially its academic setting. Dennis Quaid gives one of the two best performances in the film (the other is Daniel Stern's). But the visuals are gimmicky and sometimes distorted. A noisy rock score sabotages some of the actors' key scenes, and the film lacks the eroticism and sexuality necessary to keep the plot moving even in an attempted neo-noir remake.

There are only three really interesting scenes in the entire film. In the first, Dex realizes he is close to death and sexually bonds offscreen with Sydney Fuller (they have little in common except her adoration of him). In the second, Bernard has knocked out Dex, tied him up, and placed him in his car, to eventually kill him on Mrs. Fitzwaring's orders. He is also supposed to find Cookie and bring her home. Driving another car, Cookie sees that Dex is Bernard's prisoner and rams their car, while Dex frees himself by burning through the ropes binding his hands. He then tosses Bernard out of the car. Meanwhile, Cookie begins to drive haphazardly around the college football field (she's high on alcohol or drugs), and Bernard accidentally shoots her in the head as she tries to run him down. With Bernard on the hood, the car careens into an oil-slicked stream tossing Bernard into the muck. Dex almost drowns before he can kick out the rear window and crawl out of the car. Bernard has already crawled out of the muck, gun in hand; Dex wrestles him to the ground and knocks him back into the slime to drown. Dex's narrow escape from death is the most harrowing scene in the film. In the final scene, where Dex realizes that Hal Petersham, his colleague who wants to publish Nick Lang's manuscript as his own work, is indeed his poisoner/killer, Dex and Hal engage in a terrific fight for survival. Finally Dex shoots Hal in the chest and Hal soars through an upper-floor window, weighed down by the typewriter with which he tried to kill Dex.

The film is unique in that it creates some sort of homage to Rudolph Mate's 1950 original because the first and last scenes in the police station are photographed in glorious black-and-white. (There is an apocryphal story about a German original that was the basis for the 1950 version directed by Mate, but nobody knows the title or has seen it.) Dexter walks out of the police station, perhaps to die in a more secluded and colorful setting. The threat of his death is now missing because he has spun the entire tale on video for the police. When Edmond O'Brien keeled over in front of the desk of the police inspector, shouting "Paula!," the name of his lover, you felt involved, sympathetic. In the 1988 version, Dennis Quaid has beaten death and walks strongly down that long, long police station corridor, through a doorway into infinity. No need here to report his death and stamp that report "D.O.A.!"

FILMOGRAPHY

D.O.A. (1950), d. Rudolph Mate, United Artists, 83 min., b&w, sc. Russell Rouse and Clarence Greene, ph. Ernest Laszlo, m. Dmitri Tiomkin, v. Evergreen.

Color Me Dead (1969), d. Eddie Davis, Commonwealth United (Australia), 97 min., EastmanColor, sc. uncredited, based on the original Rouse and Greene screenplay, ph. Mick Borneman, m. Bob Young, v. not available.

D.O.A. (1988), d. Rocky Morton and Annabel Jankel, Touchstone, 100 min., CFI Color and Duart, b&w, sc. Charles Edward Pogue, based on the original Rouse and Greene screenplay, ph. Yuri Neyman, m. Chaz Jankel, v. Touchstone.

21

Night and the City (1950, 1992)

NIGHT AND THE CITY (1950)

Made in the tradition of Budd Schulberg's novel *What Makes Sammy Run?*, Jules Dassin's 1950 black-and-white film *Night and the City* stars Richard Widmark as Harry Fabian, an American expatriate, a hustler who is trying too hard to make his name famous in the (under)world of wrestling, but is always on the con. Harry is a user and is always running through metropolitan London, mostly by night (to Franz Waxman's marvelously tense score), from unknown men (and women) he has double-crossed in the recent past. The very first critical book (1955) to identify the film noir style, Raymond Borde and Etienne Chaumenton's *Panorama du film noir américain*, has a close-up photo on its cover of a very frightened Harry Fabian, his face lit by a spotlight as he runs through the London streets.

After World War II, Harry stays in London and persuades his American girlfriend, Mary Bristol (played by a woefully miscast Gene Tierney), to stay with him so he can live a life of pleasure and ease once he succeeds in the "ultimate scam": promoting Greco-Roman wrestling. He meets Gregorious (wonderfully played by Stanislaus Zbyszko) and signs him to a partnership after watching him wrestle. But Harry needs money to promote Gregorious and set up a bout at a London arena controlled by Gregorious's son, Kristo (played menacingly by Herbert Lom). So he goes to sleazy Phil Nosseros (Francis L. Sullivan), a very fat nightclub owner who sits in a metal cage (or office) suspended above his club, casting a cautious and jealous eye over his wife, Helen (Googie Withers). Nosseros advances Harry some of the necessary money, and he obtains the rest from Helen by promising he will get her a license to open her own club. Harry succeeds in arranging a bout for Gregorious with the Strangler (magnificently played by Mike Mazurki). However, the wrestlers begin to argue about Greco-Roman style and get into a fight; Gregorious bests the Strangler but dies of a stroke immediately afterward. When Kristos learns of his father's death, he sends word to every criminal in the London underworld—£1000 for the man or woman who finds Harry Fabian.

There are several subplots in the film. For example, Harry lies to Mary, steals her money, and tries to escape the London underworld. Hugh Marlowe plays Adam Dunne, an American artist who is in love with Mary but cannot declare himself until mob justice is meted out to Harry. Harry also double-crosses Helen Nosseros, who goes ahead and establishes her own nightclub but loses it when a police inspector casually inspects her license and discovers it is a fake. Helen returns to her husband, but he has committed suicide out of despair at losing her. Finally, the Strangler corners Harry on a bridge over the Thames River, chokes him, and throws his body over the railing, to meet a certain death by drowning. Kristos has had his father's death avenged, and Harry dies like the water rat he really is. And life in the city continues—in the back alleys, the slums, the factory areas, the docks, the pubs. Apparently in a last desperate attempt to redeem himself, Harry makes Mary the beneficiary of a £5000 insurance policy. As Mary watches Harry killed by the Strangler, she is consoled by Adam. These two, the only people who really know Harry, and stand apart from the rest of the characters in the film, on a higher moral ground. Certainly Nosseros, his wife, and Kristos are all losers in a society that does not tolerate outsiders (Americans) like Harry Fabian.

Richard Widmark gives the performance of his life as Harry. He has taken that giggle he created in *Kiss of Death* (1947) and uses it as a frightening cry which serves him well as a manifestation of the nervous energy he needs to survive. But his duplicitous nature does him in—he is hopelessly isolated in bars, his facial features lit with a starkness that gives the impression of a death mask. Harry is a dead man, hopelessly running in circles until he is finally stopped and given his due. His blind ambition, self-deception, and broken dreams do him in. Harry is a heel who can't live up to the code of the tough London underworld he tries to avoid. Like Sammy Glick, Harry gets what he deserves. *Night and the City* is film noir's, and the Widmark-Dassin partnership's, finest hour.

NIGHT AND THE CITY (1992)

Irwin Winkler's color remake is not an exact replication of the Dassin film, nor should it be. But it certainly is not film noir; perhaps it is neo-noir. It stars Robert De Niro as Harry Fabian, a shyster lawyer always on the con and trying to make himself a promoter in the world of professional boxing. This world is controlled by Boom-Boom Grossman (comedian Alan King in one of his menacing dramatic roles), who does not want interference in his control of New York City's fight game. Harry uses Boom-Boom's brother Al (played by Jack Warden) to enter the fighting world and create a boxing card of several teams of fighters from a local gym. He needs money to rent a huge disco and establish himself as a promoter, but cannot find any sources.

He comes to the bar owned by Phil Nosseros (played by Cliff Gorman) and tries to secure a loan of $15,000, but Helen Nosseros (played by Jessica Lange) says Phil will put up half the money if Harry finds the other half. She later shows up at Harry's apartment with a proposition. As in the original film, she wants to get away from her husband and open a bar of her own, but because of her past criminal record, she cannot obtain the necessary liquor license. Helen makes Harry a proposition—she'll give him the other half of the loan plus a cash bribe to obtain the liquor license. All Harry has to do is deliver the goods! Harry willingly takes the cash, knowing he cannot use the bribe money, and has a printer make up a counterfeit license. He secures the rest of the money from Phil. We almost believe Harry will succeed until Al Grossman fights with a black bouncer and dies of a heart attack. Boom-Boom had warned Harry, "If anything happens to my brother, you're a dead man." The fight scheme falls through when Boom-Boom tells Phil about Harry's affair with Helen (not in the original film). Harry runs from Boom-Boom's two henchman, who are out to kill him to avenge Al's death. They shoot Harry, who is taken away in an ambulance; Helen accompanies him. Harry survives in this color version, but does not deserve to!

What is basically missing in this remake is the raw motivation of the characters—psychological subtlety and colloquial dialogue are not enough. Also, the film looks too realistic and lacks the style of the 1950s noir films. Thus, despite the excellent photography and a blaring music score that sounds like a blend of source music and noise, this *Night and the City* fails to convince. Jessica Lange's Helen is not as hard or selfish as Googie Withers's portrayal in the original. Cliff Gorman as Phil is not as spidery, corpulent, and repellent as Francis L. Sullivan was in the earlier version. And fast-talking Robert De Niro is too old and all wrong for the part of Harry Fabian. Widmark was in his twenties when he made the film, and De Niro is obviously in his forties. Widmark's motivation was that of a younger man trying to break into wrestling, so he can live a life of future ease, whereas De Niro's breaking into the fight game is an act of desperation for a man nearer the end of his life who dupes everyone to get his way, no matter what the consequences. That De Niro does not die is all wrong, and Lange as a love interest simply does not work. Widmark was more credible in the role of Harry Fabian, an American trying to con his way into a hostile system where he is clearly an outsider, and dies trying. De Niro just pushes his way into the fight game, a misguided attempt to cash in on somebody else's turf that almost leads to his death. Although the one character trait common to both actors' performances is sleaziness, Widmark gives his role an urgent sense of reality, whereas De Niro's rat-a-tat delivery seems more comic than real. In view of all these differences, the 1950 version is vastly superior to its remake. Is creativity at such a low ebb in Hollywood that brilliant original material has to be recycled into pap? Read the Gerald Kersh's novel, *Night and the City*, for the superb story behind the 1950 film. It still astounds.

Perhaps the one saving grace of the 1992 version is the location photography—New York City's Greenwich Village and Soho look as dangerous in color as London's Soho does in the original. And the CinemaScope cameras catch De Niro on a Coney Island beach, with its famous boardwalk and the old Half Moon Hotel in the background, the site of the murder of the real gangster Abe Rellis. So much for the film's technical assets.

FILMOGRAPHY

Night and the City (1950), d. Jules Dassin, 20th Century Fox, 96 min., b&w, sc. Jo Eisinger, based on the novel by Gerald Kersh, ph. Max Greene, m. Franz Waxman, v. Fox.

Night and the City (1992), d. Irwin Winkler, 20th Century Fox, 108 min., color and CinemaScope, sc. Richard Price, ph. Tak Fujimoto, m. James Newton Howard, v. Fox.

22

No Man of Her Own (1950), I Married a Shadow (1982), While You Were Sleeping (1995), and Mrs. Winterbourne (1996)

NO MAN OF HER OWN (1950)

In *No Man of Her Own* (1950), film noir combines with a woman's film (melodrama)—remember the extraordinary successful *Mildred Pierce* (1945), for which Joan Crawford won a Best Actress Oscar? Randall MacDougall wrote the screenplay for *Mildred* and his female counterpart, Catherine Turney, wrote the screenplay for *No Man of Her Own*. We can expect a high-level performance from Barbara Stanwyck, an intricate plot, and a tear-jerker.

The original Mitchell Leisen film, *No Man of Her Own* has been recycled no less than three times because its author, Cornell Woolrich (under the pseudonym of William Irish), wrote a terrific short story with an intriguing plot. In the 1950 version, Barbara Stanwyck plays Helen Ferguson, a single woman from the Midwest who is working in New York City. She falls in love with Stephen Morley (Lyle Bettger), who exploits her, leaves her pregnant, and takes up with another woman, known as "Blonde" (Carole Matthews, a successful television actress in one of her early film roles). Deciding to have the baby (abortion was a forbidden option in those days), Helen buys a railroad ticket. On the train she meets Patrice and Hugh Harkness (played by stalwart character actors Phyllis Thaxter and Richard Denning). The women become fast friends, and Helen tries on Patrice's wedding ring, which bears an inscription from her husband. Seconds later, there is an enormous train wreck. Helen awakens in a hospital, and the hospital staff address her as "Mrs. Harkness." Helen tries vainly to assert her real identity, but when she learns that both Patrice and Hugh were killed in the accident, and the wealthy Harkness family is willing to accept her and her unborn child, Helen decides to find a new life of wealth for herself and security for her baby. The Harkness family had never met the real Patrice (the couple were married in Paris), so Helen believes she is safely free of her past.

In the small town where the Harkness family lives, Helen (now Patrice) moves into the lives of her in-laws, Mrs. Harkness (beautifully played by Jane Cowl), Mr. Harkness (another wonderful role for character actor Henry O'Neill) and Hugh's brother, Bill (played by John Lund). Helen falls in love with Bill, who senses she is not the real Patrice. There are clues to support his assumption scattered throughout the film, such as an incorrect signature on a check. But Helen's real shock comes when Stephen Morley arrives in town to reclaim her and their baby. However Morley's real aim is blackmail. Bill notices Patrice's mood swings, and finally she confides the truth to him (but not to her in-laws, because it would probably kill them).

As Morley smoothy worms his way into the small town's society, he gives Helen an ultimatum. She gathers the money he wants, and takes along a .45 caliber gun just in case. When Stephen takes the cash and calls it the first of many future payments, Helen decides to shoot him but cannot. Stephen slaps her, then sets the date for the next cash payment.

In a somewhat convoluted ending, on another evening a few weeks later (Stephen now has an office in a building downtown), Helen brings the cash but finds Stephen dead. But seconds before discovering this fact, she had fired several bullets into his body. Bill Harkness has followed Helen, and tries to protect her. We later discover Stephen had called the Harkness home and had spoken with the elder Mrs. Harkness, who apparently went to his office, shot him, and fled. (After her death from a heart attack, a letter is found in which she admits to the crime.) However, Stephen's blond accomplice is arrested for the murder. She, too, has several motives for killing him. Thus Helen and Bill go free to live a life of respectability. The only real casualty is the elder Mrs. Harkness, who came to love Helen/Patrice, the baby, and being a grandmother. She was willing to accept the situation (and possibly killed for it), in order to keep the family name unsullied and protect the new heir.

Barbara Stanwyck gives a vibrant performance as Helen/Patrice in a romantic melodrama with film noir overtones. Audiences are used to watching Stanwyck suffer (*Stella Dallas* [1937]), but in her Paramount films noirs, she is absolutely absorbing: *The Strange Love of Martha Ivers* (1946), *Sorry, Wrong Number* (1948), *The File on Thelma Jordon* (1949), and her pinnacle noir role as Helen Ferguson in this noir tearjerker.

I MARRIED A SHADOW (1982)

I Married a Shadow (originally titled *J'ai Epousé Une Ombre*) is the direct French remake in color (1982) of *No Man of Her Own*, and the William Irish story, "They Called Me Patricia," is given as the source of the French screenplay. Richard Bohringer plays Frank, the lover of Hélène (Nathalie Baye), who throws her out of his car and almost kills her and their unborn child. With nowhere to go (and eight months pregnant), Hélène decides to take a train ride to southern France, on the way she meets a young couple named Patrice and Bertrand Meyrand. As Hélène tries on Patrice's wedding ring, the train crashes. Of the three, only Hélène survives; she is mistaken for Patrice by the Meyrand family. Because of the trauma of the train wreck, Hélène has already had her baby, so she accepts her new identity, especially when she meets Bertrand's brother, Pierre (played by Francis Huster).

The film follows the same plot as the original and introduces a new character, Fifo (Spanish actress Victoria Abril), who vies for Pierre's attentions. But it is Bohringer as the detestable Frank who tries to blackmail the supposed Patrice (her husband was in the wine business); however, Pierre, his mother (played by the French actress Madeleine Robinson) and his father (Guy Trejan) stand by her. Patrice kills Frank after another failed blackmail attempt and, in this film, Bernard's mother signs a letter claiming responsibility for the death of Frank so that Patrice/Hélène and Pierre can marry and continue the wine business and the family name. In the original film, a letter written by Mrs. Harkness was used as a red herring to free Helen from the responsibility of killing Stephen. There is always the nagging doubt—did she really do it, or was it Blonde, Stephen's scheming last lover, who initially pulled the trigger? Whatever, *I Married a Shadow* does follow some of the story's noirish conventions, though its transposition into color and the French countryside setting makes it less faithful to its original source. Black-and-white films, especially noirish-styled ones, always have an element of danger. This is sadly lacking in *I Married a Shadow*.

WHILE YOU WERE SLEEPING (1995)

Because *While You Were Sleeping* (1995) comes chronologically before *Mrs. Winterbourne* (1996), I must acknowledge its existence, but its source is *not* related to the William Irish story (there is no screen credit indicating this), although its plot is fairly similar. Lucy (played by Sandra Bullock) works on Christmas at a Chicago train station because she has no family to go home to. She has fallen in love with Peter Gallaghan (played by Peter Gallagher), a commuter who passes her every day. On

Christmas Day, Peter is mugged on the platform, loses his balance, and falls to the tracks in the path of an approaching train. Lucy takes action, saves his life, and accompanies him to the hospital, where a nurse hears her murmuring to Peter about her desire to marry him. Suddenly Peter's family assumes Lucy is Peter's fiancée—everyone except Peter's brother, Jack (played affectingly and gently by Bill Pullman), who falls in love with Lucy. Lucy accepts Peter's family's misconception because she is a very lonely young woman—no parents, though she has sisters. Peter's family is loaded with relatives who accept Lucy into their fold. The problem is, the story has no real dramatic edge, no train wreck, no blackmail subplot, no noir stylistics. It's just a sentimental love story very loosely based on *No Man of Her Own*. *While You Were Sleeping* gets to you emotionally, but never with the raw jolt of the Barbara Stanwyck film. This is Sandra Bullock's first role as a romantic antiheroine, but it is Bill Pullman who steals the film in his role as Jack. Usually Pullman doesn't get the girl, but in this film, he succeeds admirably.

MRS. WINTERBOURNE (1996)

Mrs. Winterbourne (1996), directed by Richard Benjamin with a script by television comedy writers Phog Sutton and Lisa Marie Radano (based on the William Irish story), stars TV actress Ricki Lake as Connie Doyle, an eighteen-year-old pregnant woman who is dumped by her cold, brutal, and dangerous boyfriend, Steve De Cunzo (played by Loren Dean). After drifting into Grand Central Station, Connie boards a train and meets Hugh Winterbourne and his pregnant wife, Patricia. They strike up a conversation, and Patricia lets Connie try on her wedding ring. Just as in the original 1950 film, there is a train wreck, both Winterbournes are killed, and Connie (now called Patricia) wakes up at the hospital and is then transported to the luxurious estate of the Winterbournes. The family never met Hugh's wife, so they believe Connie to be Patricia, the mother of the Winterbournes' new heir. One new twist in the 1996 version is that the dead Hugh's brother, Bill, is his identical twin (both roles played by Brendan Fraser).

The story follows the same trajectory of the original film version, with the evil Steve trying to blackmail Connie/Patricia. Bill Winterbourne comes to suspect Patricia when she signs a check "Connie Doyle" instead of "Patricia Winterbourne." Shirley MacLaine as the matriarch is largely wasted in a role where she is required to be tough but gets most of the humorous lines. She is addicted to cigarettes and booze supplied to her by Paco, the outlandishly gay Cuban butler/chauffeur. Ricki Lake is completely clownish and unsympathetic as Patricia. *Mrs. Winterbourne* is the worst of the William Irish recyclings because it enters the province of fairy-tale romance. Its happy ending is marred by flaws in the script, the overplaying of Ricki Lake, the insipid behavior of Brendan Fraser, and the downright meanness of Loren Dean (he seems to be acting a nasty role in another film). How could Richard Benjamin make this film a heavy, predictable comedy instead of a gossamer romance?

FILMOGRAPHY

No Man of Her Own (1950), d. Mitchell Leisen, Paramount, 98 min., b&w, sc. Sally Benson and Catherine Turney, based on William Irish's story "They Called Me Patrice," ph. Daniel L. Fapp, m. Hugo Friedhofer, v. not available.

J'ai Epousé une Ombre (*I Married a Shadow*) (1982), d. Robin Davis, Sara Films, 110 min., KodaKolor, sc. Patrick Laurent, based on William Irish's story, ph. Bernard Zitzerman, m. Philippe Sarde, v. not available.

While You Were Sleeping (1995), d. Jon Turteltaub, Hollywood Pictures, 103 min., Technicolor, sc. Daniel G. Sullivan and Frederic LeBow, ph. Phedon Papamichael, m. Randy Edelman, v. Hollywood Pictures.

Mrs. Winterbourne (1996), d. Richard Benjamin, Tri-Star, 104 min., Technicolor, sc. Phog Sutton and Lisa Marie Radano, based on William Irish's story, ph. Alex Nepominaschy, m. Patrick Doyle, v. Tri-Star.

23

The Prowler (1951) and *Unlawful Entry* (1992)

THE PROWLER (1951)

Susan: You murdered my husband. You would have killed the doctor.
Webb: So what? I'm no good. But I'm no worse than anybody else.

The above is a classic noir conversation between Evelyn Keyes and Van Heflin in Joseph Losey's 1951 crime thriller *The Prowler*. One of director Losey's last American films before he fled to Great Britain to escape harassment by the House Un-American Activities Committee regarding Communist infiltration of the American motion picture industry, *The Prowler* is an impressive adult film noir about sordid people caught in sordid events. It is especially about a cop, Webb Garwood (Van Heflin), who murders the husband of lonely Susan Gilvray (Evelyn Keyes) in order to steal her money and her love. Susan is married to John Gilvray, a rich, middle-aged disc jockey (played by Sherry Hall). One evening, she calls the police because she thinks she has seen a prowler at the bathroom window of her home. Webb Garwood arrives on the scene and puts Susan at ease, recognizing her loneliness and her desirability. To obtain Susan and her money, Webb plots to "accidentally" shoot her husband, believing she will promptly marry him.

Webb cuts a hole in the screen door, to make the couple believe the prowler has returned. The Gilvrays call the police, and Webb arrives on the scene to investigate. He manages to get John Gilvray out of the house by making noise out back, shoots him, and makes it look accidental, even taking Gilvray's pistol and shooting himself with it. Susan believes Webb deliberately killed her husband, but the crime is deemed accidental. Then, through Gilvray's brother, William (Emerson Treacy), Webb gives Susan his life's savings—some $700—to ingratiate himself with her. The ruse works, and Webb marries Susan.

Within a few months, Susan becomes pregnant. Meanwhile, Webb, after resigning from the police force (and taking a Las Vegas vacation), buys a motel. To avoid unfavorable publicity and fearing Webb would still be charged with John Gilvray's murder (and Susan, as his accomplice), the couple flees to a ghost town in the desert. Here Susan learns that Webb's killing of her husband was not accidental, and, fearing he will kill the doctor who is brought to deliver the baby, Susan informs on Webb to the police. The doctor flees with the newborn infant in his car, and Webb realizes the game is over. After a wild car chase by the police, he is stopped by his former partner, Bud. Webb flees into the desert on foot and is killed by police bullets.

Van Heflin gives another of his unsavory performances as Webb Garwood (the first was in Curtis Bernhardt's *Possessed* [1947], where he played an engineer toying with a psychologically unstable Joan Crawford, and the second was in Fred Zinnemann's *Act of Violence* [1949] in which he was a U.S. POW who turned Nazi informer, hunted by Robert Ryan). At one point he says to Susan, "I was a cop. A lawyer takes bribes. I used a gun. But whatever I did, I did for you." Heflin makes the most of this unsympathetic role, but it is Evelyn Keyes who is the real surprise. She is the real victim—sensitive, morally straight, caught in a story of illicit love, premarital sex, intrigue, and murder. The plot is quite daring for 1951 because it involves an extramarital affair between a cop and a lonely married woman.

Evelyn Keyes gives many shadings to her characterization of a truly lonely woman who at last finds love and motherhood, but rebels against her lover's fatal attraction in the name of decency and sends him into the arms of justice. Evelyn Keyes is no stranger to film noir. She has given some fine performances in Columbia's *Johnny O'Clock* (1946) with Dick Powell, United Artists' *99 River Street* with John Payne (1953), and *The Killer That Stalked New York* (1950) with Charles Korvin. (The killer was smallpox.)

The Prowler is one of Joseph Losey's best films noirs of his early period: tense, moving, without unusual climactic scenes, but with unusual locales and casting against type of admirable actors playing unsavory rules in an offbeat but worthwhile story. Losey showed the underside of the American dream—his antihero is a seducer, power abuser, a failed champion basketball player (from Indiana) who became a California cop and hates his job. He has a basic contempt for others who fulfill the American dream—home, family, material wealth. You would think his love for

Susan Gilvray would have been enough, but, much like Phyllis Dietrick-son in *Double Indemnity* (1944), he is a predator with no real love for anyone but himself. His death is only a small footnote to a life zealously but uncourageously lived.

UNLAWFUL ENTRY (1992)

Not an exact remake of *The Prowler*, but definitely dealing with similar characters and situations in an unsavory story, Jonathan Kaplan's film is similar to Joseph Losey's earlier film noir. But this is a neo-noir with an expurgated story. There is no illicit sex, just the suggestion of it, but there is a "fatal attraction" between Officer Pete Davis (Ray Liotta) and Karen Carr (Madeleine Stowe). Michael Carr (Kurt Russell) is the jealous husband, the third side of the almost adulterous triangle.

In a beginning like Losey's *The Prowler*, a black intruder breaks into the luxurious home of Michael and Karen Carr, then escapes after hold-ing a knife to Karen's throat. Two policemen arrive on the scene soon after the incident. One of them, Pete Davis, is very solicitous, helping the couple install an expensive security system (to which he has the code). To thank him, the Carrs invite Pete to dinner, and in return, Pete invites Michael to go out on patrol with him. Pete and Michael come upon the prowler who assaulted Karen, and Pete offers Michael his po-lice baton to beat the man senseless. Michael refuses, and Pete takes out his aggressions on the cowering prowler, beating him unconscious. Mi-chael sees how disturbed and ruthless Pete really is, and wants nothing more to do with him. But Pete keeps inserting himself into their lives. (At one point he even enters their home while the couple is making love, on the pretext of answering an alarm.)

Karen sees Pete differently, as a man whose tendency toward violence is caused by his on-the-job proximity to criminal types. She invites him to her high school to give a lecture on police relations with the com-munity. At one point, however, Pete comes on sexually to Karen, who rebuffs him, even though she is admittedly attracted and erotically in-trigued by the sexual charge Pete exudes.

Trying desperately to seduce Karen, Pete has Michael jailed on a trumped-up charge. Michael is finally freed, and the rest of the film is a macho cat-and-mouse game between the two men. Will Michael return before Pete has his way with Karen? Who will be the victor in the final violent showdown? Of course, Michael succeeds in killing Pete. But it is Pete Davis, much like Webb Garwood, who shows his fascinating dark side to us and comes up the loser. Both cops are abusers of power and their jobs. Both want the American dream—a beautiful woman, marriage, a family, and material possessions. Both die as antiheros, loveless victims of their own predatory violence.

Ray Liotta as Pete Davis gives a wonderfully complex performance with a dangerous edge as the loose-cannon cop. Although you recognize he is a psycho from the get-go, watching his machinations unfold holds our sustained interest in his role. Madeleine Stowe is luminous, lovely, and vulnerable as the schoolteacher–wife. And Kurt Russell, whose nocturnal job is to design nightclubs, is the very model of the 1990s husband: strong but sensitive (and desperate). In fact, he has to throttle Ray Liotta twice, in one of those exasperating Hollywood "make-em-jump" endings (as in Adrian Lyne's 1987 *Fatal Attraction*). But the problem with *Unlawful Entry* is that it is completely devoid of plot twists, real sexual tension, and genuine perversity—qualities its noir predecessor, *The Prowler*, uniquely possessed.

One final note: although *Unlawful Entry* pretends to examine the dangerous stalker phenomenon, some film buffs have called its plot basically "*Fatal Attraction* in handcuffs." And it also refers pointedly to the Rodney King beating incident, which advocated the use of brutality and violence, and even the abuse of police power—what we now call "racial profiling."

Although *Unlawful Entry* lacks the noirish qualities of *The Prowler*, it has serious undertones as a social drama because we can see how average Americans can be caught defenseless by a person with serious psychological delusions. Roger Ebert makes a wonderful point in his *Chicago Tribune* review of *Unlawful Entry* (June 26, 1992). He sees Kurt Russell and Ray Liotta as "twins—one snug in a comfortable middle class home, the other wandering the night in rage and discontent." The Carrs' problem is essentially one of safety in the big city. In the noir world, no one is safe. In neo-noir, a high-tech alarm system may be the best protection against prowlers, but excessive violence between men seems to be the only way, in both noir and neo-noir worlds, to settle differences. Survival of the fittest! Susan Gilvray and the Carrs are the moral winners. Webb Garwood and Pete Davis, the cops, turn out to be the seducers and the real losers. So much for "prowling" as a recycled plot device. I do not believe there will be another remake, no matter what twists occur to screenwriters trying to recycle originally sleazy but affecting thematic material. Losey's film is the real beauty, with a wonderful social context. Kaplan's film was conceived "by the numbers," and, except for Ray Liotta's terrific performance, remains quite unmemorable.

FILMOGRAPHY

The Prowler (1951), d. Joseph Losey, Horizon-United Artists, 92 min., b&w, sc. Robert Thoeren, Hans Wilhelm, Hugo Butler, and Dalton Trumbo (uncredited), ph. Arthur C. Miller, m. Lyn Murray, v. not available.

Unlawful Entry (1992), d. Jonathan Kaplan, 20th Century Fox, 111 min., Deluxe Color, sc. Lewis Colick, John Katchmer, and George Putnam from their own story, ph. Jamie Anderson, m. James Horner, v. Fox.

24

The Narrow Margin (1952) and Narrow Margin (1990)

THE NARROW MARGIN (1952)

"A Fortune If They Seal Her Lips! . . . A Bullet If They Fail!" This is the tag line that appeared in most advertisements for this "B" film at the bottom half of double bills in American cinemas in 1952. But *The Narrow Margin* turned out to be much more than a "B" film—in fact, it is one of the favorite cult films of noir addicts and launched director Richard Fleischer's career into "A" movies. Starring Charles McGraw as Detective Walter Brown and Don Beddoe as Gus Forbes, the film begins in a sleazy part of Chicago. Brown and Forbes have orders to escort Mrs. Neall (played expertly by "B" film actress Marie Windsor) to Los Angeles to give testimony to a grand jury that may indict her gangster husband. They will travel on a crack train, keeping their witness safe until they deliver her to the Los Angeles District Attorney. Before the train trip begins, Forbes is murdered by three thugs in the employ of Mr. Neall, who is never seen throughout the film. Brown speeds Mrs. Neall away from the crime scene and sequesters her in a private compartment on the train. The events which take place on the train provide the real suspense in the film.

Charles McGraw plays a hard-boiled detective with ease, and genuinely hates the mobster's wife he is sworn to protect. His mysogynistic attitude shows even before he meets her, when he says to his partner, "What kind of a dish is she? The sixty-cent special—cheap, flashy, strictly poison under the gravy?" When Brown meets Mrs. Neall, one of their first exchanges is right on target: "You make me sick to my stomach," he says. She counters with "Yeah? Well, use your own sink!" It is barbs like these that make the dialogue in *The Narrow Margin* so spirited.

The three thugs board the train, trying to discover the identity of Mrs. Neall and which car she is riding in. To create a decoy, Brown sidles up to Ann Sinclair (played by Jacqueline White), who is traveling with her son. They even offer Brown a bribe, which he refuses. Because the thieves do not know what the real Mrs. Neall looks like, Brown knows he is putting Ann Sinclair's life in jeopardy. After several twists and turns in the plot, Marie Windsor is killed by the mob in a brutal shootout in her compartment. We then discover she is in reality a policewoman, complete with badge and gun hidden in her handbag; the real Mrs. Neall is Ann Sinclair. Brown saves the day by throttling all of the criminals, and as the train arrives in Los Angeles, there is a suggestion that the detective has now found himself a family as Mrs. Sinclair and her son walk with him out of the railroad station into bright sunlight, to testify in a clean, crime-free setting.

The film was made on a shoestring budget of $230,000. The train is the set for most of the film—there are exterior shots only at the very beginning and the conclusion. There is no music on the soundtrack except for the records Mrs. Neall (always dressed in a black negligee) plays on her phonograph. Brown spends the entire film trying to keep Mrs. Neall in her compartment and not reveal her true identity, as well as preventing her from being killed by the three thugs, who are after a payoff list that Mrs. Neall is supposedly carrying. George E. Diskant's excellent camera work, creating shadowy, confined spaces that give a wonderful sense of claustrophobia in the train scenes, is especially interesting. It was this particular style, which the French labeled "noir," that made a concise, modest, unpretentious, crime/suspense/thriller "B" movie into a minor classic that American audiences revere today. *The Narrow Margin* (1952) is the real article, with a killer hard-boiled screenplay, many plot twists, and great performances by RKO character actors—MacGraw, Windsor, White, et al. With its excellent train photography and its screenplay nominated for an Oscar, this film turned out to be one of RKO's most profitable "B" movies.

NARROW MARGIN (1990)

"It's the difference between living and dying" is the tag line for *Narrow Margin* (1990). This tepid remake of the 1952 film, in color and Panavision, cost some $21 million and has stars like Gene Hackman and Anne Archer—but does not measure up to the original. Hollywood never learns! You cannot recycle a noir into a neo-noir just by updating the material. The plot of the 1990 version is basically the same—a prosecutor is bringing a pregnant woman to testify after she witnesses a mob murder, but is trapped aboard a moving train with mobsters who are trying to do her in before she reaches her destination.

The film begins a bit differently. J. T. Walsh plays Michael Tarlow, a lawyer who seems like a real nice guy. He's dating the sophisticated divorcée Carol Hunnicut (Anne Archer). But before long, Carol sees Tarlow murdered in cold blood by Leo Watts (Harris Yulin), a notorious gangland client whom Tarlow apparently had been cheating. However, Watts does not know Carol saw the murder, so she flees to a mountain cabin in a remote part of Canada. However, she is tracked down by Caulfield (Gene Hackman as the prosecutor) who wants her testimony to put Leo Watts in prison. Unfortunately, Caulfield (Hackman played a character with the same name in Francis Ford Coppola's *The Conversation* [1974]; there he was a specialist in furtive surveillance) is tracked to Canada by Watts's group of mobsters, who try to kill both Caulfield and Carol from helicopters armed with machine guns. The two of them make their way through the woods as they duck sprays of bullets, and finally hitch a ride on a crack passenger train headed for Vancouver. Except for the brilliant scenery of the Canadian Rockies and a stunning chase literally on top of the train, the rest of the film is fairly predictable, even its conclusion. Anne Archer tries in vain to grapple with her woman-in-distress role. Gene Hackman is wonderful as the Deputy Prosecutor: incorruptible, earnest, totally straight, and heroic. But the real interest lies in the bad guys—James B. Sikking as Nelson, a hit man, is absolutely frightening in his icy approach to the role of murderer for the mob, and Harris Yulin gives a solid performance as Leo Watts, the sullen crime boss.

The major problems of the remake are in the writing, direction, and acting. You cannot take a seventy-minute original and expand it to ninety-seven minutes without losing the tautess and tension in the original screenplay. Peter Hyams's color version is bloated, with many more red herrings than Richard Fleischer's original lean screenplay. But McGraw and Windsor made their sparkling noir repartee come alive—here, one-liners suffice between Hackman and Archer. Even if there were no stunt doubles on top of that speeding train and Hackman and Archer were really up there grappling with the bad guys, Hackman is just too old (over sixty), and Archer too pregnant, to make their action scenes believable. You cannot substitute production values for a story that should be engaging the audience, full of starts and shocks. Unfortunately, Peter Hyams's remake fails on all counts. Spectacular stunt work and Canadian location photography cannot save *Narrow Margin* from a bleak outlook at the box office because it is just too cool and uninvolving, especially without even one suggestion of sex or romance in the entire film. Its 1952 predecessor seethed with sleaziness and sexuality—and jaded dialogue!

FILMOGRAPHY

The Narrow Margin (1952), d. Richard Fleischer, RKO, 70 min., b&w, sc. Earl Fenton, from a story by Martin Goldsmith and Jack Leonard, ph. George E. Diskant, m. Source, v. Nostalgia Merchant.

Narrow Margin (1990), d. Peter Hyams, Tri-Star, 97 min., Technicolor and Panavision, sc. Peter Hyams, inspired by the 1952 screenplay and original story, ph. Peter Hyams, m. Bruce Broughton, v. Tri-Star/Live Home Video.

25

The Blue Gardenia (1953) and
The Morning After (1986)

THE BLUE GARDENIA (1953)

Filmed in black-and-white by ace cinematographer Nicholas Musuraca (whose previous credits include Jacques Tourneur's *Out of the Past* [1947] for RKO); directed by the film noir expert Fritz Lang, the auteur of such great films noirs as *Woman in the Window* (1944) and *Scarlet Street* (1945); and written by Vera Caspary, author of both the novel and the screenplay of *Laura* (1944), one of the ultimate films noir of the mid-1940s, you would think *The Blue Gardenia* would be a superproduction, full of acerbic dialogue, noirish photography, and taut direction. Perhaps this is one of the films where noir style as we know it is losing its grasp both on the professionals who created it and on its audience.

The Blue Gardenia is rather a pedestrian film with some wonderful acting by Anne Baxter as Norah Larkin, a pretty telephone operator sharing an apartment with Sally Ellis (Jeff Donnell) and Crystal Carpenter (Ann Sothern). Expecting to marry her soldier fiancé, who is currently overseas, Norah receives a "Dear John" letter ending their engagement. Feeling depressed, she agrees to a date with Harry Prebble, a local bon vivant who wines and dines her. He even buys her a corsage with a blue gardenia in it.

Prebble, played by Raymond Burr, is a very talented artist who is also a serious womanizer. He gets Norah drunk, and she goes to his apartment with him. When she resists his amorous advances, she (believes) she bludgeons him with a poker from his fireplace set. Thinking

Prebble is dead, Norah flees, leaving behind the blue gardenia. The next morning, she cannot remember what happened the evening before. Of course there is a police investigation, and an affable reporter, Casey Mayo (played by the wonderful noir actor Richard Conte), looking for a story, hears Norah's confession, falls in love with her, and solves the mystery. Apparently, Norah did strike Prebble with the poker, but there was another woman in the room, an ex-lover who really did Harry Prebble in. Mayo obtains her confession, and we assume he and Norah will marry and live happily after, listening to Nat "King" Cole singing the title song of the film.

At first look, *Blue Gardenia* seems washed out, overly laden with daylight scenes whose key color is white. There are very few noir-style scenes except for the confession. But Fritz Lang's critical eye is there. His film is an indictment of the sensational journalism of the period, which brands Norah "the Blue Gardenia Murderer." She must elude the police's dragnets and their torturous questioning even as she asks herself whether she really committed the crime. She decides to trust Casey Mayo, who had transformed her into such a notorious figure; he discovers the real murderer and writes a particularly venomous story about Prebble and his murder. Through Casey, Fritz Lang condemns the kind of journalism that feeds the public's thirst for blood, exposure, and ruin. What could have been a severely critical film seems restricted by casting, production values, a fairly weak story, and a happy ending. Lang's first film of his "newspaper trio," which includes *While the City Sleeps* and *Beyond a Reasonable Doubt* (both 1956, for RKO), *The Blue Gardenia* is clearly the weakest of the three, perhaps out of fear of the House Un-American Activities Committee attacks on the motion picture industry and also because his later films were at RKO, where he was allowed to express the full range of his talent. Warner Bros. was eager to exorcise communism from the film industry, so its films of the period have a well-laundered look. Such is the case with *The Blue Gardenia*.

THE MORNING AFTER (1986)

Perhaps James Hicks, author of the screenplay for *The Morning After*, did not realize it, but this film is a remake of *Blue Gardenia*, written some thirty years after the original. Expressly, it is a new vehicle for Oscar-winning Jane Fonda (*Klute*, 1971), teaming her with the new hot lead Jeff Bridges. Fonda plays Alexandra Sternbergen, a former actress given to bouts of drinking and sex with men she picks up at parties. One morning, she awakens with a dead man in her bed (knife in his chest), wonders if she committed the crime, and goes to great efforts to remove all evidence that would incriminate her. She takes off for Los Angeles and promptly meets ex-cop Turner Kendall (Jeff Bridges), a divorced man who lives in a garage and is an avid reader who buys books by the pound. Naturally Alex and Turner fall in love, and Turner helps her to solve the crime. The problem is, no one really seems to care "who done it," even if it was . . . Isabel Hardy (played by Diane Salinger). It seems Joaquin Manero (Raul Julia as Fonda's ex-husband) is in love with Hardy and her society background—her father is a judge. So Joaquin planted the body of Bobby Korshak (Geoffrey Scott, seen only in a video at the beginning of the film) in his ex-wife's apartment to make her think she committed the murder. Apparently Korshak had nude photographs of Isabel with which he was trying to blackmail her father. Clearly, Isabel would have been ostracized from Los Angeles society if these photos were ever made public. Sounds a bit like *Murder, My Sweet* (1944) crossed with *The Big Sleep* (1946)—both Chandler films with similar story lines. Also, you never really get to know the victim of the crime (in contrast to *Gardenia*'s Harry Prebble). He's just a stud who deserved to be killed.

The real star of the film is director Sidney Lumet. *Morning After* is his first film shot outside of New York in years. He and his photographer have given Los Angeles a very jazzy, modern look, and his actors move in wide, colorful spaces against interesting backgrounds. It looks like he had every location shot repainted to emphasize the pastel colors of Los Angeles. But the thriller aspect of the screenplay is so skewed (apparently the director shot two different endings) that one simply gives up the mystery in favor of the characterizations. Also, Jane Fonda's role is sadly neglected. We really never get the story of her decline as an actress and her descent into alcoholism. Nor do we understand why she married hairdresser Joaquin Manero or the blossoming of her relationship with Turner Kendall. The psychological underpinnings are as nonexistent as the mystery. If *Morning After* is indeed a remake of *Blue Gardenia*, its political ambience is totally missing. Also, Fonda never looked better at the beginning or the end of the film. So much for a realistic portrayal of alcoholism and its effects, and a thriller-cum-murder mystery gone sour.

FILMOGRAPHY

The Blue Gardenia (1953), d. Fritz Lang, Warner Bros., 90 min., b&w., sc. Charles Hoffman, based on a story by Vera Caspary, ph. Nicholas Musuraca, m. Raoul Kraushaar, v. Kino International.

The Morning After (1986), d. Sidney Lumet, 20th Century Fox, 103 min., Deluxe Color, sc. James Hicks (James Cresson), ph. Andrzej Bartowiak, m. Paul Chihara, v. Fox.

26

Inferno (1953) and *Ordeal* (1973 [TV])

INFERNO (1953)

Shot in 3-D (Three Dimension) and Technicolor, this experimental effort from 20th Century Fox, directed by Roy Baker and starring Robert Ryan as millionaire Donald Carson, Rhonda Fleming as his scheming wife, Geraldine, and William Lundigan as her lover, Joseph Duncan, *Inferno* was Fox's only film made in this process. (The following year, Spyros Skouros and Darryl F. Zanuck brought out CinemaScope, which revolutionized the motion picture industry with its wide screen and projection and seven-channel stereophonic sound.) Nevertheless, *Inferno* is an excellent color noir, with a terrific story line that could have been filmed in any wide-screen process—and is one of the "A" films shot in 3-D that shows off the value of the process and spins a good tale without sacrificing its story line to special effects.

The film opens in the American Southwest, in an unnamed desert (probably the Mojave), where Donald Carson has broken his leg during a bout of drinking while on a prospecting trip for manganese with his wife, Geraldine, and Joseph Duncan. Apparently Duncan and Geraldine had become lovers two nights earlier, and plan to leave Carson in the desert to die. Saying they will go for help, they leave Carson with some food, water, and a gun, then drive to the opposite side of the desert, where they pretend to be stranded and are rescued by local police. They say Carson ran off, drunk, into the desert, and tire tracks and faked footprints seem to corroborate their story. The police send out search parties for Carson, and the lovers pray for rain to cover evidence of their deception.

The rest of the film deals with Carson's attempts to put his broken leg in a cast, climb down a cliff, gather food and water, and just survive with only one thought—revenge against his wife and her lover. In one of the best scenes, the starving Carson shoots a rabbit and scrambles downhill to retrieve it, only to see it carried off by a coyote. "It's my rabbit! Get your own," he shouts helplessly. He later kills a very young deer. We watch Carson trudge along, discover water by digging deep into an old sandy pool, and menaced by a rattlesnake. Finally Geraldine and Joe decide to drive out to the place where they left him, and Joe begins to track Carson. He almost shoots him when a prospector, Sam Elby (played by character actor Henry Hull) picks Carson up and saves his life. Geraldine has been watching all of this through binoculars. Thinking the jig is up, she turns the car around to flee, but manages to break the crankcase. When Joe returns, he knows she was going to leave him in the lurch, so he decides to trek toward Mexico, with Geraldine following. Joe finally takes pity on Geraldine and gives her his canteen when he spies the prospector's cabin.

Believing he can have Geraldine and Carson's money, too, Joe knocks out the prospector and begins shooting at Carson. The latter, after pretending to be dead, ambushes Joe with a 2 × 4, and the two fight to the death. The cabin catches fire after the men topple the potbelly stove, and Carson knocks Joe out with a blow to the head, then faints. The prospector awakens outside and, seeing Carson at the cabin door, pulls him out of the inferno. Joe regains consciousness on the floor in the middle of the cabin, seconds later, the flaming roof falls on him and burns him to death. The next morning, as Carson and the prospector are driving to town, they pick up Geraldine, who has the choice of going with them or waiting for the sheriff. She goes with them, and "The End" appears on the screen as Carson, a wry smile on his face, is on the way to hand his wife over to the law for plotting to kill him. Terrifically noir!

The film is a wonderful suspense yarn with sharp (although somewhat stereotypical) cutting between desert and hotel scenes. For example, as Cameron is searching for water in the desert, cut to Joe drinking a large gin and tonic at the hotel. Several cuts like these throughout the film hold our interest but are a bit simpleminded. Nevertheless, the direction is taut and Robert Ryan is totally believable as the spoiled millionaire who uses his inner resources to fight off the desert and take vengeance on his would-be killers. The climactic fight scene is beautifully staged, with burning beams hurtling at the audience and a metal coffee pot being thrust into your face (actually Cameron's face as he steps back to throttle Joe). Perhaps the metaphor of the title is lost or a bit trivialized because

Cameron survives the desert inferno, but Joe dies in a man-made fire he helped to create, a victim of his own lust and greed. One would have liked to see this film in the old 3-D process, but 90 minutes of those uncomfortable glasses was enough for me to prefer the flat, single-camera version.

Inferno is one of the best offerings filmed in the 3-D process that did not wholly depend upon its special effects to keep the audience watching. The triangle of Ryan, Fleming, and Lundigan keeps us engaged throughout the film. Rhonda Fleming was no stranger to film noir, having played the beautiful but cold Meta Carson in Jacques Tourneur's *Out of the Past* (1947), and Robert Ryan is a real noir icon, having done most of his best work at RKO in the late 1940s and early '50s; *Crossfire* (1947), *The Set-up* (1949), and *On Dangerous Ground* (1951). But William Lundigan was really cast against type as Fleming's lover. He projected the necessary malice and sexuality, but was not believable. He played only "good guy" roles after that.

ORDEAL (1973 [TV])

Directed by Lee H. Katzin, and written by Francis M. Cockrell (who also wrote the original story for *Inferno*) and Leon Tokatyan, this remake stars Arthur Hill as Richard Damian (the Robert Ryan role), Diana Muldaur as his wife, Kay (played originally by Rhonda Fleming), and James Stacey as Andy Folsom, her lover (originally played by William Lundigan). *Ordeal* is a close remake of the 1953 original. *TV Guide* described it thus: "An arrogant businessman injured in a fall, abandoned and left to die in a desert by his wife and her lover, fights desperately for survival in order to exact his revenge and discovers an inner strength that changes his life."

With an excellent performance by Arthur Hill (not as gritty as Robert Ryan's), a capable one by Diana Muldaur (she is not as spidery as Rhonda Fleming), and a respectable one by James Stacy as her lover (Stacy makes more sense in the role than Lundigan did), this is a capable remake for the small screen: nothing more, nothing less. It is interesting to note the name changes of the characters, especially the villain, Joseph Duncan (played by Lundigan) becoming Deputy Sheriff Joe Duncan in the remake. Except for a star turn by Macdonald Carey as Eliot Frost, Damian's business manager (originally played by Larry Keating as Emory) and a capable bit by Michael Ansara as the sheriff, *Ordeal* is just a total recycling—it even has the original producer, William Bloom. Obviously it was made for the money it would bring in, and not for its artistic values. Once again, the original was the better film.

FILMOGRAPHY

Inferno (1953), d. Roy Ward Baker, 20th Century Fox, 83 min., Technicolor and 3-D, sc. Francis M. Cockrell, ph. Lucien Ballard, m. Paul Sawtell, v. not available.

Ordeal (1973), d. Lee H. Katzin, 20th Century Fox Television, 73 min., color, sc. Leon Tokatyan and Francis M. Cockrell, based on Cockrell's original story, ph. William K. Jurgensen, m. Patrick Williams, v. not available.

27

I, The Jury (1953, 1982)

I, THE JURY (1953)

Vengeance, violence, and sex. These are the three key motives in most of the novels of Mickey Spillane, especially in his first one, *I, The Jury* (published in 1947). Spillane had created private detective Mike Hammer, a World War II veteran with a penchant for both honesty and brutality. Producer Victor Saville thought this novel, made in film noir style in black-and-white, and utilizing the new 3-D photography, would be a winner commercially. He introduced a very young unknown actor, Biff Elliot, as Hammer. Supported by Peggie Castle as the villainous psychiatrist, Dr. Charlotte Manning; Preston Foster as Captain Pat Chambers (one of his last roles); Margaret Sheridan as Velda, his sexy secretary; and a roster of character actors from 1940s noir films, such as Elisha Cook, Jr., as Bobo and John Qualen as Dr. Vickers, the film comes alive with veteran John Alton's specialist noir cinematography (remember Anthony Mann's *Raw Deal* [1948]?).

Backed by a stunning jazz score by Franz Waxman, *I, The Jury* tells Mike Hammer's story of murder, deception, and punishment. Hammer acts as executioner, a role he also plays in subsequent novels and film versions written by Spillane. The film opens at Christmas, and we hear "Hark, the Herald Angels Sing!" on the sound track. The atmosphere is broken as a gunman brutally shoots Jack Williams (played by Robert Swanger), a helpless amputee. Williams crawls toward his own gun and retrieves it, but the murderer finishes him off. When Hammer gets news of Williams's death, he vows to seek vengeance. Apparently Williams saved Hammer's life during World War II, and Hammer never forgets a friend, least of all his savior. Warned by Captain Chambers against using illegal means to find the killer or take vengeance, Hammer checks out everyone who saw Jack at a Christmas party he gave before he was killed. Among the guests were Jack's former fianceé, Myrna (Frances Osborne), a heroin addict; a beautiful blonde psychiatrist, Dr. Charlotte Manning (Peggie Castle); loved-starved twins, Mary and Esther Bellamy (played by Tani Guthrie and Dran Seitz); and George Kalecki (Alan Reed), a shady art collector and fight promoter.

As Hammer moves through this sleazy world of junkies, nymphomaniacs, and drug dealers, he comes across several murders. He discovers Kalecki is a drug dealer and kills him, believing him to be Williams's murderer. During the hunt for clues, he falls in love with Charlotte Manning, and they plan to marry. However, Hammer discovers Manning was responsible for a few murders herself, and wanted to wrest control of the drug ring from Kalecki. He confronts her with the facts. Beginning to disrobe so she can use her sexual charms on him, Charlotte grabs Hammer in an embrace. As they move into a kiss, a gunshot is heard. Charlotte looks into Hammer's eyes and asks, "How could you do it?" He answers, "It was easy." Charlotte slumps over, mortally wounded in the stomach, as Hammer says in a voice-over, "Then she went down like a soft rope, and there was only one thing to do—order a basket." Hammer knew Charlotte was reaching for a hidden gun to do him in, so he acted first.

The opening and closing scenes are stunningly executed and brilliantly brutal. Williams's murder to the strains of a Christmas carol and Charlotte's death at Hammer's hand are both chilling for early 1950s cinema. Apparently World War II (especially Hammer's service in the South Pacific) is responsible for turning a cautious detective into a brutal man living by a violent code of honor that calls for seeking vengeance even if it means killing someone he loves. When he kills Charlotte, he fulfills the promise of the novel's (and film's) title—*I, The Jury*—and spends the rest of his days justifying his act to the police and his friends. Unlike other detectives before him—Philip Marlowe and the like—Hammer does not turn the murderers over to the police, but executes them himself. He is more than just brutal; Hammer has lost his belief in the judicial system and his own innocence. His newfound hardness and brutality will serve him well in other fictional and cinematic situations. Ralph Meeker, in Robert Aldrich's production of Spillane's novel *Kiss Me Deadly* (1955), played the quintessential Hammer, incorporating all of Hammer's good and bad qualities.

Despite all the good production values and performances, the center of *I, The Jury* is weak and generally mediocre. Biff Elliot's performance is poor, and the raw sex that defines most of the characters in the novel is absent from this film version (with the exception of Peggie Castle's attempt to seduce Hammer at the conclusion). Because of strict censorship codes, the film lacks the intense sadism and sexuality that are in the novel. One could blame the producer for his casting of sophomoric Biff Elliot as the toughest detective of the early 1950s and the writer/ director Harry Essex, whose work is conventional and completely off the mark. Except for the opening and closing scenes, the film comes off as pretty dull, with Mike Hammer as a pretty dull "continental op." Perhaps the only qualities of the novel that come through are Hammer's dislike of homosexuals, his machismo, and his misogyny. The suggested sadism appears in the opening murder scene and the closing execution by Hammer—but Spillane novels are loaded with sadism and violence and sexuality—the charge needed to resurrect this film from the oblivion it now deserves.

I, THE JURY (1982)

The 1982 remake of I, The Jury is certainly as hard as nails. What was missing from the 1953 version has been restored, perhaps as a result of the relaxation of censorship codes and the new rating system. I, The Jury was released in 1982 with an "R" rating because of the scenes of nudity and violence, and in Great Britain it received an "X" rating, making it forbidden to anyone under twenty-one years of age. Armand Assante incarnates the macho Mike Hammer as best as he can. He is dark, muscular, and hairy, and acts with an ironic (and sometimes sadistic) edge.

The story of the 1982 version has been updated from the original novel and screenplay. Dr. Bennett is still a psychiatrist, but now is in charge of a sex-therapy clinic; a new character, Romero (played by Barry Snider), a former CIA operative, has been added, Captain Pat Chambers (played by Paul Sorvino) is there, keeping Hammer from acting outside of the law; another new character, Charles Kendricks (played by Judson Scott), is a knife-wielding psychopath, interested in killing redheads; Velda, Hammer's secretary (played by Laurene Landon), returns and does her sexy star turn; and, finally, the twin nymphomaniacs (played by Lee and Lynette Harris) are resurrected from the earlier film. The story differs slightly in that Hammer's friend Jack Williams is a one-armed cop killed on duty, and Hammer seeks vengeance for his murder. (Williams was a buddy of Hammer's in Vietnam who saved his life.)

By the time we get to the conclusion—after many red herrings, a couple of car chases in the Bear Mountain area, the storming of the ex-CIA agent's mountain retreat, and a multitude of corpses—I, The Jury lives up to the promise of its title. In a spectacularly filmed nude scene, Dr. Manning (played by gorgeous Barbara Carrera) uses her sexuality to seduce, then kill, Hammer, but he beats her to the draw. In fact, if you watch each concluding scene of the "execution" separately, the 1982 version is an almost exact re-creation of the 1953 film that I remember. The novel is still more spectacular, because you can use your imagination regarding Charlotte's demise.

But for all of the good production values—script, direction of the updated version, Assante and Carrera working up a sexual storm, the nudity, the frankness, the immorality, the sadism, the violence, the jaunty music score of Bill Conti—the 1982 *I, The Jury* fails to convince as a hardboiled detective movie in the tradition of film noir. You might put it in the "new noir" category, but it lacks the violent and urgent atmosphere of the Spillane novel and even of the 1953 film version. If you do not retain the "noirish atmosphere" even in color, the film just shines on the surface; but there is no foreboding, no shadows that breathe atmosphere into each scene. This *I, The Jury* has the graphic violence, nudity, and sexuality, but it is a disappointment, even though it is interesting because of its parodic, almost cartoonlike portrayal of detective fiction.

FILMOGRAPHY

I, The Jury (1953), d. Harry Essex, United Artists, 87 min., b&w, 3-D, sc. Harry Essex, from the Mickey Spillane novel, ph. John Alton, m. Franz Waxman, v. not available.

I, The Jury (1982), d. Richard T. Heffron, 20th Century Fox, 111 min., color, CinemaScope, sc. Larry Cohen, based on the Mickey Spillane novel, ph. Andrew Laszlo, m. Bill Conti, v. Fox.

28

Rear Window (1954, 1998 [TV])

REAR WINDOW (1954)

"The most unusual and intimate journey into human emotions ever filmed" is the tag line for the Paramount's 1962 rerelease (in VistaVision) of Alfred Hitchcock's celebrated 1954 thriller *Rear Window* (from an original story by noir mystery writer Cornell Woolrich). Although critics do not usually include this film in the noir category, its theme—voyeurism—and the darkness of the minds of its protagonists, despite the clarity of its photography and color in VistaVision, qualify it as a "noir classic." *Rear Window* has a very simple story: L. B. Jeffries (played by veteran Hitchcock actor James Stewart), a top action photographer, is confined to his Greenwich Village apartment because of an accident that has left him in a leg cast.

To amuse himself between visits from his nurse, Stella (played by Thelma Ritter), Jeffries gazes out the rear window at the opposite buildings. Thanks to a high-powered lens attached to his very expensive camera, he takes pictures of his neighbors, who almost never have the shades down, day or evening. He even gives them names: Miss Torso, a ballet dancer (Georgine Darcy) who is always practicing her art to the strains of Leonard Bernstein's *On the Town*; a songwriter (Ross Bagdasarian) who is composing the song "Lisa" (Franz Waxman's song for Grace Kelly, the film's female star) and always giving parties; "Miss Lonelyhearts" (Judith Evelyn), who sets an extra place at her candlelit dinner table, then dines alone; and the Thorwalds (Raymond Burr and Irene

Winston), a mysterious couple who seem to argue at all hours—Lars Thorwald ends up storming out of their apartment, then returns several hours later, when his wife is asleep. There are other minor characters within Jeffries's field of vision, such as a newlywed couple who always leave the shades down and an older couple always on their fire escape, trying to beat the heat of a New York summer. But Jeffries seems most interested in the Thorwalds.

Feeling trapped, physically powerless, and virtually impotent, Jeffries receives regular visits from his nurse and his girlfriend, Lisa Fremont (played airily by Grace Kelly dressed in Edith Head's haute couture). Lisa is a breath of fresh air and is very sophisticated. Although Jeffries has not asked her to marry him, she brings an overnight case, complete with negligee and slippers, and will probably do the asking herself! One evening Jeffries believes he sees or dreams Lars Thorwald killing his wife and then dismembering her body, packing it in suitcases, and carrying out some luggage each day. He calls in a friend, Lieutenant Thomas J. Doyle (played by noir icon Wendell Corey), who at first does not believe Jeffries, but then asks him to get hard evidence.

The film is divided into three neat sections. The first presents the entire set of characters within Jeffries's purview. The second lets us observe the "murder" that occurs while Jeffries is dozing or fully asleep. The last is the most thrilling—immobile Jeffries and mobile Lisa team up with the police lieutenant to find clues to Mrs. Thorwald's death. In the Thorwalds' apartment, Lisa discovers Mrs. Thorwald's handbag, wedding ring inside—no woman would leave her wedding ring behind if she went on vacation (as Lars Thorwald claims). As Lisa holds up the bag and ring, Thorwald returns and catches her, but Lisa twists out of his grasp and flees back to Jeffries, dropping the handbag but slipping the ring on her finger. Thorwald (played by beefy noir actor Raymond Burr) realizes Lisa was looking across the courtyard, and stares directly into Jeffries's telephoto lens. Frightened, Jeffries calls for police aid, but to no avail. In the early morning hours Thorwald invades Jeffries's apartment, in search of his wife's wedding ring, knowing Jeffries is alone. Struggling with Jeffries, whose only defense is setting off flash bulbs from his camera, Thorwald finally grabs him—and, as the police arrive, Jeffries is hanging outside his apartment window. He finally lets go and falls to the ground. In the next scene, Lisa Freemont is giving solace and food to Jeffries, who is now in a *double* leg cast up to his waist. The camera wanders out the window into the courtyard, to the strains of Franz Waxman's song "Lisa." The End.

Apart from Hitchcock's experiment, shooting all his scenes from Jeffries's point of view (with the exception of the "sleeping" sequence and the shot of Jeffries hanging out the window after almost being pushed to his death by Thorwald), *Rear Window* has some real noir chills—

mostly in the darkness, as our photographer voyeuristically spies on his neighbors with his telephoto lens from his darkened apartment. And when Thorwald invades his apartment, Jeffries further darkens the room, then uses periodic flashes of extreme light to blind his assailant. Although the film may be a bit slow-moving, even chatty, we discover the foibles of the protagonists—Jeffries's cantankerous unpleasantness and his "uncomfortable" situation; Lisa's perfect charm, wit, and sophistication, and her annoyance at Jeffries' male chauvinist attitudes. (She still wants him to propose!) Even Mrs. Thorwald's nagging voice (we never really hear what she says) and Thorwald's resistant body language to her voice are indicative of frustration and murder in the air. If it were not for the excellent star performances and unusually tight direction by Alfred Hitchcock, with its restricted space premise, this film could have been a real disaster. As it turned out, it was certainly a winner. In fact, it underwent restoration in 1998 (adding Dolby sound and heightened color), the same year as the television remake starring Christopher Reeve.

REAR WINDOW (1998 [TV])

A *Variety* review by Ray Richmond (May 26, 2000) said, "ABC's remake of the 1954 Hitchcock classic is so different in style and focus from its predecessor that it's scarcely accurate to call it a redo.... Comparisons are futile." Starring actor Christopher Reeve (left a quadriplegic after a horseback riding accident in 1995) as Jason Kemp, this television version differs in many ways from the original. It begins with an auto accident that leaves Jason paralyzed and cuts to a hospital room full of the amazing technology that will help to get him out of bed. When he returns to his small New York apartment, all of the gadgetry and high-tech video cameras installed for his safety (and voyeuristic entertainment) are unleashed upon his neighbors—a musician, a computer programmer, a gay couple, the blonde wife of a sculptor—who always leave their shades open. Because Jason is paralyzed from the neck down, he is an extremely vulnerable target for Julian Thorpe (played by Ritchie Coster), a sculptor who has throttled his wife, Ilene (played by Allison Mackie), and dismembered her. The murder was seen by Jason. Thus this updated version keeps the Cornell Woolrich noir subtext intact but concentrates more on the difficulties of a quadriplegic.

When Thorpe discovers Jason's voyeurism, he hunts Jason down in the film's climactic scene. He confronts Jason, mocking both his condition and his vulnerability. There is a palpable sense of danger. Jason survives the ordeal, and the suspense is in keeping with the original. But the film is also testimony to a quadriplegic's efforts to cope with his limited world. So where investigation of a crime was the determining motivation of the actors in the 1954 film, here it is the failure of technology (respirator pop-offs causing Reeve to choke because of a lack of oxygen) that becomes part of the everyday struggle for survival. Also, the love interest (Daryl Hannah) is less sexual and more caring. The film leaves you with the conclusion that even a quadriplegic can find love, despite all of his infirmities.

Although some of the Hitchcockian touches come through in the updated version, and Reeve's performance is quite riveting because of his physical limitations, most viewers felt the 1998 *Rear Window* should have been called *Side Window* because the film is an untense spin on the original. Jason's additional motivations—doing "normal" things like getting out of bed, walking, eating successfully, lying down comfortably—bring down the suspenseful aspect of the film. And Daryl Hannah is no Grace Kelly! The film also has an additional but necessary character—Ruben Santiago-Hudson as Antonio, Jason's West Indian male nurse. Their chit-chat is amicable but barely moves the plot along. One hopes Christopher Reeve will find other projects to accommodate his artistic potential without necessarily calling attention to his physical condition. But, as a first effort, his acting is quite remarkable. And, as television films go, this one is better than average.

FILMOGRAPHY

Rear Window (1954), d. Alfred Hitchcock, Paramount, 112 min., Technicolor, VistaVision, sc. John Michael Hayes, from a story by Cornell Woolrich, ph. Robert Burks, m. Franz Waxman, v. Universal.

Rear Window (1998), d. Jeff Bleckner, Hallmark Entertainment/ABC, 90 min., color, sc. Eric Overmeyer and Larry Gross, based on a short story by Cornell Woolrich, ph. Ken Kelsch, m. David Shire, v. ABC.

29

Les Diaboliques (1955), Reflections of Murder (1974 [TV]), House of Secrets (1993 [TV]), and Diabolique (1996)

LES DIABOLIQUES (1955)

"The Great Suspense Film That Shocked The World . . . And Became a Classic" is the tag line for the very, very infamous French film noir *Les Diaboliques* (1955), directed by Henri-Georges Clouzot, that was the inspiration for no less than three remakes of much lesser quality. Clouzot was a top director of French film noir during the 1940s and '50s, and is most renowned internationally for *La Salaire de la Peur (The Wages of Fear)* 1952, which made international stars of Yves Montand and Charles Vanel. Vanel is a star of *Les Diaboliques*, playing Inspector Ficher, who investigates the disappearance of Michel Delasalle (unctuously played by Paul Meurisse) from a surburban boys' school. Simone Signoret stars as Nicole Horner, a teacher who was a former mistress of Delasalle, and Vera Clouzot (the director's wife) is Christina Delasalle, wife of the headmaster. Christina, the owner of the school, is constantly humiliated by her brutish husband, especially when he takes up with women who work at the school. Nicole and Christina realize they have more in common than Michel's bad treatment of them—they detest him so much that they plot his disappearance and murder. Their bonding also suggests a possible lesbian relationship, which is never depicted on screen.

The women decide to go off with Michel on a weekend away from the school. Perhaps Michel is thinking of a ménage à trois with his wife and ex-mistress. They arrive at Nicole's home in the country and promptly get

Michel drunk on wine laced with sedatives. They fill the bathtub and drown Michel, who offers little resistance. Nicole and Christina load his body, wrapped in a shower curtain, into a large wicker basket and return to the school. Late in the evening they dump Michel's body into the dirty swimming pool outside of the school, and believe they have accomplished their mission.

But the women come to suspect Michel may be alive when the suit he was "drowned" in mysteriously turns up at the school, delivered by a local dry cleaner. Then students say they have seen the headmaster walking around the school in the late evening. Christina orders the pool to be cleaned and drained. Voilà, the body of Michel is gone. She calls the police to search for Michel and Inspector Fichet arrives on the scene, suspecting, but not being able to prove, wrongdoing by Nicole and Christina.

One very dark evening, Christina awakens, believing she hears Michel in the school. With a candelabra in her hand, she investigates. She returns to her apartment and hears water running in the bathroom. Opening the door, she spies Michel underwater. The "corpse" begins to rise and, screaming, Christina is literally scared to death. (She has a weak heart.) Nicole appears in the bathroom as Michel removes some plastic eye coverings which made him look "dead," and embraces him. The lovers have accomplished their aim—the death of Christina and Michel's inheritance of the school and her wealth. Of course, Inspector Fichet tumbles to the plot and the lovers are arrested. Watching the last minutes of the film is the real hook for noir addicts. In fact, when the film was advertised in France and America, Clouzot urged that every ad campaign include the statements "Do not reveal the ending to anyone!" and "No one will be seated the last 30 minutes of the film!"

The 1955 *Les Diaboliques* still is as thrilling as when it was first released internationally, chiefly because the original screenplay, based on the novel by Pierre Boileau and Thomas Narcejac, is quite wonderful. (When Alfred Hitchcock saw the film, he asked the authors to write something for him. It turned out to be *Vertigo* [1958].) The performances are all superb: Simone Signoret as Nicole, a blowsy blonde always wearing dark sun glasses to hide the black eyes given to her by Michel; Paul Meurisse as Michel, a particularly odious, self-interested, truly evil, and wretched human being (especially when he serves rotten fish to the students) and has no concern for the boys' education or physical well-being; Vera Clouzot as Christina, in the performance of her life, looking fragile yet strong, but succumbing to the insidious plot of the lovers. The film was restored and rereleased in the United States in 1996, with the same power to shock. It is one of the best suspense noir thrillers ever made!

REFLECTIONS OF MURDER (1974 [TV])

Based upon the original script of *Les Diaboliques*, *Reflections of Murder* (1974) is a slick made-for-television color film with Tuesday Weld in the role of Nicole (now called Vicky), Joan Hackett in the role of Christina (now Claire Elliot) and Sam Waterston in an unusually unsavory role as Michael Elliot (Michel in the original). *Reflections* is set in Maine at the all-boys Island School. The initial triangle is there—Michael hates children, the school, and his wife, and wants the latter to sell the school to a group of builders of vacation condominiums for $3 million; Claire hates Michael because of his affair with Vicky and wants to keep the school she inherited from her grandfather, and the island, intact—no condo development; Vicky hates Michael's brutalization of her and Claire, and wants the latter to help her kill Michael so the two can run the school their way. There is the same hinted-at lesbian relationship—unrequited on Claire's part. There is basically the same set of events in the first half of the film: the women drag a huge wicker basket to Vicky's aunt's house, and Claire phones Michael, asking for a divorce and promising $1.5 million for each of them. Michael drinks the scotch laden with sedatives. The women force him underwater in a bathtub, using a small statue to weigh him down, and then place his body, wrapped in a shower curtain, in the wicker basket.

Vicky and Claire spend the evening off the island, return the following evening, and ease Michael's body out of the basket and into the leaf-covered swimming pool. Expecting his body to pop up in a few days, the women wait. When it fails to appear, Vicky finds a reason to drain the pool—she tosses her keys to a student poolside, but purposely misses him, and the keys sink to the pool's bottom. A student strips and dives in after the keys, but comes up with the headmaster's lighter. Claire has the pool drained, and when she sees that the pool is empty, she faints.

One cold and dark evening, Chip (Lance Kerwin) visits Claire. She confesses to the boy that she murdered Michael, but of course Chip does not believe her. The television film is filled with the same clues as the original: Michael's hunting jacket, the one he is drowned in, is delivered to the school by the dry cleaners. When a school photograph is taken, Michael is shown staring out of one of the upper windows of the school building. On the same evening as her confession to Chip, Claire believes Michael is alive and in the house. She finds a cigarillo burning in an ashtray and hears movement in the house. She flees to her bedroom and, thinking she hears running water, she enters the bathroom. The bathtub is filled with water, and Michael's body rises from the water. Claire is so startled that she has a heart attack and sinks to the floor. Michael pops false plastic eyes from his eye sockets and checks Claire's pulse. He lowers her eyelids and goes into their bedroom. Vicky then enters and kisses Michael full on the mouth. Their plan has succeeded—with Claire out of the way, Michael can inherit her estate and sell everything off to the developers.

There are some slight twists from the original film. Michael reappears on the last day of school dressed in mourning clothes, and so does Vicky. There is no detective investigating the case, so you feel they get away with murder. Only Chip knows the truth, and he tearfully leaves the campus, driven away by his parents. But there is one little boy who loves to hunt quail with his slingshot. When Vicky asks where he obtained the weapon, which had been taken away by the headmaster, he says the headmistress gave it back to him the other day. Vicky remonstrates with the boy, saying Claire has been dead for at least two weeks. Then we hear the strains of Bach played on Claire's piano. Vicky and Michael look at each other. Can Claire be alive?

Although *Reflections of Murder* is very well scripted, directed, and acted, it still does not measure up to the original *Les Diaboliques* of 1955. Perhaps color and the Maine setting tend to soften the shocks of the original black-and-white film. And the French original was far more sensual, sexual, and brutal, given the subtleties of filming in the French language. Nevertheless, this made-for-telvision movie boasts excellent production values and a cast that makes it an interesting and extremely watchable remake.

HOUSE OF SECRETS (1993 [TV])

Crediting the writing team of Boileau and Narcejac for the screenplay, along with Andrew Laskos, this second remake of *Les Diaboliques* is a credible version with less-known actors than the 1974 TV version. Melissa Gilbert stars as Marion Ravinel, Bruce Boxleitner as Dr. Frank Ravinel, and Kate Vernon as Laura Morrell. Although the geographical setting has been changed, *House of Secrets* is the same old story of *Les Diaboliques*. Marion Ravinel is trapped in an abusive marriage. She forms a plan with her husband's former lover to kill him. However, the outcome is more than she planned on—she begins to believe that her husband has come back from the grave to take revenge. This is especially true after the two women have carried out an elaborate murder scheme, yet several people remark that they have seen Dr. Ravinel alive. Is he really dead?

House of Secrets is a very loose remake of *Les Diaboliques*. The differences are minor but numerous. The setting is now New Orleans, and Marion runs a sanatorium in an antebellum mansion. Her doctor husband, Frank, has several sexual dalliances with a recreational therapist, Laura Morrell, who feels abused and suggests to Marion that they drown Frank to end their mutual problem.

This television version hints at a blackmail scheme and removes any sexual relationship between the female conspirators. Because of its setting, there is a Mardi Gras parade and elements of voodoo. The story is told in flashback from the point of view of a family retainer, Evangeline (played by Cicely Tyson), who, like Cajun (Joseph Chrest), a nosy neighbor, is a new invention of the scriptwriters. And Michael Boatman, playing a dapper police sergeant investigating the disappearance of Frank Ravinel, is an improvement over Charles Vanel in the original film. The writers and director follow the original script to a similar conclusion, adding some supernatural elements via Evangeline, but the conclusion remains and is a satisfying shocker. As television movies go, this reworking of the original plot falls farthest from the mark, but it is still within the realm of fairly good entertainment (even though it lacks the nastiness and perversity of the original film).

DIABOLIQUE (1996)

"Two women. One man. The combination can be murder"—this is the tagline for *Diabolique* (1996), the third version of *Les Diaboliques*, filmed in color and sporting an "R" rating for violence, sex, and language. It stars Sharon Stone as Nicole (the Simone Signoret role), Isabelle Adjani as Mia (the role Vera Clouzot created as Christina), and Chazz Palminteri as Guy (the role of Michel played by Paul Meurisse in the original). The original story has been kept intact (almost), but the conclusion is different.

The setting is St. Anselm's School for Boys, outside of Pittsburgh. Guy Baran is the abusive headmaster who beats Nicole, his former mistress, and his wife, Mia. The women plot his death and drown him in a bathtub. And, as in the original, the body disappears from the swimming pool and the women wonder if somebody is going to blackmail them. The film has been updated to include a disrobing by Mia, so audiences can view her beauty, and there is a definite lesbian attraction between Mia and Nicole (it was suggested in the original and hinted at in *Reflections of Murder*).

Unlike the last two previous remakes, this one includes a detective (Kathy Bates as Shirley Vogel, a male-bashing investigator who wanders into the case of the disappearing husband). As in the original, Guy's body, after disappearing from the pool, turns up in a bathtub inside the school and comes to life. Mia suffers a heart attack and it is revealed Nicole and Guy have been plotting her demise for her money—but Mia survives. At first she does not want to murder Guy again, but she soon changes her mind, and the two women collaborate in Guy's "genuine" murder. Shirley Vogel, who has figured it all out, helps Mia and Nicole cover up their crime. She is also in at the conclusion—remarkably different from the original—when Guy has a rake embedded in his skull during a struggle with Nicole. Shirley gives her blessing to this murder instead of carting the culprits off to jail. Nicole's character has been changed. She has undergone a sort of reformation—throughout the film she has been playing a "bad" woman, but in reality she is Mia's savior.

This last remake is so poor, so pedestrian. The acting is quite dreadful, especially Sharon Stone, who tries to look tough, a cigarette always dangling from her mouth. The direction and screenplay are also quite poor, and the three leading players seem like cartoons of the originals. When you trash the original ending of the 1955 film, creating something quite unoriginal, throwing in an updated "slasher" element just for the sake of being "original," the film loses its integrity as a remake and even on its own dramatic terms.

Diabolique (1996) follows the original for almost two-thirds of its length, uses the original conclusion, then repudiates and ultimately trashes it in favor of an ending that can be considered sheer travesty. The ending, suffering from the coarseness that is common in the films of George Romero, takes place at the swimming pool, a scene of clichéd horror and mindless gore. The strength of the original *Les Diaboliques* depended on the constant element of surprise. The director and his protagonists wanted to fool the audience. Jeremiah Chechik is not even duplicitous. When the sexual tension between the women is eliminated in favor of "female solidarity," a very nineties concept, the relationship between the former nun (Adjani) and the tough math teacher (Stone) loses its credibility. Bisexuality, not homosexuality, is operating here. One hopes, after this version, that we never see another remake unless it has a really expert director, screenwriters, and actors. Only Alfred Hitchcock could have done this remake and given it the respect it really deserves. Legend has it he asked the French authors of *Celle qui n'etait plus* (The Woman Who Was Dead) to remake *Les Diaboliques,* but they came up with *D'entre les Morts* (From Among the Dead), which later became the 1958 color noir classic, *Vertigo.* If only Hitchcock had been encouraged to make his version of *Les Diaboliques,* we would have had a courageous film true to the original, not this fearful, hackneyed film which undercut Clouzot's brilliance.

FILMOGRAPHY

Les Diaboliques (1955), d. Henri-Georges Clouzot, Filmsonor, 114 min. (some older U.S. prints run 107 min.), b&w, sc. Clouzot, Frédéric Grendel, Jerome Geronimi, and René Masson, based on the Pierre Boileau-Thomas Narcejac novel *Celle qui n'etait plus,* ph. Armand Thirard, m. Georges Van Parys, v. Cinémathèque Française.

Reflections of Murder (1974), d. John Badham, 20th Century Fox Television, 100 min., Color by Deluxe, sc. Carole Sobieski, from the Boileau-Narcejac novel, ph. Mario Tosi, m. Billy Goldenberg, v. not available.

House of Secrets (1993), d. Mimi Leder, Multimedia Productions, 100 min., color, sc. Andrew Laskos, from the Boileau-Narcejac novel, ph. Thomas Del Ruth, m. Anthony Marinelli, v. not available.

Diabolique (1996), d. Jeremiah S. Chechik, Morgan Creek, 107 min., Technicolor, sc. Don Roos, from the 1955 screenplay of the Clouzot film, based on the Boileau-Narcejac novel, ph. Peter James, m. Randy Edelman, v. ABC/Morgan Creek.

30

The Desperate Hours (1955) and Desperate Hours (1990)

THE DESPERATE HOURS (1955)

The 1950s novel by Joseph Hayes has been recycled as a stage vehicle for Paul Newman and Karl Malden (1955), then a film noir (1955) starring Humphrey Bogart and Fredric March (who replaced Spencer Tracey when the latter and Bogart argued about top billing), and finally remade as a neo-noir starring Mickey Rourke and Anthony Hopkins in 1990. *The Desperate Hours* was a hot property in the 1950s because its theme was a home invasion by escaped criminals, and how the family succeeded in maintaining home and hearth during the ordeal, which ended in the criminals' capture by the police.

Humphrey Bogart reprises his breakout role of Duke Mantee (*The Petrified Forest* [1936]), now as Glenn Griffin, a career criminal protective of his younger brother, Hal (Dewey Martin) and in league with the brutish Sam Kobish (Robert Middleton). After the trio breaks out of an Indianapolis jail, they search for a suburban home in which to roost while waiting for Glenn's sweetheart (unseen in this film) to send cash for the group's escape from the country. They spy the Hilliard home and, thinking no one is home, they knock at the door. Eleanor Hilliard (Martha Scott) lets the criminals in. Once they are inside, the trio wait for the rest of the family to return—her son, Ralphie (Richard Eyer); her daughter, Cindy (Mary Murphy); and her husband, Dan (Fredric March).

The rest of the film consists of a cat-and-mouse game between the Hilliards and the criminals. After their initial shock and bewilderment at the invasion of their home and of their privacy wear off, the Hilliards unite, using their wisdom and courage (qualities they didn't know they possessed) to thwart the criminals and hand them over to the police.

There are several subplots: (1) Ralphie believes his father is cowardly when Glenn Griffin threatens him with his gun (Dan is just using common sense and his cool-minded courage to defeat the criminals); (2) Hal Griffin falls in love with Cindy and regrets his life of crime (later, Cindy is spirited out of the house by her boyfriend, Chuck [Gig Young], who wants to prove he really loves her while risking his personal safety— and the safety of the entire family); (3) when the police realize the Hilliard family is being held captive, they encircle the area and the sheriff (sensibly played by Arthur Kennedy) clearly wants to capture the convicts—without endangering the hostages.

All of these are resolved favorably: (1) Dan proves his courage to Ralphie by throwing Glenn Griffin out of his house, into the arms of the police and a barrage of bullets; (2) earlier, Hal tries to escape from his brother's influence and dies under the wheels of a truck during a police chase; (3) Cindy is reunited with her family and realizes Chuck's love for her is the real article; and (4) Eleanor and Dan, initially frightened by the invasion of their home, summon up the necessary courage, substance, and strength to beat the criminals at their own game, and forge a stronger marital bond.

The Desperate Hours was Paramount's first black-and-white film in VistaVision. Although called a film noir by most critics essentially because of its themes, there is a kind of whitish grayness of film stock and intense clarity of vision of the VistaVision process which works against the popular "shadowy" atmosphere of a true film noir. Many scenes are too brightly lit, and Bogart's reprise of his Duke Mantee character is a bit surreal, because he has aged noticeably (probably due to his fight with cancer, which took his life in 1957). And the novelty of a bad-talking mobster with a gun as a convention of crime cinema had obviously worn thin by 1955. Only Fredric March, Arthur Kennedy, and Martha Scott, actors in their professional prime, are the major-league winners here. March reprises his Academy Award-winning role as father (*The Best Years of Our Lives* [1946] in an Oscar nomination performance). Arthur Kennedy and Martha Scott, two admirable character actors, are winning in their respective roles as the sheriff and as the mother of the beleaguered family—especially Scott, who at times is near hysteria, but generally is in control and courageous. Bogart comes off tough, snarling, capable of murder to ensure his own preservation even if he has to kill an entire family. If one had to describe this 1955 film in a word, "classy" would be it, essentially because of William Wyler's good taste and professionalism in choosing solid actors, filming a tautly written script, and directing it with gusto. He brings out the best performances from all of the principal players through probing close-ups that reveal the gestures of seem people caught in a vortex of crime and personal stress.

Wyler and film composer Gail Kubik should be complimented on their sparse use of music to heighten the reality of the action on screen. Unlike the scoring of Max Steiner—each note reflects each action of a leading character, even echoing their thoughts—here are a composer and a director who agree: less is more. The film is based upon a real incident, and to this end, Wyler wanted to make a film in keeping with the realities of the experience.

DESPERATE HOURS (1990)

This remake of the 1955 film, starring Mickey Rourke in the Bogart role (now Michael Bosworth, a sadistic criminal with dandyesque qualities, who leads the invasion of the Cornell household and the terrorizing of an innocent family) is similar to the original but too far over the top to be taken seriously as based on real events.

In this version, directed by Michael Cimino (well known for his excessively overbudgeted *Heaven's Gate* [1980]), what was once a household invasion by career criminals has become an overwrought melodrama with listless, unbelievable dialogue delivered by a wonderful cast badly directed. Bosworth escapes from a local jail when his lawyer, Nancy Beyers (Kelly Lynch) smuggles a gun into the jail. After breaking out, he brutalizes her (she should have known better than to get sexually involved with a career criminal), then meets up with his brother, Wally (Elias Koteas), and his boyhood friend, Albert (hulking David Morse in the Kobish role). The trio heads for the suburbs of Salt Lake City, looking for a place to wait for a cash shipment to be delivered that will fund the criminals' flight into Mexico.

Anthony Hopkins plays Tim Cornell, a man who is estranged from his wife, Nora (played by Mimi Rogers), and their two children May and Zack (Shawnee Smith and Danny Gerard). Whereas the 1950s version dealt with one family's fear and their wisdom in controlling the results of a household invasion, this neo-noir shows Hopkins as a surburban Rambo type who ultimately uses his formidable intelligence and skills to halt the terrorizing of his family. One of the biggest problems the film has is that the Cornells are not believable as husband and wife. Mimi Rogers and Anthony Hopkins are totally miscast, but even more unbelievable is their reconciliation when Rogers has to trust her philandering husband in this situation. It brings her back to her senses and inspires admiration for her husband's courage.

This color version of *Desperate Hours* winds down to the same predictable conclusion but makes a mess of the law's attitude toward protecting the family from the criminals. Also miscast is Lindsay Crouse as an FBI agent who provokes arguments with the local police and decides upon a "containment" scheme when she finds out Bosworth is in the house—a scheme barely understandable to the police and probably beyond the audience. It's is too bad the movie is all style and flash and that the actors fail to involve the audience in the action because of poor direction from an even poorer script. Some of the scenes in the house between the hostages and the criminals involve shouting matches, screaming, threats and promises, and struggles that are so overacted they are hardly believable. One wonders how the actors could keep straight faces while struggling through this ridiculous dialogue.

But the worst sin of all is casting Mickey Rourke in a screen role that belonged to Humphrey Bogart. (John Garfield played a similar role, taking Shelley Winters, Wallace Ford, and Selena Royle hostages in John Berry's 1951 film noir, *He Ran All the Way*; it was Garfield's last great film, and it would be equally disturbing if Rourke was cast in the remake.) When Bosworth demands that the family feed him, and he comes downstairs to the dining room in a borrowed tuxedo, looking like a dandy, you have to laugh at the director's vision. The assumption that a mad-dog killer could indulge in this kind of behavior is ultimately insulting to the audience, to Bogart's (and Garfield's) memory, and to the novelist, Joseph Hayes, although he supposedly had a hand in fashioning the updated screenplay. Once again, updating classics or trying to fit classical roles to different actors or to the persona of the actor in the remake just does not work—another nail in the coffin for the derivative and unentertaining 1990 *Desperate Hours*. If you want to see a truly professional original, try the 1955 version (now available on video from Paramount).

One last note. According to *Variety*, there was an ABC 120-minute television version of *The Desperate Hours*, directed by Ted Kotcheff and written by Clive Exton (based on the Joseph Hayes novel). It starred Teresa Wright and Arthur Hill as the Hilliards, Yvette Mimieux as Cindy, and George Segal as Glenn Griffin, and was shown in December 1967. Its credits were listed in the October 20, 1990, edition of *Variety*, and it was reviewed on December 20, 1967. Apparently Clive Exton's teleplay "destroyed the character evolution and turned the novel into a two-bit thriller." The Arthur Hill character was turned into a sadist, stomping and kicking Glenn Griffin until he fled the house, to be killed in a hail of police bullets. The TV version was considered "mediocre." No actor or member of the production team lists *The Desperate Hours* television show among their credits.

FILMOGRAPHY

The Desperate Hours (1955), d. William Wyler, Paramount, 112 min, b&w, Vista-Vision, sc. Joseph Hayes, based on his novel, ph. Lee Garmes, m. Gail Kubik, v. Paramount.

Desperate Hours (1990), d. Michael Cimino, MGM/UA, 105 min., Technicolor, sc. Lawrence Konner, Mark Rosenthal, and Joseph Hayes, based on Hayes's novel, ph. Doug Milsome, m. David Mansfield, v. MGM/UA.

31

Night of the Hunter (1955, 1991 [TV])

NIGHT OF THE HUNTER (1955)

"The wedding night, the anticipation, the kiss, the knife, BUT ABOVE ALL . . . THE SUSPENSE!" This is the tag line of the poster art for the first film directed by actor Charles Laughton, which shows Robert Mitchum (as Rev. Harry Powell) holding the lovely Shelley Winters (as Willa Harper) in his arms on their wedding night. On his right fingers are tattooed the word "Love"—on his left fingers, the hand in which he holds a switchblade (unknown to his new bride), "Hate." Based on the David Grubb novel and with a screenplay supposedly written by James Agee (and by Laughton, without credit), *Night of the Hunter* is a true masterpiece of film noir, compelling as a thriller, imaginative, dreamlike, expressionistic, idiosyncratic, chilling in its black-and-white photography (by ace cameraman Stanley Cortez) and also a tribute to D. W. Griffith, whose haunting pictorial images inspired Laughton's film noir style. Laughton called the film "a nightmarish Mother Goose tale" that went against the grain of contemporary Hollywood productions in Cinema-Scope and color. It was a critical and commercial failure at the time of its release, but it has been elevated to cult status by audiences responding to the performances of Robert Mitchum and Lillian Gish (D. W. Griffith's leading player), as well as to the technical wizardry of Stanley Cortez, especially his ability to create painterly images that stick in the mind long after the film ends. (One of the most thrilling images is of Shelley Winters underwater, tied behind the steering wheel of a car, her throat slit, her eyes closed, her hair floating to the rhythms of the currents of a river.)

The plot of the film is relatively simple. Ben Harper (Peter Graves) has stolen over $10,000 from a bank and is caught by the police. (He is later convicted and sentenced to hang.) Before being taken to jail and eventually executed for killing two people during the robbery, he hides the cash in the rag doll of his daughter, Pearl (played by Sally Jane Bruce), and makes his son, John (Billy Chapin), promise never to reveal the whereabouts of the money, especially to their mother, Willa (beautifully played by Shelley Winters).

While in prison, Ben Harper meets up with the Rev. Harry Powell and reveals that he has hidden the bank loot, but never discloses the exact location. When Harry is released from prison, he returns to Ben's hometown, marries Willa (but refuses to have sexual relations with her), and eventually kills her because she has discovered his interrogation of her children concerning the whereabouts of the money. The children flee downriver and wind up on the property of Rachel Cooper (played by Lillian Gish), who protects all of God's children. In fact, Gish practically inhabits Whistler's portrait of his mother—but this time she's holding a shotgun!

Powell searches for the children, finds them, and tries to intimidate Rachel into returning them to his care, but she will not do so? (In an earlier scene, Powell had gotten the children alone and Pearl had told him where the money was hidden, but the children then escaped their father's old skiff and began the trip downriver.) When Powell reaches for the doll, Rachel Cooper wounds him with her rifle, and he retreats to her barn. The police drag him out and arrest him for the murder of Willa. When little John sees Powell arrested, he grabs Pearl's doll and starts to hit Harry with it. The hidden money flies out. "Here, here, take it back. I don't want it. It's too much!" cries John, and collapses. Rachel gathers him into her arms and takes him into the house.

The film ends in a tranquil Christmas setting. Looking at her brood, Rachel declares, "They abide and they endure!"

There are many wonderful moments in *Night of the Hunter*, some of them symbolic of the thoughts of the protagonists. For example, at the beginning of the film, when Powell stares at a stripper, his libido is aroused and a pocketknife opens threateningly—a phallic symbol as he thinks what he might do to this sinful woman. He says, "There are too many of them . . . can't kill the world."

When Powell arrives at the Harper farm, John is telling a story to Pearl about a king who was taken away by bad men. Just then, a huge shadow of the preacher's head covers the wall of the children's bedroom, symbolizing his evil character. The shadow is actually the result of the preacher's being next to a huge street lamp in front of the Harper house as he eerily sings, "Leaning, leaning, leaning on the everlasting arms."

The bedroom where Harry and Willa consummate their marriage looks much like the nave of a church. In a scene lit from below, Harry rises up over Willa, his arms outstretched, rising like a crucifix over her, ready to penetrate her body, but then refrains from any sexual activity with the very sexually repressed and jittery Willa—possibly Shelley Winters's best performance since George Stevens's 1951 film, *A Place in the Sun*. Harry reduces Willa to a shivering mess praying for cleanliness, and redirects her repressed sexual energies into becoming a religious fanatic who condemns her sinful past with wayward, thieving Ben Cooper. Similar to this scene is Willa's murder by Harry. In their bedroom, which looks like the corner of an A-frame church, Willa lies on her back, arms crossed over her chest, and confesses she heard Harry questioning Pearl and John about the money. Harry opens his switchblade and ritualistically murders Willa. Later he claims she ran away that night, driving a Model T Ford.

Another nightmarish, hypnotically fascinating scene is Willa underwater, reeds bending in the current, her long, blonde hair tangled among the reeds, her throat slashed. Uncle Birdie (James Gleason) discovers the body while fishing but is afraid to tell anyone about it because the townspeople would think he killed Willa after having his way sexually with her, then drove her car into the river. Birdie finally confides the discovery to his wife, who eventually informs the law about the murder.

Another beautifully photographed scene is the children's escape aboard their father's boat. Powell comes after them full tilt, knife held high, lunging after the skiff, which glides beyond his reach. He lets out a blood-curdling scream, venting his rage as the boat floats downstream on moonlit water, under a sky full of glittering stars. The scene is observed by night creatures—croaking frogs, hooting owls, bleating sheep, slow-moving turtles—all symbolic of the children's innocence and vulnerability. The black-hearted preacher follows the children on a white horse.

When Lillian Gish speaks the lines "I'm a strong tree with branches for many birds. I'm good for something in this world, and I know it, too," you know that the preacher is in for a bumpy ride trying to retrieve those children. The film does a lyrical about-face here—the noir frissons are lost in favor of brightly daylit scenes of the children in their newfound happiness. This is short-lived, for Harry arrives, and, lurking outside the farmhouse, sings "Leaning, leaning . . ." We hear an owl attack a rabbit offscreen as Rachel shoots Powell—the Devil incarnate (Harry), a false prophet, battling with a true, strong Christian woman (Rachel). Mitchum's performance as the homicidal evangelist with a mellifluous Southern accent is one of the most thrilling in the world of film noir.

(His role as a career criminal in J. Lee Thompson's 1962 film *Cape Fear* is his second most chilling performance in film noir.) It is the only time Robert Mitchum ever acted outside of himself—that is, there is little of Mitchum in the persona of Harry Powell. (It was reported that Mitchum helped Charles Laughton direct the children, a task for which Laughton had little patience. Also, Laughton goes uncredited for a large portion of the screenplay because James Agee was continuously inebriated, or so the story goes.)

Much can be said about the film's style, which is as much noirish as it is allegorical. It is also loaded with great themes—sexual repression, fanatical religious observance and its repercussions, innocence versus promiscuity. But it is the unusual direction by Charles Laughton and the beautiful photographic images of Stanley Cortez (he was Orson Welles's chief cinematographer for the 1942 RKO production *The Magnificent Ambersons*), wonderfully low-lit scenes shot from low-angled camera setups, that make the film the eccentric, idiosyncratic, and marvelous work it is. Laughton also obtained the best performances possible from Lillian Gish, Robert Mitchum, Shelley Winters, and the children. *Night of the Hunter* is a marvelous noirish visual fantasy with a timelessness and a haunting quality that still thrill more than forty years after it was filmed. No director has ever made anything quite like it.

The music score by Walter Scharf has an oratorio quality that completely captures the visual lyricism onscreen as well as the rural America of the 1930s. Its folk themes are exactly right (no "Red River Valley" here!), supporting Stanley Cortez's allegorical cinematic approach and Charles Laughton's direction. *Night of the Hunter* deserves its cult status—it was not appreciated by the public in 1955, but one hopes it will find a new video audience in the new millennium.

NIGHT OF THE HUNTER (1991 [TV])

The 1991 TV version of *Night of the Hunter* is based on the 1955 film, is directed by David Greene. It stars Richard Chamberlain (of television's *The Thorn Birds* and *Dr. Kildare* fame) as Harry Powell, Diana Scarwid as Willa, Ray McKinnon as Ben, Amy Bebout and Reid Binion as Pearl and John, Burgess Meredith as Uncle Birdy (certainly a casting coup for this great 1940s star), and Mary Nell Santacrose as Willa's employer.

Chamberlain certainly looks like an aging and hardened ex-convict who hears a dying prisoner's confession about a robbery and decides do go in search of the money. The telefilm is now set in the rural South of the 1950s, updated from the Depression era setting of the American Midwest of the original. The plot follows the 1955 original up to a point—complete with tattoos on Chamberlain's fingers—"Love" on the right hand and "Hate" on the left. In search of the money, Harry Powell goes to the small town where Willa lives with her children, and even marries her—the ultimate con—to get the money. But the teleplay short-circuits the original story, having Chamberlain caught for the murder of Willa early on. Eliminated are the Rachel Cooper character (Lillian Gish in the original), the escape of the children downriver, and the original ending. The main drawback of the teleplay is its opting for a quick ending, leaving lots of strings untied for the characters, especially the children.

There are only two aspects of the 1991 television film that are worthwhile: (1) the indictment of small-town Southern society, as the poor and uneducated blindly toil and turn to religion for relief from their hard lives, and (2) Chamberlain's spine-chilling performance. His tight slits of eyes, peering out from under a large-brimmed black hat, are enough to scare the daylights out of you. Chamberlain seems to be wearing ashen makeup and a slight gray mustache and beard, which add to the ghostliness of his face.

Several details from the original have been changed. In the 1991 version, Willa's husband, Ben, robs a local store and is shot while escaping. He hides the money in a drainpipe, telling only his son its whereabouts. When Harry is released from jail, he shows up at Ben's funeral and tells the family Ben wanted to make amends by returning the money. (In 1955, Harry wanted to use it to further God's work—and his own sick brand of evangelism). But no one will tell where the money is, and the rest of the film becomes a cat-and-mouse chase between John and Harry, putting the entire family in mortal danger. Bad guy Harry reveals his true nature and is undone in the last scene.

An anonymous viewer of the telefilm felt "this TV movie should be erased from existence"; he/she called it a "TV movie monstrosity," and Chamberlain's performance, "ridiculous." Television producers should think many times before remaking even a failed film classic. With the 1955 *Night of the Hunter* they came up against an incomparable, formidable, enduring motion picture made with great art and sophistication, qualities lacking in this poor remake. The 1955 original looks even better today in comparison with its color television remake, despite the latter's top production values. Although Richard Chamberlain's performance is strong, it can in no way compare to the frissons and shadings of Robert Mitchum. Watch the artful original at a rerun theater or on a videocassette. It is truly a wonderful experience.

FILMOGRAPHY

Night of the Hunter (1955), d. Charles Laughton, United Artists, 93 min., b&w, sc. James Agee, based on the novel by David Grubb, ph. Stanley Cortez, m. Walter Scharf, v. MGM/UA.

Night of the Hunter (1991), d. David Greene, ABC-TV, 100 min., color, sc. Edmond Stevens, based on David Grubb's novel, ph. Ron Orieux, m. Peter Manning Robinson, v. not available.

32

A Kiss Before Dying (1956, 1991)

A KISS BEFORE DYING (1956)

Released by United Artists and directed by German actor Gerd Oswald, *A Kiss Before Dying* (1955), a Robert L. Jacks production in Color by Deluxe and CinemaScope, is really a 20th Century Fox film with Fox casting and production values. Why it was released through United Artists is a mystery. Nevertheless, it is a trenchant tale of greed, duplicity, and murder based on the Ira Levin novel. Teen idol Robert Wagner (fresh from his triumph in Fox's CinemaScope epic *Prince Valiant* [1954]) is cast against type in a role as a duplicitous murderer, Bud Cort. At an unnamed California college campus, we discover Dorothy Kingship (Joanne Woodward in an early role) is pregnant by fellow student Bud Cort. Bud would like to marry Dory, but if her father, the mining magnate Leo Kingship (played by George Macready), knew she was pregnant, he would disown her. Bud has his eyes on the Kingship mining fortune more than on Dorothy—so when he goes to town and spots the Municipal Building, where couples can be married quickly, he thinks this would be the ideal way to solve his problem.

After she is duped into writing a "suicide" note (Bud claims he needs a translation in English from a Spanish text), Dory buys something old, something new, and something blue in preparation for their wedding the next day. The couple leaves campus early the following morning, but finds that the office where they will be married opens at noon. Bud suggests they go up to the roof and wait. He positions Dory in front of a low ledge, then asks her to kiss him. Dory steps forward and Bud pushes her hard, with both hands, over the ledge to her death.

Dorothy's older sister, Ellen (played by Virgina Leith in uninspired fashion), had talked to her the day before, and Dory was happy. Suspecting foul play, Ellen has the investigation into her sister's "accidental fall" reopened while she is being courted by a new boyfriend—Bud Cort. Bud is after the family fortune, any way he can get it! He removes anyone who knew about his relationship with Dory. He kills a fellow student who works in a local hamburger joint and whom Ellen suspects might be the murderer, making his death look like a suicide because of his love for Dory. Ellen is not convinced, and finally discovers it was Bud who courted her sister, made her pregnant, and probably killed her. Ellen is ready to go to the police when Bud tries to throw her off a cliff—and dies in the attempt.

There are some wonderful performances in the film. Robert Wagner as Bud is particularly good because of his youthful looks that hide a truly black heart. His desire to move into a higher level of society does him in. Mary Astor, playing Bud's mother, is excellent as the manipulated parent, unaware of her son's misdeeds. George Macready as Leo Kingship is just right as the wealthy father who is completely out of contact with his daughters. Jeffrey Hunter, as a detective/university lecturer named Gordon Grant, figures out the mystery behind Dory's death and saves Ellen from Bud. However, he is not convincing in the role and does not shine in this film, as he did in the Fox *Seven Angry Men* and *Seven Cities of Gold* (both 1955). In one scene in *A Kiss Before Dying*, Hunter and Wagner are dressed almost exactly alike, leading one to believe Wagner's dark side has an opposite—the morally straight Hunter as his doppelgänger.

The film succeeds as a color noir thriller and is a cleverly executed murder mystery. It even has a title song (sung by Dolores Hawkins)— this was usual for films in this period, such as *Peyton Place, A Certain Smile, Love Is a Many-Splendored Thing, Three Coins in the Fountain*. However, the title song from *Kiss* . . . never found real popularity. But Lionel Newman's jazzy film score supports the visuals admirably—especially using 1950s source music in the malt shop and other scenes in the film. Why it took some forty years to put the original film version on videotape is a mystery to this writer. It certainly is more deserving than some of the newer films without style or class. *A Kiss Before Dying* has both, and deserves to be seen by new audiences.

A KISS BEFORE DYING (1991)

"Loving him was easy. Trusting him was deadly." This is the tag line from the advertising for the 1991 remake of the original 1955 film, now

starring Matt Dillon in the Bud Cort role (now called Jonathan Corliss),
Sean Young (playing both Dorothy and Ellen, now surnamed Carlsson),
Max van Sydow as her (their) father, Thor Carlsson, and Diane Ladd as
Mrs. Corliss.

Writer James Dearden (of *Fatal Attraction* fame), now director, has
opened out Ira Levin's 1950s crime novel and updated it brilliantly. We
begin with Jonathan Corliss as a child, living in a small Pennsylvania
town, watching the Carlsson Mining Company railroad cars roll by. Even
as a child, he wants to enter the Carlssons' world of money and luxury.
The film then cuts to Jonathan as a college student at the University of
Pennsylvania. His mother has worked hard to send him to an Ivy League
University. Jonathan uses his charm and sexuality to seduce young and
demure Dorothy Carlsson. As in the earlier film version, when he finds
out Dory is pregnant, he throws her over a ledge to her death and covers
his tracks.

Moving to New York and changing his name to Jay Faraday, Jonathan
pursues Dorothy's twin sister, Ellen (a clever casting move by the director), who does not believe Dorothy committed suicide. Ellen is a social
worker, and Jonathan shows up at the center where she works. He is an
enormous success at the center, helping Ellen to organize activities and
solve problems. Ellen falls in love with him, and they soon marry. But
she is still fixated on resolving the death of her sister. There are several
close calls when Jonathan is almost recognized as Dory's former beau.
When Ellen begins to investigate Dory's death, she discovers the murderer was Jonathan Corliss—her own husband, under another name.

In the film's final scenes, Ellen goes to Jonathan's childhood home,
meets his mother, and enters his bedroom, where she discovers some of
Dory's personal effects. Jonathan has followed her, and attempts to kill
her because he is now Mr. Carlsson's right-hand man—and does not
want to lose his chance to obtain the Carlsson fortune for himself. In an
electrifying final scene, as Ellen realizes her husband has murdered her
own sister, she flees along the railroad tracks. Jonathan pursues her but
is killed by an oncoming train like the ones he used to watch as a child.

This updated remake is certainly twisty and much more exciting than
the original. In fact, after *Drugstore Cowboy* (1989), Matt Dillon has the
second best role of his film career in *A Kiss Before Dying*. Dillon is a
natural for the camera. His handsome good looks—those dark eyes and
knitted eyebrows, that innocent, angelic face—work wonderfully to hide
the maladjusted man that he really is. And Dillon brings off the performance sharply and believably. Max van Sydow gives an equally capable
performance as the millionaire "Copper King"—but one wonders how
such a clever businessman could be duped so easily into making his son-
in-law second in command. Finally, there is Sean Young in the dual role
of Dorothy/Ellen. Although I like her as an actress, she seems more

credible as Ellen than as Dorothy. However, she doesn't seem to be convinced that Jonathan is dangerous and capable of killing her, which mars the movie's conclusion. Diane Ladd as Mrs. Corliss is exceptionally good, providing the right touch of psychological complexity and lack of comprehension of her son's problems as Mary Astor, who inhabited the role some thirty years before.

The *New York Times* critic Vincent Canby, in his April 26, 1991, review of the film, said: "*A Kiss Before Dying* is not *Crime and Punishment*. It is pop moviemaking to be enjoyed without guilt." So do not look for logic or credibility. However, I did enjoy one interesting touch at the very beginning of the film—Jonathan as a young boy, played by James Bonfanti. Bonfanti has Dillon's good looks in his child's face. But as the film comes full circle, you glimpse young Jonathan's obsessional behavior, a poor young kid who just wants to get ahead and get away from his mother. James Dearden's remake is certainly worth watching as a neonoir and, with minor reservations, it adds fuel to the argument for remaking films noirs, especially those about psychopathic killers.

FILMOGRAPHY

A KISS BEFORE DYING (1955), d. Gerd Oswald, United Artists, 94 min., Color by Deluxe, CinemaScope, sc. Lawrence Roman and Ira Levin, from the Levin's novel, ph. Lucien Ballard, m. Lionel Newman, v. MGM/UA.

A KISS BEFORE DYING (1991), d. James Dearden, Universal, 95 min., Technicolor, CinemaScope, sc. James Dearden, from Ira Levin's novel *A Kiss Before Dying*, ph. Mike Southon, m. Howard Shore, v. Universal/MCA.

33

Ransom (1956, 1996)

RANSOM (1956)

Filmed in glorious black-and-white, *Ransom* (1956) stars Glenn Ford, one of Hollywood's most dependable and durable actors, as David G. Stannard, inventor and president of a portable vacuum company. Donna Reed plays his good-natured wife, Edith, and Bobby Clark is their son, Andy. They live in a spotless Midwestern suburb in luxurious surroundings with a maid (Juanita Moore) and a butler (outstandingly played by character actor Juano Hernandez). The camera pans into this genteel environment, which is upset when Andy does not come home from school at the usual hour and the Stannards receive a telephone call from the boy's abductors, demanding $500,000 in cash.

After notifying the local police and FBI, Stannard initially agrees to hand over the ransom in exchange for the safe return of his son. Chief Jim Backett (Robert Keith) goes along with the scheme and everyone is ready to obey the demands of the kidnappers. Then, suddenly, Stannard announces that there is no guarantee the boy will be returned after he hands over the money. He goes on local television, saying the kidnappers will never receive a red cent from him, and if the boy is not returned unharmed, he will use the money to hunt the criminals down until they are caught.

Ransom is based on a live television program called *Fearful Decision*, presented by the Theatre Guild in 1954 and written by the screenwriters of the 1956 film. It was fifty-seven-minute TV drama starring Ralph Bellamay as the father, Sam Levene as the reporter, and Meg Mundy as the mother. It received excellent reviews and was directed by Alex Segal. Now it has been expanded to 109 minutes and contains a lot of padding. For example, the newspaper reporter, Charlie Telfer (Leslie Nielsen), wants to publish the story of the abduction and is continually fighting with the father, who fears the story might endanger his son's life. Edith Stannard has a nervous breakdown that puts her into bed and at odds with her husband, who had to make the "tough decison" not to pay the ransom. Stannard even gets some flack from his brother (and partner), Al, who would rather pay the ransom and not put Andy's life at risk. In a wonderful scene, after many hours have gone by, Stannard breaks down tearfully, believing his son to be dead; he collapses into the arms of his butler, Jesse, who tells him he made the right decision. And as MGM would have it, little Andy is set free and walks into the house, where he is embraced by his anxious and loving family.

In this 1956 film, the kidnapping takes place offscreen. We never see the kidnappers—only parts of their bodies while they are making telephone calls. Glenn Ford portrays Stannard as an executive of a prosperous manufacturing company who must constantly make hard decisions— and his most fearful one, not paying the ransom, he feels will give his son a better chance for survival. The audience identifies with Stannard as a father and champions his decision, hoping it was the right one! The camera hardly ever leaves the Stannard home, which is the center of the action. There is no violence, no gunfire, no gore—only the drama of a family caught in the vortex of a kidnapping, aided by police and awaiting the outcome.

Although the film is believable on an intellectual and emotional level, many law enforcement officers would disagree with Stannard's decision not to pay the ransom. Ford and Reed give agonizing, realistic performances that avoid the pitfalls of theatricality. Reed could be seen as saccharine, but accurately represents a 1950s woman who has been protected all of her life and cannot endure stress. Only Charlie Telfer seems out of control, with too much power over police. His intrusiveness almost results in the child's death. Perhaps the writers are criticizing the power of the media. I am certain that *Ransom* was more successful as television drama, because it was tautly written. The 1956 screenplay suffers from its expansion to almost double the original television running time. Its noirish aspects are diminished because most of its scenes are daylit. Perhaps *Ransom* falls into the "police procedural" category of melodrama, and its happy ending may forecast the ending of an era of black-and-white, cynical, noir-styled films.

RANSOM (1996)

"Someone is going to pay." This is the tag line for the second version of *Ransom* made exactly forty years after the original, in a twistier version in color and CinemaScope, shot on Manhattan locations. The story line is based on the 1956 version but completely updated. We have come a long way from the 1950s—into the age of computers, cell phones, and video cameras. And surveillance techniques have improved dramatically. This new version of *Ransom* takes into account all of these technological advances, and more. Directed by Ron Howard, it stars Mel Gibson as Tom Mullen, an extraordinary wealthy airline owner, a self-made man who is ruthless in his business dealings, especially with unions. Rene Russo plays his wife, Kate, and Brawley Nolte, his son Sean, who is kidnapped on the family's outing to a science fair in Central Park.

In this version, we become familiar with the kidnappers. They are Detective Jimmy Shaker (Gary Sinise), a renegade cop who wants to make a $2 million score with the aid of his girlfriend, Maris Conner (Lili Taylor), a caterer's assistant who worked for the Mullens and knows the family's schedule; two grungy brothers, Clark and Cubbie Barnes (Liev Schrieber and Donnie Wahlberg) and Miles Roberts (Evan Handler), a computer whiz/drifter. The film runs for 117 minutes (a video release, the director's cut, ran much longer—139 minutes).

The 1996 *Ransom* is a true neo-noir, an action thriller with noirish overtones. When Sean is kidnapped, we follow the kidnappers to an undisclosed location, where the boy is held captive in a small, windowless room, handcuffed, and blindfolded. From this location, the group makes its ransom demand. Mullen calls in the FBI, and FBI agent Hawkins (Delroy Lindo) advises him to pay the money. Mullen agrees, but as time goes by, he starts to believe his son is dead. He reverses his decision to pay, stunning his wife and fellow executives of Endeavor Airlines, and gives a convincing live television speech about how the $2 million will be used for the capture of the kidnappers if the boy is not returned unharmed. Everything depends on Mullen's hunch that his child is doomed anyway.

There is an interesting subplot about Mullen bribing a union official and not taking the fall for that crime. Shaker knows about the bribe and realizes Gibson is buying his airline's way out of trouble. Shaker expects Mullen to pay the $2 million ransom. There are also many false stars and red herrings in the film—for example, when Gibson agrees to drive to pay the ransom, an FBI helicopter interrupts the drop and Sean is put into jeopardy. In another case, the Barnes brothers are trapped by police and killed in yet another attempt by Gibson to pay the ransom. Shaker even kills his girlfriend, acting the role of good cop when the police are tipped to the location of the kidnappers and the boy. Sean is finally freed, and Shaker sets himself up to receive the $2 million now offered as a reward by Tom Mullen. He comes to the Mullen's town house, and Sean has trouble sleeping after the visit. He hears Shaker's voice from his bedroom and recognizes it as belonging to one of the kidnappers. Shaker goes to the bank, where he will wait for the $2 million electronic transfer; Tom Mullen, after hearing his son's story, sets out after him. The two of them battle to the death outside the bank, and Shaker is shot dead by police.

Perhaps the ending is a conventional one, but the film is loaded with shudders throughout. Violence, blood and gore, nudity, and profanity contribute to its "R" rating. The film's pace is fast, fast—full of car chases, intruding helicopters, shoot-outs, and such. But it is Shaker's unshakable resolve that Mullen will pay and his seeing himself as striking a blow for the hardworking against the rich that form the emotional fuel propelling him to get the $2 million, killing his partners in crime and risking personal exposure. Sinise is a wonderful actor to watch as a villain, and Mel Gibson's sexy, not-so-good guy is his match. Rene Russo is certainly no Donna Reed, and although she has little to do, you feel she would *not* have a nervous breakdown over the kidnapping; rather, she would provide her own solution, probably going after the criminals with a gun. It is also interesting to note that Japanese director Akira Kurosawa based his 1962 black-and-white TohoScope film, *High and Low*, on a similar story from an Ed McBain novel about kidnappers who believe they have a millionaire's son, but have taken the chauffeur's boy instead. The moral problem there was: Should the millionaire ransom an employee's son?

Needless to say, it is difficult to compare the *Ransom* of 1956 and its remake of 1996 because the films are so different. The 1956 version is more of an adult drama: low-key, with a straightforward story and an unexpected conclusion. The color and CinemaScope 1996 version could be seen by teenagers and adults alike because of its extensive production values and twistier plot. But the one common link is their indictment of the media for rushing to action and putting a family into jeopardy. The Stannards are small-town folk, straightforward and somewhat repressed. The Mullens are complex people living in a metropolis, movers and shakers, not easily intimidated and at the top of their game. The Mullens relish a personal family crisis being turned into a media event (Tom Mullin appears in ads for his airline), whereas the Stannards want to remain in their private, small town world. Just think of the differences in communication of the respective eras—the multiple-propeller heavy aircraft of the 1950s versus the superfast, lighter jet planes of the 1990s, the dial telephone of the earlier period versus the cell phone and E-mail as standard modes of 1990s communication. In fact, the ransom demand of the remake was received in an unsigned E-mail! *Ransom* (1996) could not be a better example of the new noir in its updated state, just as the 1956 version was a testament to its own noir style and era. Let them coexist, and let's enjoy both for their respective cinematic and entertainment values.

FILMOGRAPHY

Ransom (1956), d. Alex Segal, MGM, 109 min., b&w, sc. Cyril Hume and Richard Maibaum, ph. Arthur L. Arling, m. Jeff Alexander, v. not available.

Ransom (1996), d. Ron Howard, Columbia, 117 min., Technicolor and Cinema-Scope, sc. Richard Price, Jonathan Gold, and Alexander Ignon, based on the original by Hume and Maibaum, ph. Piotr Sobocinski, m. James Horner, Billy Corgan (songs), v. Columbia.

34

Vertigo (1958) and Mirage (1995)

VERTIGO (1958)

"Alfred Hitchcock engulfs you in a whirlpool of terror and tension." This is the tag line for the advertising posters of Hitchcock's celebrated color noir, *Vertigo*, made on location in San Francisco from the novel *D'entre les morts* (From Among the Dead) by Pierre Boileau and Thomas Narcejac. The poster shows James Stewart (as John "Scottie" Ferguson) hanging onto the drainpipe of a high-rise apartment building, looking down as police scramble across a slate roof to rescue him before he falls to certain death. When the film begins, Scottie is chasing a man across a rooftop with police following close behind. Gunfire is heard. The man tries to jump from one building to another, and succeeds. Scottie follows, then slides down on the slate roof and grabs the drainpipe. A patrolman tries to rescue him but falls to his death. Scottie watches in horror. He is eventually rescued offscreen, but the experience leaves him with deep psychological scars and a tremendous fear of heights. The San Francisco newspapers publish the story and Scottie leaves the police force. In semi-retirement, he works as a private detective.

One day Scottie is summoned to the office of an old college friend, Gavin Elster (played by Tom Helmore), a shipping magnate. Elster is worried about his wife, Madeline (Kim Novak), because of her strange and self-destructive behavior. So Scottie follows her all around San Francisco—to her grandmother Carlota's home, to Carlota's grave, to a hotel where Madeline registers under Carlota's name, to a museum where

Madeline sits in front of Carlota's portrait. (Carlota went mad after her husband left her, taking their only child, and then committed suicide.)

One day, Scottie follows Madeline to the edge of San Francisco Bay. For no apparent reason, she dives into the water. Scottie plunges in after her, saves her life, and takes her to his apartment to dry off. Fascinated by her, Scottie starts to fall in love with her, and they take car rides together. One day, Madeline confides one of her dreams to Scottie: she is running up the stairs in a bell tower, then leaps to her death. They drive to San Juan Bautista (where Carlota jumped to her death), and Scottie makes Madeline confront the realities of life versus her dream world. However, he cannot prevent Madeline from running into the bell tower. Scottie tries desperately to reach the top, but his fear of heights gets the better of him. He hears a scream, and watches Madeline sail past him, an apparent suicide he was helpless to prevent. Scottie falls apart from this trauma and is committed to an asylum. His longtime friend Midge (sympathetically played by Barbara Bel Geddes) visits him, and finally Scottie is released. He returns to San Francisco.

On a San Francisco street, Scottie notices a brunette who bears a re-markable resemblance to the blonde Madeline. He learns that her name is Judy. He wants to date her, but at first Judy puts him off; later she succumbs to his obvious charm. Scottie begins a Pygmalion-like refash-ioning of Judy, making her into the Madeline of his dreams. He picks out her clothes, her hair style, her hair color—finally, one evening, she is transformed into Scottie's image of Madeline. Bernard Herrmann's music captures the moment as the camera circles the actors as they em-brace and the set rotates like a diorama, casting images of Scottie's dreams and thoughts of Madeline and the places they visited together.

Judy and Scottie go out on a date. As she puts on a necklace (a replica of the one worn by Madeline and shown in Carlota's portrait), Scottie realizes he has been duped. As they drive to San Juan Bautista, he forces a confession from Judy—that she was Gavin Elster's lover and was paid to impersonate Madeline so the real Madeline, who was already dead, could be thrown from the bell tower and Elster could collect on a sizable insurance policy on her life. In a flashback, as Judy tells the story, we see Elster and Judy at the top of the bell tower, where Scottie could not climb, safe after committing their crime and using Scottie as a reliable witness to an apparent suicide. In San Juan Bautista, Judy and Scottie climb the bell tower steps to the very top: Scottie has mastered his vertigo and fear of heights. Judy admits she came back to San Francisco because she fell in love with Scottie, and is about to embrace him when suddenly a figure in black rises up. Judy is so frightened that she falls to her death. (The figure in black is a nun who heard voices that called her into the tower.) Scottie stands on a ledge at the edge of the tower, looking shell-shocked, his hands outstretched, Christ-like, a figure in pain. He has loved and lost twice.

Vertigo is probably one of the three best films Alfred Hitchcock ever made. It is certainly one in which the director brings out the finest performances from James Stewart and Kim Novak, who is remarkable as the elusive Madeline and the earthy Judy. It is the first time Hitchcock cast one of his "icy blondes" in a sympathetic role. *Vertigo's* story is remarkable and twisty. This is the film Boileau and Narcejac wrote specially for Hitchcock when he asked them to do a remake of *Les Diaboliques*. *Vertigo* is much better. Hitchcock used San Francisco locations to fine advantage: the camera wanders into Ernie's Restaurant, where we see the elegantly dressed Madeline having dinner with her husband; then to Nob Hill, where Madeline lives in an exclusive apartment building; then to the Art Museum, the Palace of the Legion of Honor in Golden Gate Park; then to Old Fort Point under the Golden Gate Bridge, where Madeline tries to commit suicide; then to Muir Woods; and finally to Mission Dolores at San Juan Bautista, where the hair-raising conclusion takes place.

Because *Vertigo* was filmed in VistaVision, High Fidelity, there is a clarity of vision unparallel in any other Hitchcock noir thriller. The 1958 film underwent a complete restoration in 1996 in wide screen and THX digital sound, and looks even more thrilling than the original print. And that haunting film score by Bernard Herrmann has got to be one of the ten best sound tracks ever composed or recorded for a film. Just listen to the music behind the main titles, the rooftop chase sequence, and the Scottie/Judy love scene sequence. Absolutely thrilling! *Vertigo's* score has been recorded many times, but the real beauty is the one on a Mercury LP or CD orchestrated by Herrmann, with Muir Matheson leading the London Philharmonic. *Vertigo* was the last great American noir in color, competing with Orson Welles's *Touch of Evil* (1958) and Robert Wise's *Odds Against Tomorrow* (1959) as the cultural and historical marker for the end of the film noir style until its revival in the 1960s. *Vertigo* is such a brilliant work that it defies any attempt to remake it. It is a true original, artful and incomparable!

MIRAGE (1995)

"Love Is the Deadliest Illusion" is the tag line from the video advertising *Mirage*. Written by actor/writer James Andronica (who stars as Lieutenant Richie Randazzo), *Mirage* is the poor man's version of *Vertigo*. No acknowledgment is given to the original film, nor is screenplay credit given to Boileau and Narcejac, who wrote the novel on which *Vertigo* is based. *Mirage* is a complete rip-off, but interesting in its change of details, locations, and performances. It tells virtually the same story as *Vertigo*. It is characterized as a "plot-twisted suspenser" in which Mateo (Matt) Juarez, an ex-Palm Springs cop (Edward James Olmos), is hired by Donald Gale, an environmentalist/director Paul Williams), to protect his beautiful wife, Jennifer/Shannon, (played by Sean Young), who is suffering from multiple personality disorder.

The film opens in a bar in Coachella, California, a sleepy, undeveloped town where drunks can easily lose their entire lives in drink, untroubled by the outside world. Such is the life of Matt Juarez, who resigned from the Palm Springs police force after accidentally shooting a female teenage hostage of a kidnapper and killing the abductor. Matt is recommended by Richie Randazzo to follow the wife of Donald Gale, who has two distinct personalities: the very proper Jennifer and the blonde stripper Shannon. Gale's greatest concerns are to save the Salton Sea and to protect his wife. Matt follows her everywhere and saves her twice—first, from a man who tries to beat her after she gives a strip performance in a local bar, and second, as she almost jumps off a cliff, raising her arms like a bird ready to take flight. They fall in love, but just before they consummate their relationship, Jennifer/Shannon returns home, finds a servant murdered, and is surprised by the man who had tried to beat her. Holding a shotgun to her head, he pulls her into the kitchen. Matt loads his own gun but finds it hard to follow them because of what had happened in Palm Springs. He hears gunfire and finds that Randazzo has shot the abductor, who supposedly had killed Jennifer (she has gunshot wounds to the head that make her unrecognizable). We see a woman, wearing the same pink dress as the victim, flee out the door. Jennifer is cremated, and then her husband scatters her ashes from a seaplane, over the Salton Sea.

One year later, we find Matt in the same condition as at the beginning of the film—drunk, sinking into depression, alcoholism, and self-blame. He wakes up in his favorite bar, and sees a new female barkeep who resembles Jennifer. She says she is an Irish immigrant and has worked at the bar only three weeks. Matt begins to date her. Even after they sleep together, Matt is still suspicious. One day the barmaid gets in her car and travels to the place where Jennifer/Shannon tried to fly like a bird. Matt stops her, then realizes she is really Jennifer and holds her over the precipice until she admits the truth. At that moment, Randazzo shows up, apparently in cahoots with Jennifer and Donald Gale. Randazzo is thrown over the cliff to his death in a fight with Matt, and Donald Gale is shot to death by Jennifer. She turns to Matt and says, "I know where the money is [the insurance money from the death of Donald Gale's wife]. Do you turn me in, or do we get married?" Fade out on Matt's face, which is a blank mask. Like Judy in *Vertigo*, Jennifer returns to Coachella because she really did fall in love with Matt, and wants to share her life with him. The multiple-personality story is a ploy created by Gale to use Matt as a witness to the death of Gale's wife (as it was in *Vertigo*). We wonder: Will Matt turn Jennifer in, or will they live happily ever after?

All the principals in the cast give good performances—but this is certainly a seedy version of *Vertigo*. First, the color is poor and grainy—probably because Agfacolor was used. Second, although Olmos has a lived-in, expressive face, he looks just a tad too old to attract, much less sleep with, luscious Sean Young. The actress does very well in three roles—Jennifer, Shannon, and the Irish barkeep. She has a sauciness and piquancy that really work. She is in control of all the men in the film.

There is some nudity in the film, some violence, and some really filthy language (which may update the appeal of the film to American audiences) which thus has an "R" rating. *Mirage* is a really lowbrow remake. As far as I know, it appeared only on video; there are no reviews of the film in any of the leading periodicals. This film did nothing to improve the careers of any of the actors, the writer, or the director. Watch the original *Vertigo* for everything that *Mirage* should be, but is not.

FILMOGRAPHY

Vertigo (1958), d. Alfred Hitchcock, Paramount, 129 min (additional 100 min. in restored version) Technicolor, VistaVision, sc. Alec Coppel and Samuel Taylor, from Boileau and Narcejac's novel *D'entre les morts*, ph. Robert Burks, m. Bernard Herrmann, v. MCA/Universal.

Mirage (1995), d. Paul Williams, Tigertail Flicks/Shonderonsa & Olmos Productions, 92 min., Agfacolor, sc. James Andronica, ph. Susan Ellen Emerson, m. David Richard Campbell, v. Tigertail.

35

A Bout de Souffle (aka Breathless, 1960)
and Breathless (1981)

A BOUT DE SOUFFLE (1960)

When Jean-Luc Godard's first film, *A Bout de Souffle*, was shown in New York City in 1961, it was a mesmerizing experience for viewers and critics alike. It had vitality, spontaneity, and effervescence that were rooted in the American tradition of 1940s film noir—in fact, one can find influences of Joseph Lewis's *Gun Crazy* (1949) and Nicholas Ray's *They Live by Night* (1949), both American noir classics. Godard dedicated his film to Monogram Pictures, one of the "B" studios along "Poverty Row" that had made such excellent films noirs as *Dillinger* (1945), *Suspense* (1946), and *The Gangster* (1947).

The film's plot is quite simple. Michel Poiccard (played stunningly by Jean-Paul Belmondo in his first cinema role) is a petty automobile thief who likens himself to the great Humphrey Bogart. He dangles a cigarette from his mouth, wears a hat in the Bogart manner, and believes himself to be one of the best cocksmen of all time, especially with his girlfriend, American student/*Herald-Tribune* peddler Patricia Franchini (played by the American actress Jean Seberg). When the film opens, Michel is in Marseilles and steals a car, heading for Paris. He is pursued by a motorcycle cop, whom he kills with a gun he finds in the car's glove compartment. Once in Paris, he steals money from a friend and goes off to find Patricia, his girl, who usually sells newspapers on the Champs-Elysées. Patricia who agrees to let him hide out from police in her small apartment. They spend two days together, having fun, smoking, making

love. Michel's plan is to steal several more cars, sell them, take the proceeds, and go with Patricia to Rome. However, Patricia has other ideas.
She is independent, and wants to continue her studies (as a journalist)
and separate herself from Michel. She informs the police of Michel's
whereabouts, and in a startling conclusion, Michel is shot dead by police.
Patricia watches Michel running with the police in pursuit, and sees him
stagger, then fall to the ground face up. She goes over to him, and he
mutters, "Dégalasse. Dégalasse." She asks the surrounding police what
he said, she receives no answer. But we know he said "Dirty rotten
bitch!"

A Bout de Souffle is a terrific French film noir which deserves its cult
reputation, and it is certainly one of the most exciting films to come to
America that is based on our own traditions of film noir. Godard must
be praised for many things: his hiring of ace cameraman Raoul Coutard,
whose use of jump cuts, hand-held cameras, and grainy black-and-white
texture bring a realistic grittiness to the Paris location shooting that is so
indispensable to this story; his realizing the brilliance of François Truffaut's original screenplay (of course, Truffaut had a brilliant career of his
own in French and American cinema); and, most important, his willing-
ness to take a chance on two virtually unknown actors—Jean-Paul Belmondo (who had had a minor career in boxing) and Jean Seberg (an Otto
Preminger discovery for his film *Saint Joan* [1957]). Godard's greatest
innovation was the incorporation of the film's title "Breathless" into the
camera work and the aesthetics of the film. With lightning editing and
unresolved camera movements, Godard brings out the very essence of
Michel's lifestyle: living fast and for the moment, and pushing everything to the limit. "To Live Dangerously Till the End!" says one of the
posters on his wall—very much in the style of another American icon,
James Dean as Nicholas Ray's *Rebel Without a Cause* (1955).

A Bout de Souffle conveys an emotionally erratic story about a not-so-
handsome hero who falls in love with a hypnotic, deceptive woman.
Both characters are devoid of any moral nature, living frenetically for
the moment; moving their ragged relationship from one nerve-tattering
day to the next; constantly threatened by discovery but uncaring; im-
pudent, arrogant, and belligerent. Belmondo's imitation of Bogart's
swaggering American is poignant at times, but barely touches the emo-
tionless Jean Seberg, whose Patricia Franchini is impervious to morality
or sentiment; her sensitive nature has been abused in the past, torn by
disappointments and loneliness. Seberg was perfect for this role because
she projects a bland woman—an immobile mask of a real woman—cold,
calculating, destructive, and self-defensive in the irrational, heartless
world of urban Paris, 1959. All of these qualities are caught in Raoul
Coutard's jump-cutting, which *New York Times* film critic Bosley
Crowther called "pictorial cacaphony," and in Martial Solal's nervous

music score with erratic tonal qualities that support Godard's grainy images in black-and-white. This is strong stuff. Crowther also said, "It is more of a chunk of raw drama, graphically and artfully torn with appropriately ragged edges out of the tough underbelly of [the] modern metropolitan life [of Paris]." It is exactly that.

BREATHLESS (1981)

"He's the last man on earth any woman needs—but every woman wants." is the tag line for the advertising posters of the remake of Jean-Luc Godard's *A Bout de Souffle*. First-time director Jim McBride and his cowriter, L. M. "Kit" Carson, were so thrilled by the original that they wanted to do an American version of it—so they transposed the location to Los Angeles and starred Richard Gere as Jesse Lujack, a small-time car thief who falls in love with Monica Poiccard (Valerie Kaprisky in her first role)—which turns out to be a fatal mistake, as in the original film. But the remake has a whole different feeling and aesthetic.

The film begins in Las Vegas, where Jesse has just murdered a cop and hides out with Monica, a beautiful but cold woman. Now, in Los Angeles, Monica is on track with her studies and Jesse carries his criminal past with him. She is no longer certain she wants to continue her affair with Jesse and run off to Mexico. En route, she calls the police from a roadside phone booth, and as Jesse meets her with the money he has earned selling hot cars, the police arrive. Gere, hands in the air, sings a pop ballad, mouthing the words of Jerry Lee Lewis. A pal of Jesse's had given him a gun, which is lying on the ground. Monica declares her love for Jesse and begins running toward him. Jesse wheels around, picks up the gun, then turns toward the police. "The End." Quite a different conclusion from *A Bout de Souffle*. In fact, the remake is a very different film in many ways.

First, color makes *Breathless* more of a neo-noir. And Gere is not just a car thief but a male hustler as well. The former "sexiest man alive" wears shirts open to his belly button or goes shirtless. And both Gere and Kaprisky have scenes of full frontal nudity.

Second, *Breathless* is certainly more sexy and erotic; it also has a great set of rock tunes that have been imaginatively selected by the director in order to bolster the images of the pop culture of the early 1980s.

And, finally, this remake has an exciting visual style apart from the color and location shooting. There is one scene where Jesse and Monica are making love, seen in silhouette against a theater screen where Joseph Lewis's *Gun Crazy* is playing. McBride also used fabulous locations to heighten the film's exaggerated visual style—an enormous auto graveyard, seedy bars, a procession of Venice, California, murals, and the famous Bonaventure Hotel as an architectural pop icon. With its loud colors, innovative set designs, and fashions of the era, *Breathless* is a lively film marred only by its impotent ending. Nevertheless, it is a sharp remake of a classic by a talented new director whose career deserves our attention.

FILMOGRAPHY

A Bout de Souffle (1960), d. Jean-Luc Godard, Imperial/SNC, 89 min., b&w, sc. Jean-Luc Godard, from a story by François Truffaut, ph. Raoul Coutard, m. Martial Solal, v. Cinémathèque Française.

Breathless (1981), d. Jim McBride, Columbia/Orion, 100 min., Color by Deluxe, sc. Jim McBride and L. M. "Kit" Carson, from the story by François Truffaut, ph. Richard H. Kline, m. Jack Nitzsche, v. Columbia.

Conclusion

In the course of writing this book, over sixty years of American cinema have been examined, with the intention of discussing film noir originals and their remakes. There have been some minor detours along the way for television remakes of original noir films as well as explorations of French noir. But we have had major theatrical releases under scrutiny for the majority of films under discussion.

Even at this point, one cannot make any sweeping generalizations regarding original noirs and their remakes. Cinema purists might always consider the original film better than any remake, no matter what proof of the opposite we may give. However, there are several exceptions that defy this belief. *Broken Lance* (1954), *Thieves Like Us* (1974), *Farewell, My Lovely* (1975), *Body Heat* (1981), *I, the Jury* (1982), *No Way Out* (1987), *Johnny Handsome* (1989), *A Kiss Before Dying* (1991), and *Ransom* (1996) are noir remakes that broke the mold and improved in some way upon their predecessors. They represent roughly 25% of the group of remakes examined in this book. This percentage reflects my own opinion of the originals, which were made in a different era, utilizing different technology, and directed to a vastly different audience—the moviegoing public of World War II and after. In that era, story lines were more important. Quality, charismatic actors and actresses were working under seasoned, capable directors in a studio system. The group of remakes singled out above utilized color and CinemaScope, advanced lensing techniques, and stereo or digital sound. These films are more commercially oriented, seeking a wider audience—from teenagers to older adults. Story values and charismatic actors are still extremely important, but Hollywood's heroes and heroines have changed. The star system is gone. Also gone are Barbara Stanwyck and Lana Turner—replaced by Jessica Lange and Kathleen Turner (no relation to Lana). Among the men, no more Van Heflin or Ray Milland—they have been replaced by Kurt Russell and Kevin Costner. A new breed of sexy male (and female) stars has arrived. The studio system has been gone for nearly forty years, and with it, the directors and technicians who had a particular style which characterized their work for the studios that employed them. You could easily recognize a Paramount noir or a Warner's noir or a Fox noir. Nowadays, it is hard to keep track of which films are made by which directors and for which studio or releasing corporation or business conglomerate. Lawrence Kasdan is certainly no Billy Wilder (Paramount's supreme noir director), Bob Rafelson is no Tay Garnett (MGM's noir expert), Taylor Hackford is no Jacques Tourneur (RKO's supreme noir stylist), and Jim McBride is certainly no Jean-Luc Godard (one of France's top noir filmmakers).

In the last thirty years, the noir directors of the 1940s and '50s have retired, died, or moved on. We have a new group of talented directors, nurtured by commercial conglomerates, who have tried to adapt past successes into neo-noir formulas of their own in order to succeed as filmmakers in today's Hollywood. Consider for a moment the concept of censorship. In the 1940s and '50s, the motion picture industry was regulated by the dated 1930s Hays Code. Stories involving sex and violence were told obliquely—much of the action that was censorable happened offscreen. The breakdown of censorship came in the late 1950s with Otto Preminger's releases of *The Moon Is Blue* (1953) and *The Man with the Golden Arm* (1955). He dared to use adult language and chose previously forbidden themes, like drug addiction, in his films. From the 1960s on, directors could tell their stories more openly. There was a greater use of salty language and more nudity on screen. Notice the differences between *Double Indemnity* (1944) and *Body Heat* (1981). *Body Heat* is *Double Indemnity* with explicit sex and nudity thrown in. Noir productions of the 1980s and '90s were more honest, more faithful to realities of modern life than the obliquely told tales of the 1940s and '50s, where you had to use your imagination to figure out what was going on between men and women. And yet, with all of this relaxation of censorship rules and a new rating system, there have been three times as many neo-noir failures in the last decade of the twentieth century than successful remakes, despite the attempt at frankness and honesty on the big screen. Eric P. Nash, in his May 28, 2000, short take from the *New York Times Book Review* of criminologist Nicole Rafter's *Shots in the Mirror*, says, "Film noir is still in the pink . . . because it provides (as Rafter says) 'routes into the enticing but forbidden underworlds of crime, access to the secrets of the prison, the joys of identifying with heroic rebels, the gratifications of vengeance and the satisfaction of moral certainty.' " And as we enter the new millennium, the noir style continues to surface—call it "neo-noir" or "new noir" or "film après noir," there will always be a woman dragging a weak man down, using her sexuality as a weapon to make him commit criminal acts—and he won't get the money or the dame, just punishment, legal or self-inflicted, for his stupidity. Film noir and its permutations will go on as long as there are men, women, and conflicts over love, money, or power.

APPENDIXES

The appendix section of this book is divided into two parts, A and B. Appendix A consists of filmographies of a dozen groups of films, early pre-noirs whose roots were in plays, mysteries, melodramas, thrillers, crime films, and gothic and detective dramas from the 1920s, '30s, and '40s. Some of the original titles were kept for the remakes, others were discarded to update the original version. Rarely did these films succeed as remakes beyond 1955, but it is interesting to trace the history of both originals and remakes from one genre to another and to their eventual demise. All titles will be very briefly described, sometimes because of their relative obscurity, other times because they were in the formative stages before noir erupted as an American style of filmmaking in the early 1940s. It is also interesting to note the French influences on early 1940s and '50s American film as well as the frequency of remakes of some themes. I deliberately excluded *Rebecca*, *The Maltese Falcon*, and *High Sierra* from the main body of the book, according to my criteria (presented in the Introduction). Yet because of their noirish elements, I have included them in Appendix A.

Appendix B deals with films made between 1960 and the present. Emanating from thrillers, horror films, caper and suspense films, and neo-noirs, they have been recycled as new noir remakes, and deserve recognition as such. Here, too, the titles will be described briefly, not because of their obscure nature but because these titles first appeared in the late noir or post-noir period and have been successfully remade in the 1990s, to fine effect. I have deliberately not included "serial noirs" like *Dirty Harry*, *Magnum Force*, and the rest of the Clint Eastwood films about Detective Harry Callahan, or sequels like *Terminator* and *Terminator 2*, or the sequels to *Chinatown* and *48 Hours*. They could be the subject of another volume.

APPENDIX GUIDE

Appendix A. From Plays, Mysteries, Melodramas, Thrillers, Pre-Noir to Film Noir

The Letter (1929, 1940, 1982 [TV]) and *The Unfaithful* (1947)

La Chienne (The Bitch) (1931) and *Scarlet Street* (1945)

The Criminal Code (1931), *Penitentiary* (1938), and *Convicted* (1950)

The Maltese Falcon (1931, 1941), *Satan Met a Lady* (1936), and *Hell's Island* (1955)

La Bête Humaine (1938) and *Human Desire* (1954)

Blind Alley (1939) and *The Dark Past* (1948)

Rebecca (1940; 1948, 1950, 1962, 1978, 1997 [TV])

I Wake Up Screaming (1941) and *Vicki* (1953)

High Sierra (1941), *Colorado Territory* (1949), and *I Died a Thousand Times* (1955)

Suspicion (1941, 1987 [TV])

The Falcon Takes Over (1942) and *Murder, My Sweet* (1944)

Time to Kill (1942) and *The Brasher Doubloon* (1947)

Appendix B. From Thriller, Horror, Caper, Suspense, Neo-Noir to New Noir Remake

Plein Soleil (Purple Noon) (1960) and *The Talented Mr. Ripley* (1999)

Psycho (1960, 1998)

Cape Fear (1962, 1991)

Point Blank (1967) and *Payback* (1999)

The Thomas Crown Affair (1968, 1999)

The Getaway (1972, 1994)

Day of the Jackal (1973) and *The Jackal* (1997)

La Femme Nikita (1990) and *Point of No Return* (1993)

Appendix A

From Plays, Mysteries, Melodramas, Thrillers, Pre-Noir to Film Noir

THE LETTER (1929, 1940, 1982 [TV]) AND *THE UNFAITHFUL* (1947)

The Letter (1929), d. Jean de Limur, Paramount, 65 min., b&w, sc. Monta Bell, Jean de Limur, Mort Blumenstock (titles), based on the play by W. Somerset Maugham, ph. George J. Folsey, v. not available.

An early sound film with Jeanne Eagels making her debut in the role of Leslie Crosbie; Reginald Owen as her husband, Robert; Herbert Marshall as Geoffrey Hammond, Leslie's lover; O. P. Heggie as her lawyer, Howard Joyce; Irene Browne as Mrs. Joyce; and Li-Ti as Lady Tsen Mei, Hammond's common-law wife, this is the first cinema version of the celebrated stage play that was remade no less than four times.

The Letter (1940), d. William Wyler, Warner Bros., 95 min., b&w, sc. Howard Koch, from the novel by W. Somerset Maugham, ph. Tony Gaudio, m. Max Steiner, v. MGM/UA.

This most celebrated version of Maugham's story stars Bette Davis as Leslie Crosbie, who utters the famous line "I'm still in love with the man I killed." This time Herbert Marshall plays her husband, Robert; James Stephenson, Howard Joyce, the lawyer who defends Leslie, knowing she is guilty of murder; and Gale Sondergaard, Hammond's common-law wife (called Mrs. Hammond in this version). The film is set in Malaysia. In the moonlit opening scene, Geoffrey Hammond runs out of the Crosbie house with Leslie following, pistol in hand. She empties the entire gun into her lover as he falls down the porch stairs to his death—perhaps one of the best opening scenes ever filmed. Max Steiner's wonderful score accentuates the themes of adultery and revenge. After buying back a letter that would prove her guilty, Leslie is set free by an English court, then is killed by Hammond's wife. Terrific early noir.

The Unfaithful (1947), d. Vincent Sherman, Warner Bros., 109 min., b&w, sc. David Goodis and James Gunn, from the W. Somerset Maugham novel, ph. Ernest Haller, m. Max Steiner, v. not available.

In this update of Maugham's novel *The Letter*, Ann Sheridan plays Chris Hunter, the wealthy wife of an architect, Bob Hunter (Zachary Scott), who is returning home from military service after World War II. She is supposed to meet him at the airport. But the previous evening an intruder forced his way into the Hunter home and, after a struggle, Chris shot him dead, supposedly in self-defense. Lew Ayres plays her attorney, Larry Hannaford. It is revealed that the intruder was Michael Tanner (Paul Bradley), a sculptor who had been having an affair with Chris while sculpting a bust she commissioned. His wife (Marta Mitrovich) accuses Chris of murder and tries to blackmail her by selling the statue to Hannaford. Chris is found innocent, but when Bob finds out about the affair after seeing the bust sculpted by Tanner, he asks for a divorce. Their lawyer proposes a deal whereby they might put all this behind them and start afresh. Ann Sheridan, Lew Ayres, and Zachary Scott bring depth and conviction to their roles, aided by a wonderfully sensitive script by noir novelist David Goodis and with an appropriate noirish score by Max Steiner.

The Letter (1982), d. John Erman, PBS Television, 96 min. color, sc. Lawrence B. Marcus, m. Laurence Rosenthal, v. not available.

Apparently this is the second television version of *The Letter*. The first was produced in England in 1969 and starred Peter Bowles. (There is no other information on this production.) The 1982 version, set in Malaysia, is formidable because of its casting and production values. Lee Remick stars as Leslie Crosbie, wife of Robert Crosbie (Jack Thompson), who had an affair with Geoff Hammond (Ian MacShane), the husband of a notorious Chinese woman (Kieu Chinh). Leslie is brought to trial for murdering Geoff by Officer Withers (Christopher Cazenove) and is defended by Howard Joyce (Ronald Pickup). She is found innocent of the crime after Joyce buys an incriminating letter Leslie wrote to her lover on the day of the shooting. However, justice is served when Leslie dies at the hands of the Chinese woman. It's the old story of sin, murder, redemption, and justice meted out to adulterous lovers. Remick gives a luminous performance.

LA CHIENNE (THE BITCH) (1931) AND *SCARLET STREET* (1945)

La Chienne (The Bitch) (1931), d. Jean Renoir, Gaumont, 95 min., b&w, sc. Jean Renoir and André Girard, based on the Georges de La Fouchardiere novel and André Mouzey-Eon play, ph. Theodor Sparkuhl, m. Eugenie Buffet, v. Cinémathèque Française.

Lucienne Pelletier (played by Janie Mareze) is a prostitute called Lulu who is controlled by her lover/pimp, Dede (played by Georges Flamant). Maurice Legrand (marvelously played by Michel Simon) is a henpecked bank teller who will do anything for Lucienne's love. When Maurice discovers Lulu has been two-timing him with Dede, he kills her with a dagger and Dede is blamed for the crime. Maurice loses his job and family, and becomes a *clochard* (beggar) as Dede goes to the gallows for a crime he did not commit. There are two subplots. First, Maurice apparently was not legally married to Adele (Madeleine Berubet); her supposedly ex-husband turns up and wants to blackmail Maurice regarding his bigamy. Second, Maurice is an amateur painter who uses Adele's dislike of his hobby to rent an apartment for Lulu, work there, and sleep with her. Lulu sells off the paintings and gives the money to Dede. When Maurice finally discovers the truth, he murders Lulu and lets Dede take the blame.

Scarlet Street (1945), d. Fritz Lang, Universal, 103 min., b&w, sc. Dudley Nichols, based on the novel *La Chienne* by Georges de La Fouchardiere and the play by André Mouzey-Eon, ph. Milton R. Krasner, m. Hans J. Salter, v. Universal.

If *La Chienne* was an exact reproduction of the La Fouchardiere novel, *Scarlet Street* is almost an exact remake of the film *La Chienne*, with Lang's famous film noir touches. Produced by Walter Wanger for Diana Productions (a company he formed with his wife, actress Joan Bennett), *Scarlet Street* tells the same story as *La Chienne*, with Edward G. Robinson playing Christopher Cross, an accountant who is totally henpecked by his wife, Adele (Rosalind Ivan in one of her bitchiest roles), and is reduced to wearing aprons and doing "feminine" household chores. His only escape is the time he devotes to his oil painting. Joan Bennett plays Kitty March, the prostitute he rescues from a beating by Dan Duryea (in one of his slimiest roles as her lover/pimp Johnny Prince). Kitty persuades Chris to rent an apartment for her where he can do his painting. When she and Johnny begin to sell the paintings and Chris finds out Kitty is cheating on him, he murders her with an ice pick and lets Johnny take the blame. We see Robinson as a hobo, broken by the dream of a tainted love he could not possess. He wanders, unknown, with a guilty conscience as Johnny goes to the electric chair for Kitty's brutal murder.

There is one wonderful scene that shows Chris's enslavement to Kitty—he is seen painting her toenails as she lies provocatively on their bed in a flimsy negligee and boa. Kitty is trash, but Chris can see only her (cheap) beauty. It was Joan Bennett's role of a lifetime as the two-timing femme fatale Duryea calls "Lazy Legs," and possibly Dudley Nichols's best screen adaptation from the original film. But it is Fritz Lang, the German Expressionist director, who really shines, making *Scarlet Street* into a film that pulls no punches—a film noir that uses the song "Melancholy Baby" to emphasize the grittiness of the story and the baseness of its elemental emotions. And the wonderful low-key lighting on those rain-soaked streets—what wonderful noir atmosphere to create the tensions between the characters that lead to their uniquely individual tragedies, which are due to their lust, greed, weakness, and cruelty. Lang's direction and Milton Krasner's photography are the true stars of this terrific film noir.

THE CRIMINAL CODE (1931), *PENITENTIARY* (1938), AND *CONVICTED* (1950)

The Criminal Code (1931), d. Howard Hawks, Columbia, 95 min. b&w, sc. Seton I. Miller and Fred Niblo, Jr., from the Martin Flavin play, ph. James Wong Howe and Ted Tetzlaff, v. not available.

District Attorney Brady (played by Walter Huston) gets a ten-year sentence for Robert Graham (played by Phillips Holmes), who killed in self-defense. Several years later, Brady becomes the prison warden and is told by the prison physician, Dr. Rinewulf (John St. Polis), that Graham has spent six years working in the jute mill and is not a hardened criminal. Brady sympathizes with Graham and has him transferred to his home, where he does odd jobs. Graham falls in love with Mary Brady (Constance Cummings), and life seems more tolerable. Then he finds out about a murder plotted by Ned Galloway (Boris Karloff), but refuses to tell the warden what he knows about it because it would be a violation of the criminal code. Nevertheless, Mary and Robert marry, and Robert finally gets out of prison to lead a new life. D.A. Brady finally accepts Robert's innocence as a "victim" of multiple circumstances—the original bar brawl and his honesty in keeping silent regarding the criminal code—and gives consent to his daughter's marriage. The criminals deservedly die in a shootout and Robert does not need to reveal their identities. *The Criminal Code* is certainly pre-noir, played totally straight without any pretensions of a photographic style. It has all the ingredients of the usual criminal film of the era—"convict buddies, a paternalistic warden, a cruel guard, a craven snitch, a bloodthirsty convict, and a young hero," as Nicole Rafter describes the film in her book *Shots in the Mirror*. It is a formula that has endured in the genre of prison films.

Penitentiary (1938), d. John Braham, Columbia, 74 min., b&w, sc. Seton I. Miller and Fred Niblo, Jr., ph. Lucien Ballard, v. not available.

Starring Walter Connelly as District Attorney Matthews; Jean Parker as his daughter, Elizabeth; John Howard as William Jordan, unjustly convicted of murder; and Robert Barrat as Grady, a criminal out for revenge, this film is practically a scene-by-scene remake of *The Criminal Code*, but has no charisma in performances and is much less dynamic.

Convicted (1950), d. Henry Levin, Columbia, 91 min., b&w, sc. William Bowers, Seton I. Miller, and Martin Flavin, based on Flavin's original play *The Criminal Code*, ph. Burnett Guffey, m. George Duning, v. not available.

This third recycling of *The Criminal Code* has much to offer, essentially because of the performances of Glenn Ford as Joe Hufford, convicted of manslaughter after the man he beat in a barroom brawl dies. Warden George Knowland (Broderick Crawford), the district attorney who convicted Hufford, has become more sympathetic to him since his trial. Hufford starts to work at the warden's home, where he meets and falls in love with Kay Knowland (played by Dorothy Malone). Just as he is about to be paroled, he witnesses the killing of an informer by a convict named Malloby (Millard Mitchell). He refuses to be a stool pigeon, following the criminal code, even if it means jeopardizing his parole. The murderer is finally caught, and Joe and Kay run off to marry. The greatest change from the 1931 version is the attractive noir style in which the film is photographed. *Convicted* is a wonderful example of "prison noir," and Ford's and Crawford's excellent performances make the film a tight, exciting crimer.

THE MALTESE FALCON (1931, 1941), SATAN MET A LADY (1936), AND HELL'S ISLAND (1955)

The Maltese Falcon (1931), d. Roy del Ruth, Warner Bros., 80 min., b&w, sc. Maude Fulton, Lucien Hubbard, and Brown Holmes, from the Dashiell Hammett novel, ph. William Rees, v. not available.

Ricardo Cortez stars as private detective Sam Spade, who is hired by Ruth Wonderly (Bebe Daniels) to find her sister. What she is really searching for is the Maltese Falcon, a jewel-encrusted statue that disappeared en route from Turkey to San Francisco. Other parties are interested in the black bird as well: art connoisseur Caspar Gutman (Dudley Digges), who is traveling with his henchman Wilmer (Dwight Frye), and the effeminate gentleman from Turkey, Joel Cairo (Otto Mathieson). Spade sends his partner, Miles Archer (Walter Long), who is immediately killed on the job. Sam and his secretary, Effie (Una Merkel), are devastated. Iva (Thelma Todd), Archer's wife, seeks comfort in Sam's arms, but he is spending his time (probably in bed) with Ruth Wonderly. Finally, Captain Jacobi (Agostino Borgato) brings the statue to Spade's apartment after playing a cat-and-mouse game with all of the interested parties. The falcon turns out to be a colossal fake. But someone has to pay for the murder of Miles Archer, and Sam hands Miss Wonderly over to Lieutenant Polhaus (J. Farrell MacDonald)—and the gas chamber. Roy del Ruth directs the mystery in a straightforward fashion—no frills. Spade comes off as a hard man, ruthless and selfish. He has been used by Ruth Wonderly, and sex does not save her from Tehachapi and the gas chamber. If Warner Bros. had used the alternate title for the film, *Dangerous Female*, the mystery would have been easily solved. There is no real noir style in this first version of Hammett's complex novel.

Satan Met a Lady (1936), d. William Dieterle, Warner Bros., 75 min., b&w, sc. Brown Holmes, based on *The Maltese Falcon* by Dashiell Hammett, ph. Arthur Edeson, m. Leo Forbstein, v. MGM/UA.

This is probably the worst version of the Hammett novel ever made. The changes are considerable. Bette Davis plays Valerie Purvis, the femme fatale to Warren Williams's Ted Shane, private investigator. The black plaster bird filled with jewels is now a ram's horn that the villains are searching for. The other actors—Marie Wilson as Miss Murgatroyd (the Effie role), Arthur Treacher as Anthony Travers, Alison Skipworth as Madame Barabbas, and Winifred Shaw as Astrid Ames—find themselves in an unfunny farce, acting at breakneck speed in a lunatic film that makes little sense. Hammett should be thankful the producers did not place the title of his novel on this terrible, terrible remake.

The Maltese Falcon (1941), d. John Huston, Warner Bros., 101 min., b&w, sc. John Huston, based on Dashiell Hammett's novel, ph. Arthur Edeson, m. Adolph Deutsch, v. MGM/UA and Warner Bros.

This second remake of the 1931 version is, for this writer, a mystery with many noir elements—call it "transitional noir," not full-fledged noir. With Humphrey Bogart's sensational performance as Sam Spade and Mary Astor's equally excellent femme fatale, Brigid O'Shaughnessy (aka Miss Wonderly), the film is noirish, especially in its night scenes and in the black hearts of its villains. But their evil natures are generally dissipated by too much dialogue and the use of both red herrings and logic to discover the whereabouts of the infamous black bird, so that one loses interest in the human drama—up until the very end. When Sam tells Brigid, "I am sending you over [for the murder of his partner, Miles Archer (Jerome Cowan)]," you know he means it! Brigid has used Sam sexually, and she expected Wilmer (Elisha Cook, Jr.) to take the fall for Archer's death. As Sam hands her over to Lt. Polhaus (Ward Bond) and the two disappear from view, going down in an art deco elevator, you know Sam will not sleep for several nights. But you have to do something when someone kills your partner.

The script is much tighter than the 1931 version and the photography, especially during night scenes, uses low key lights and diverse angling of shots, very common to film noir. The cast is simply superb—Gladys George as Iva, who kisses Sam full on the mouth and invites him to her bed after the death of her husband, his partner, Miles Archer; Lee Patrick as Effie Perrine—lovely, efficient, and supportive of her boss; the trio of villains: Sidney Greenstreet as Caspar Gutman, homosexual art connoisseur, his "boy" or "gunsel," Wilmer; and perfumed, effete Joel Cairo (Peter Lorre), a Turkish art worshiper who does not like to be betrayed. And the film score by Adolph Deutsch, its themes laden with mystery, helps support the visuals and is not intrusive. This *Maltese Falcon* is the best one of all! And what was it all about? The pursuit by several people of a fake black bird, willing to kill for the wealth they thought they could possess. Detective Polhaus asks Sam, looking at the falcon, "What is it?" Sam answers, "The stuff that dreams are made of." And he goes down the staircase, carrying the falcon, past that art deco elevator with that resonant, dark music in the background.

Hell's Island (1955), d. Phil Karlson, Paramount, 84 min., Technicolor, VistaVision, sc. Maxwell Shane, William H. Pine, and William C. Thomas, from a story by Martin Goldsmith and Jack Leonard, ph. Lionel Lindon, m. Irvin Talbot, v. not available.

Hell's Island is a rip-off of *The Maltese Falcon* without screen credit given to Dashiell Hammett or his novel. It stars John Payne as Mike Cormack, a Las Vegas bouncer who is hired by Barzland (Francis L. Sullivan in the Sydney Greenstreet role) to find a ruby that was stolen from him and probably is in the possession of either Eduardo Martin (Paul Picerni) or his wife, Janet (Mary Murphy in the Brigid O'Shaughnessy role). Mike was once engaged to Janet, and Barzland figures that through him he can more easily find out where the elusive ruby is. Somewhat of a color noir, the film begins with Cormack lying on an operating table, apparently shot by Barzland, telling the whole story in flashback. We learn that Janet, the femme fatale, has the ruby. She murders a confederate, Paul Armand (played by Arnold Moss), in order to keep the ruby and arranges her husband's incarceration on an island, and his eventual murder when Cormack goes to rescue him. Janet is finally arrested by Inspector Peña for involvement in several murders and committing one herself, and Barzland dies in his wheelchair, tumbling over a cliff into oblivion. Cormack thinks he has fallen so low, he cannot go anywhere but up. He won't go back to Janet, and is at last free of the past—and probably $5,000 richer for finding the ruby.

John Payne, a song-and-dance man of the 1940s, revived his acting career when he took on tough guy roles at Paramount and United Artists during the 1950s. *Hell's Island* may not have been his best showcase (Karlson's *99 River Street* [1953] was a much better film), but Payne did become a noir icon. It's unfortunate that *Hell's Island* did not live up to its promise as a remake or an adulterated version of the Hammett original.

LA BÊTE HUMAINE (1938) AND HUMAN DESIRE (1954)

La Bête Humaine (1938), d. Jean Renoir, Paris Films, 100 min., b&w, sc. Jean Renoir, from the novel by Emile Zola, ph. Curt Courant, m. Joseph Kosma, v. Cinémathèque Française.

Jean Gabin plays Jacques Lantier, an alcoholic who is subject to epileptic seizures, works as a locomotive engineer. One evening, he witnesses a murder aboard his train. Robaud (Fernand Ledoux), a stationmaster for the railroad, kills his boss (also his wife's lover)—with the help of his wife, Severine (Simone Simon). Severine finds it impossible to be with her husband after the murder, so she takes a new lover—Jacques, in order to silence him and also to help her do away with her repulsive husband. They murder Robaud, but then Jacques, in an epileptic seizure brought on by excessive drinking, kills Severine. Through Zola's novel, Renoir proves it is impossible to escape your destiny, the result of heredity and environment. Renoir was one of the filmmakers responsible for the school of French "poetic realism," certainly a forerunner of film noir.

Human Desire (1954), d. Fritz Lang, Columbia, 90 min., b&w, sc. Alfred Hayes, based on the novel by Emile Zola, ph. Burnett Guffey, m. Daniele Amfitheatrof, v. Columbia.

Gloria Grahame ("She was born to be bad . . . to be kissed . . . to make trouble!") plays Vicki, the wife of stationmaster Carl Buckley (Broderick Crawford), a moody, depressed, and violent man who, with his wife, has just killed her former lover aboard a train. Jeff Warren (Glenn Ford) witnessed the murder. Vicki insinuates herself into Jeff's life, trying to protect herself from her wildly jealous husband and to use her new lover to kill her husband. In this version Jeff does not take the bait, and Vicki is murdered by Carl. Jeff goes off with the daughter of his landlord and finds true happiness with a good woman. Although the style of this film is certainly noirish, with those wonderful Langian touches and Gloria Graham's pouting sexuality (the most indecent femme fatale seen on screen up to that time), the upbeat ending is more in keeping with post-World War II America's desire to capture the positive dream. Most Lang films of the 1950s have happy endings despite their noir trappings, and *Human Desire* belongs to that group.

BLIND ALLEY (1939) AND THE DARK PAST (1948)

Blind Alley (1939), d. Charles Vidor, Columbia, 68 min., b&w, sc. Michael Blankfort, Albert Duffy, Philip MacDonald, and Lewis Meltzer, based on the play by James Warwick, ph. Lucien Ballard, m. Morris Stoloff, v. not available.

Chester Morris plays Hal Wilson, a gangster who has broken out of a penitentiary an assorted group of fellow prisoners. They break into the house of a psychiatrist, Dr. Shelby (played by Ralph Bellamy), interrupt a dinner party, and proceed to wreak havoc in the household until Shelby begins analyzing Wilson while being held hostage. He diagnoses Wilson's illness—the mania to kill—by probing his subconscious, so that Wilson is ready to give himself up to the police because of his new understanding of himself and his motives. *Blind Alley* contains many pre-noir elements and vaguely suggests the scenario for William Wyler's *The Desperate Hours* (1955). In fact, it was one of the first attempts by Hollywood to illustrate psychological ideas.

The Dark Past (1948), d. Rudolph Maté, Columbia, 75 min., b&w, sc. Michael Blankfort, Albert Duffy, and Philip MacDonald, with a new adaptation by Oscar Saul and Marvin Wald, based on the James Warwick play, ph. Joseph Walker, m. George Duning, v. Columbia.

Almost a scene-by-scene remake of *Blind Alley*, *The Dark Past* shows killer Al Walker (William Holden) breaking into Dr. Andrew Collins's hunting lodge with a group of assorted hoods and his girlfriend, Betty (a very young Nina Foch). The pipe-smoking doctor, a psychiatrist (astutely played by Lee J. Cobb), analyzes Walker, proving his troubled childhood and life of juvenile delinquency made him a killer. There is much conversation between Walker and Collins, and Walker has a series of bad dreams. At one point, Walker shoots one of the hostages in Collins's home, which causes the good doctor to probe further into Walker's psyche and his dark past. But once Collins has analyzed his patient, Walker can never kill again. As directed by Rudolph Maté, a former photographer, the film has a noir look, a darkness that masks the psychological abyss of the leading character. Several rain-filled scenes and flashbacks give this film its unique noir style.

REBECCA (1940; 1948, 1950, 1962, 1978, 1997 [TV])

Rebecca (1940), d. Alfred Hitchcock, Selznick International, 133 min., b&w, sc. Robert E. Sherwood and Joan Harrison, based on the Daphne du Maurier novel, ph. George Barnes, m. Franz Waxman, v. Key and others.

French critic Patrick Brion, in his famous volume *Le Film Noir*, cites Alfred Hitchcock's *Rebecca* as the first true film noir made in America in 1940. (He conveniently forgets about Boris Ingster's *Stranger on the Third Floor* as the real beginning of noir.) Whatever, *Rebecca*, is Alfred Hitchcock's first American film, is one we could call "gothic noir." It stars Laurence Olivier as Maxim de Winter, an English aristocrat whose wife died in a boating accident, and Joan Fontaine, who narrates the film. She meets Maxim in the South of France, falls madly in love, and is whisked into a fast marriage to become the new mistress of Manderly. The film contains layer upon layer of intrigue. We discover Rebecca is alive for Mrs. Danvers (Judith Anderson), who worships her even in death. We find out about Rebecca's affairs and her pregnancy by a man not her husband. Jack Flavell (played by George Sanders), Rebecca's cousin, tries to blackmail Max, thinking he killed her. We later learn that Rebecca had cancer and that she scuttled her own craft, to avoid suffering a painful death. The film climaxes with the spectacular fire at Manderly that burns down the entire estate. Mrs. Danvers, trapped on an upper floor, prefers to die with her dreams of Rebecca than to see Maxim and his new wife happy there. Max and his second wife drive off as Manderly crumbles behind them.

One may consider Rebecca a kind of femme fatale—her presence is everywhere in the film. She is Joan Fontaine's main antagonist. She lives for Mrs. Danvers. Curtains blowing in her room keep her presence alive, and the monogram "R" everywhere, her portrait, her perfume testify to her power. All this is reinforced by the haunting Franz Waxman score and the visuals of George Barnes. But *Rebecca* is not a true noir, nor is it a ghost story. It is a very, very moody romantic film with fine cinematography, a wonderful script, a terrific music score, and taut direction by Alfred Hitchcock. It has many dark, gothic elements in its story line and setting, and the notable use of a first-person narrative in flashback, but it is certainly not a true film noir in any sense. It is probably one of the best films that paved the way for the noir style to take hold of American audiences in the mid-1940s. But if one considers this film to be the one with the most "noirish" elements, then every subsequent remake falls far from the mark.

Rebecca **(1948)**, *Philco Television Playhouse*, October 13, 1948. No reviews or cast listing can be found.

Rebecca **(1950)**, *Robert Montgomery Presents*, May 24, 1950. No reviews or cast listing can be found.

Rebecca **(1962)**, *NBC Television Theatre*, April 11, 1962. This color version starred James Mason as Maxim de Winter, Joan Hackett as his new wife, and Nina Foch as Mrs. Danvers.

Rebecca (1978), PBS. This four-part, 205 min. version starred Jeremey Brett and Joanna David. It was directed by Simon Langton, and had a script written by Hugh Whitemore with original music by Ron Grainer. Anna Massey played Mrs. Danvers and Elspeth March, Mrs. Van Hopper.

Rebecca (1997), PBS, 1997. This two-part, color version starred Charles Dance as Maxim, and Emilia Fox as his second wife, Faye Dunaway as Mrs. Van Hopper (played by Florence Bates in the original film), Diana Rigg as Mrs. Danvers, and Jonathan Cake as Jack Flavell. Despite fairly good reviews, the specter of the Hitchcock film is always present.

I WAKE UP SCREAMING (1941) AND *VICKI* (1953)

I Wake Up Screaming (1941), d. H. Bruce Humberstone, 20th Century Fox, 82 min., b&w, sc. Dwight Taylor, from the novel by Steve Fisher, ph. Edward Cronjager. m. Cyril J. Mockridge, v. Key Video.

Definitely a noir mystery, *I Wake Up Screaming* opens with Alfred Newman's famous *Street Scene* theme playing as black-and-white titles flashing on Broadway marquees. Victor Mature plays publicity agent Frankie Christopher, who wants to promote model Vicki Lynn (Carole Landis in one of her bitchiest roles) to stardom and to high society. She is murdered just as she's headed for Hollywood. The film is told in flashback. Inspector Ed Cornell (Laird Cregar) wants to pin the murder on Frankie, but Jill (Betty Grable), Vicki's sister, has found evidence that will convict—of all people—Inspector Cornell. While visiting Cornell's apartment, she and Frankie discover a shrine he has made, candles and all, to Vicki. Cornell takes poison rather than face prosecution, and Frankie and Jill run off, probably to marry. Minor roles are played by Allan Joslyn as a nosy reporter and Elisha Cook, Jr., as an elevator operator who could have killed Vicki Lynn. Edward Cronjager's low-key photography and a script containing flashbacks about the death of a femme fatale put this film in the early noir category. According to Darryl F. Zanuck, the film would have done better at the box office if it had a musical number showing Betty Grable's famous legs. The film did pretty well without a number from Grable, but Zanuck never showcased her again in a "serious" film.

Vicki (1953), d. Harry Horner, 20th Century Fox, 85 min., b&w, sc. Dwight Taylor, based on Steve Fisher's novel, ph. Milton R. Krasner, m. Leigh Harline, v. not available.

This film, told in flashbacks with noir stylistics, is a faithful remake of the 1941 version, about an obsessed detective who attempts to pin the murder of a conniving model he loved on the press agent who made her into a possible Hollywood star(let). It is directed by Harry Horner from a similar script by Dwight Taylor (based on Steve Fisher's novel). Jean Peters plays Vicki Lynn; Jeanne Crain is her sister, Jill; Elliott Reid is Steve Christopher; and Richard Boone is Lt. Ed Cornell. Clearly Elliott Reid is not as charismatic as Victor Mature, and Richard Boone is a poor substitute for Laird Cregar, who made us shudder with his creepy noirish performance. And at every turn Carole Landis trumps Jean Peters, who is quite unsuited to the role of bitchy model-cum-starlet-cum-social climber. Fox showcased her much better in subsequent films.

HIGH SIERRA (1941), COLORADO TERRITORY (1949), AND I DIED A THOUSAND TIMES (1955)

High Sierra (1941), d. Raoul Walsh, Warner Bros., 100 min., b&w, sc. John Huston and W. R. Burnett, based on Burnett's novel, ph. Tony Gaudio, m. Adolph Deutsch, v. Key.

High Sierra was Humphrey Bogart's breakout film as a romantic gangster-hero who falls for the wrong woman, fails at a robbery, and is killed, while fleeing, on top of a mountain in the High Sierras of California. Many critics place this film in the "noir" category, but I would call it a film "gris," because it is really another Burnett gangster story of a killer gone wrong, looking for the wrong woman and meeting his fate in daylight. No femme fatale here, no expressionist photography, no urban atmosphere—only those looming High Sierras and a wonderful score by Adolph Deutsch to support those bright white-and-gray visuals.

Bogart plays Roy Earle, nicknamed "Mad Dog" because of his reputation as a killer-bank robber. He has been on the run since Big Mac (Donald MacBride) helped break him out of a California prison. Mac also set up a job for Roy—robbing the safe of a resort managed by Louis Mendoza (Cornel Wilde in a very early screen role). Roy links up with Babe Kozak (Alan Curtis) and Red Hattery (Arthur Kennedy), who bring along ex-show girl Marie Garson (Ida Lupino in one of her best tough girl roles). Roy wants her to leave, but Marie convinces him that her presence is necessary. On the road, Roy meets the Goodshoe family and is taken with their beautiful daughter, Velma (Joan Leslie in her first screen role). He plans to settle down with her after the robbery, and he gives the parents the money they need for her corrective foot surgery. The robbery goes very badly, but Roy and the gang escape. He sees Velma one last time, as she is dancing jive with local men, and wants to make her his own, but she does not love him. Roy leaves with Marie and their mutt, Pard. Marie is in love with Roy and she throws her lot in with him, for better or worse. They probably have one night together before they are hounded by the media and the police, chased on mountain roads into the High Sierras. Roy urges Marie to take Pard and get on a bus. She does, but when she learns Roy is trapped on top of a mountain, she returns. Pard runs up the mountain to Roy, and as he is reaching for the dog, a sharpshooter fires the shots that kill him. Marie runs up, cradles the dead Roy in her arms, and says, "He finally broke out—he's free, free!"

Bogart and Lupino have excellent roles in this gangster film that is known for its speed, excitement, suspense, and suggestion of futility which culminates in irony and, perhaps, even poetry. *High Sierra* is a wonderful film, but it is not really a film noir.

***Colorado Territory* (1949)**, d. Raoul Walsh, Warner Bros., b&w, 94 min., sc. Edmund H. North and John Twist, based on the W. H. Burnett novel *High Sierra*, ph. Sidney Hickox, m. David Buttolph, v. not available.

This film follows *High Sierra* as closely as a remake can, except that it has been turned into a western starring Joel McCrea as Wes McQueen (the Roy Earle role), Virigina Mayo as Colorado Carson (the Marie Garson role), and Dorothy Malone as Julie Ann Winslow (the Velma role). McQueen is broken out of prison by confederates to help them pull one last train robbery that will set them up for life. When he meets Julie Ann, just arrived from the East, he feels she is the girl for him and wants to set up housekeeping with her and her father. But there is a $10,000 reward for his capture, and when the train robbery goes wrong, McQueen is forced into the desert, into an Indian cave dwelling where he holes up with Colorado Carson, who declares her love for him. Unable to avoid his destiny, McQueen is shot dead and Colorado is taken to jail. Sad ending for this pseudo-western noir remake.

***I Died a Thousand Times* (1955)**, d. Stuart Heisler, Warner Bros., 105 min., WarnerColor, CinemaScope, sc. W. R. Burnett, from his novel *High Sierra*, ph. Ted D. McCord, m. David Buttolph, v. Warner Bros.

In this recycling of *High Sierra*, Jack Palance is surprisingly touching as Roy Earle, especially in his scenes with Shelley Winters as Marie Gibson, the tough ex-dance hall gal who is in love with him. Roy is still setting his sights on "good girl" Velma (played by Lori Nelson), to whom he has given money so she can have surgery to reverse her club foot condition. As in the original, she spurns Roy after she has the surgery. The robbery also goes badly, and Babe (Lee Marvin), Red (Earl Holliman), and other gang members scatter when the police are informed by Louis Mendoza (Perry Lopez) that Earle's gang committed the robbery. Marie casts her lot with Roy, who now realizes he loves her, and returns to him—after Roy has sent her away—when she finds out he is holed up in the High Sierras, a target for police. The ending of the film is exactly the same as the original. Color and CinemaScope help somewhat to tell this small story on the wide screen, but, as *New York Times* critic Bosley Crowther so rightly said, "It is an insult to the audience's intelligence to take a mythologized hero [Bogart] and put him on top of the high Sierras again." The film goes wrong early on when there is too much dissention among the gang members and too much talk, talk, talk that leads virtually nowhere. Only the quiet moments with Palance and Winters are worth savoring in this most un-noirish of color remakes.

SUSPICION (1941, 1987 [TV])

Suspicion (1941), d. Alfred Hitchcock, RKO Radio Pictures, 99 min., b&w, sc. Samuel Raphaelson, Joan Harrison, and Alma Reville, from the Francis Iles's novel *Before the Fact*, ph. Harry Stradling, m. Franz Waxman, v. Key and Vid-America.

The setting is rural England. Johnnie Aysgarth (played by Cary Grant) is a handsome bounder with no money but lots of charm. He meets mousy Lena McLaidlaw (Joan Fontaine) on a train. Her father, General McLaidlaw (Cedric Hardwicke), is well-to-do and a man of position in society. Johnnie romances Lena and sweeps her off her feet into a marriage she starts to regret. Sums of money are missing from the bank where Johnnie works. And the death of Beaky (Nigel Bruce) is suspect, because Johnnie and he were partners in a real estate scheme and Johnnie stands to profit from his death. He also knew Beaky's weakness for liquor, which could have killed him. Lena now suspects Johnnie is after her money. In one scene, Johnnie brings a glass of warm milk up a dark staircase to Lena. Hitchcock put a lightbulb in the glass and focused the camera on it, giving it a lethal glow in the darkness. In the novel, Lena drinks the milk and dies happy because she has had Johnnie as a lover and has been extremely happy. But Hollywood could not cast Cary Grant as a murderer who gets away with it—and so, in the film version, Lena does not drink the milk.

Lena tries to run off the next morning—but Johnnie accompanies her in their roadster. Just as the car is speeding around a curve, the car door accidentally opens on her side. Johnnie grabs Lena, pulling her to safety, and the two talk (we can't hear what they say) as the car turns around. We realize Johnnie and Lena have reconciled. Perhaps it was an unsatisfying cinematic ending, but according to the Production Code of the period, you could not get away with murder. Fontaine is particularly luminous in the film, revealing her thoughts in her facial expression, and Grant is equally good as the suspected rotter/playboy. Nigel Bruce, Cedric Hardwicke, Dame May Whitty, and Leo G. Carroll supply adequate support. The tag line for the film was "Each time they kissed . . . there was the thrill of love . . . and the threat of murder!" Except for the marred ending, *Suspicion* did provide adequate thrills.

***Suspicion* (1987)**, *American Playhouse* (PBS), d. Andrew Grieve, 90 min., color, sc. Jonathan Lynn and Barry Levinson, based on the 1941 screenplay by Joan Harrison, Alma Reville, and Samuel Raphaelson, ph. Brian Morgan, m. Larry Grossman, v. not available.

Anthony Andrews and Jane Curtin play the roles originally written for Cary Grant and Joan Fontaine. The color film has been updated to the late 1980s, and Jane Curtin plays an American heiress who is the stepdaughter of General McLaidlaw (Michael Hordern) and his wife (Betsy Blain). The television script follows the original screenplay in all other aspects, down to the conclusion, but without the original suspense provided in black-and-white by Alfred Hitchcock. Andrews's Johnnie comes off smug, and Curtin uses Fontaine's expressions in a dead reading of the part of Lena. A television critic called the telefilm "much diminished and director Grieve deserves the blame for permitting the unoriginal approach" of letting Andrews and Curtin play Grant and Fontaine. "The improvements [in color, autos, clothes, and furnishings] offer no solace" (*Variety Television Reviews*, June 8, 1988). Another poor television remake.

THE FALCON TAKES OVER (1942) AND MURDER, MY SWEET (1944)

***The Falcon Takes Over* (1942)**, d. Irving Reis, RKO Radio Pictures, 62 min., b&w, sc. based on Raymond Chandler's novel *Farewell, My Lovely* and characters created by Michael Arlen, adapted by Lynn Root and Frank Fenton, ph. George Robinson, m. Mischa Bakaleinikoff, v. not available.

Starring George Sanders as Gay Lawrence, The Falcon, this film is one of the best in the entire "Falcon" series made by RKO through the 1940s. Taking Chandler's story from his novel, director Reis uses the Michael Arlen detective instead of Chandler's Philip Marlowe to solve the mystery of the missing jade necklace and the whereabouts of Velma (now Diana; played by Helen Gilbert). Tracking down her former, employer when she worked as a "B" girl, Jesse Florian (Anne Revere) Lawrence also discovers Diana's former lover, Moose Malloy (played by Ward Bond), and who murdered Marriot (Hans Conried). Of course it turns out to be the femme fatale who was trying to escape her shady past by marrying into respectable society. Lynn Bari as Ann, a reporter, helps Sanders chase down the criminals. James Gleason and Allen Jenkins provide comic relief as Detective O'Hara and Goldy Locke, The Falcon's chauffeur. The first version of *Farewell, My Lovely* cannot be taken seriously as a definitive version of Chandler's novel, perhaps only as a comic one. Sanders, who seems to be acting above the material, probably considered the paycheck admirable, but the film is a complete waste of time. Chandler's convoluted plot was simplified by the writers, but this original adaptation of the novel falls far from the mark of its great film noir successor.

Murder, My Sweet (1944), d. Edward Dmytryk, RKO Radio Pictures, 95 min., sc. John Paxton, from the Raymond Chandler novel *Farewell, My Lovely*, ph. Harry J. Wild, m. Roy Webb, v. Nostalgia.

For an extended critique of this film, see Chapter 2 of this book. Needless to say, this is the definitive (remake) film noir of the period that showed Chandler's seedy milieu of Los Angeles to fine effect. It contains the usual blonde femme fatale (played by Claire Trevor), two wonderful expressionistic dream sequences, fascinating low key lighting, and a host of sleazy characters, including private investigator Philip Marlowe (former crooner Dick Powell, cast against type), gargantuan Mike Mazurki playing Moose Malloy, Esther Howard as bordello owner Jessie Florian, and Otto Kruger as the proprietor of a sanatorium. *Murder, My Sweet* is the definitive noir of 1944 (other than Billy Wilder's *Double Indemnity*), which is the real article. Even the 1975 remake pales by comparison. The Dmytryk version is classic film noir at its most profound.

TIME TO KILL (1942) AND *THE BRASHER DOUBLOON* (1947)

Time to Kill (1942), d. Herbert I. Leeds, 20th Century Fox, 61 min., b&w, sc. Clarence Upson Young, based on Raymond Chandler's novel *The High Window* and the character Michael Shayne, created by Brett Halliday, ph. Charles Clarke, m. Emil Newman, v. not available.

Starring Lloyd Nolan as Michael Shayne, P.I. (in one of seven films he made for Fox), this was the first of the "B" programmers in which Shayne is substituted for Philip Marlowe this time, to solve the case of the missing Brasher doubloon as well as a murder and the whereabouts of a ring of counterfeiters of rare coins. It is a "bottom of the bill" feature and is directed with little vigor and zest by Leeds. Nolan gives a capable performance but always arrives at a murder scene when the police do, and is weighed down by the explanations of the crimes. The supporting cast, including Ethel Griffies as Mrs. Murdock, the chief villain, and Heather Angel as Myrle Davis, her secretary who mistakenly believes she committed a crime, are capable but do little to offset the Irish blarney (and music) behind the entire film.

The Brasher Doubloon **(1947)**, d. John Brahm, 20th Century Fox, 72 min., b&w, sc. Dorothy Bennett and Leonard Praskins, from Raymond Chandler's novel *The High Wall*, ph. Lloyd Ahern, m. David Buttolph, v. not available.

Although it is categorized as a film noir, this is one of the lightest remakes of Raymond Chandler's *The High Window*. Bringing Philip Marlowe back into the fold, famous noir director John Brahm does what he can with a mediocre story and the minor talents of George Montgomery (a handsome song-and-dance man) as Marlowe; Nancy Guild (her first film) as Merle Davis, the secretary of Mrs. Murdock (magnificently played by Florence Bates as a bad, bad woman); and the old reliable German silent film villain Fritz Kortner as Vannier. Art dealer Sidney Janis's son Conrad makes his debut as Leslie Murdock, the son who is stealing from his mother. Marlowe is hired by Mrs. Murdock to find the Brasher doubloon, a quite valuable ancient Dutch coin missing from her collection. (It was stolen by her son, who owed huge gambling debts.) Some murders are committed, and we discover in a home movie that it was Mrs. Murdock who pushed her husband out of a window to his death, in order to gain control of his fortune. However, she convinced her mentally unstable secretary, Merle, that she committed the crime (which defies explanation). Marlowe solves the crime, and he and Merle go off toward the bright horizon of a 20th Century Fox happy ending. Although the style of the film is definitely noir, Nancy Guild is no femme fatale. She spends most of the film rebuffing Montgomery's sexual advances because she believes she is mentally ill. But once she discovers the truth, she becomes a sexy, warm-hearted, available woman. The real darkness of the film resides in the heart of the murderer, Mrs. Murdock, and the night-lit scenes, where dangerous transactions of money and crimes take place. But otherwise, *Brasher* is rather a bore and often too mysterious for its own good. When it is called upon to deliver on the sinister promises made in the trailer, it reneges completely. "Faux noir" is a better way to describe it.

Appendix B

From Thriller, Horror, Caper, Suspense, Neo-Noir to New Noir Remake

PLEIN SOLEIL (PURPLE NOON) (1960) AND THE TALENTED MR. RIPLEY (1999)

Plein Soleil **(Purple Noon) (1960),** d. René Clement, CCFC, 125 min., Eastmancolor, sc. René Clement and Paul Gegauff, based on the Patricia Highsmith novel *The Talented Mr. Ripley,* ph. Henri Decae, m. Nino Rota, v. Miramax (restored version with yellow subtitles).

As we enter the 1960s, film noir, as a style in black-and-white, ceased production in both America and Europe. However, there are occasional films in 1960 and after that take "noirish" stories written before 1960 and mount them into a new noir style. *Purple Noon* is one of these stories, filmed in Eastmancolor and wide screen, that has a black-hearted villain who is photographed in lush Italian surroundings, commits most murders in bright daylight, and finally gets his just deserts through a twist of fate.

Alain Delon plays Tom Ripley, supposedly an old college chum of Phillip Greenleaf (exultantly played by Maurice Ronet), is hired by Greenleaf's father to persuade his wastrel son to stop spending money lavishly, give up his relationship with Marge (Marie Laforet in her film debut), and come home to the United States and behave like a responsible person. When Phillip discovers Tom has designs on his girlfriend and his fortune, Tom stabs Phillip to death aboard the latter's yacht in what is perhaps the film's most violent scene. The rest of the film is a cat-and-mouse game played between Marge, the police, and Tom as everyone suspects Phillip's disappearance was the result of foul play. In this French version, when the yacht is brought out of the water so it can be sold to settle Phillip's estate, his body, wrapped in a old sail, is found wired to the ship's rudder. We never see Tom again, and the film ends with this image, though we know justice will be done—offscreen. Young Alain Delon plays Tom with the seductive charm of a true psychopath but also repels us through his brutality. Tom is an intelligent murderer with a sinister edge that he hides behind partly closed eyes that see everything through a guileless mask which makes him dangerous. Phillip is the poor dupe who gets sucked into Tom's spontaneous plot, but Marge clings to her love for Phillip and is repelled by Tom's presumption that he could replace her lover. *Purple Noon* (aka *Lust for Evil*) is a terrific new noir set in the Mediterranean, a variation on American films noirs of stolen identities with the added touch of sexual ambiguous lead characters.

The Talented Mr. Ripley (1999), d. Anthony Minghella, Paramount, 139 min., color, CinemaScope, sc. Anthony Minghella, based on Patricia Highsmith's novel, ph. John Seale, m. Gabriel Yared, v. Paramount.

Starring Matt Damon (wearing glass frames and clothes of the 1950s) as Tom, sexy English actor Jude Law as the rich, spoiled "Dickie" Greenleaf, and Gwyneth Paltrow as his girlfriend, Marge, this neo-noir remake contains the same chills as the original French version but adds many more interesting characters and a homosexual murder from which Tom Ripley cannot escape. The 1999 American film follows the script of the 1960 French film rigorously, except that it opens out the story and gives a wider range for supporting players to shine with the stars. Lovely Cate Blanchett plays Meredith Logue, a former flame of Dickie's, and is part of the cat-and-mouse game to find him after his disappearance. Also involved are Philip Seymour Hoffman as Freddie Miles, one of Dickie's expatriate friends, and Peter Smith-Kingsley as Jack Davenport, a gay music teacher living in Venice who mistakenly befriends and falls in love with Tom, discovers the truth of Dickie's disappearance and murder, and is killed by Tom aboard a liner bound for the United States.

Although the ending is somewhat ambiguous, as is Tom's sexuality throughout the film, we know he will be caught at the end of the voyage because Meredith saw Tom and Jack together aboard ship (and no doubt Jack's body will be found in the closet of the stateroom the two of them shared). The interesting ending in the newer version delays Tom's exposure regarding Dickie's death, for we never know if Dickie's body is found attached to the yacht's mechanical screw as it was in *Purple Noon*. Another big difference between the films is that in the original French version, Tom's murder of Phillip was spontaneous, rather than the fumbled but premeditated murder of Dickie in the American version. Tom wants to be Dickie, and take his fortune and girlfriend for himself. Assuming someone else's identity leads to disaster, as it led Jack Nicholson to his death in Michelangelo Antonioni's great Italian noir, *The Passenger* (1975), a film of true genius. Switching identities is a noirish theme—*Purple Noon* exploits it thoroughly, but most of the time *The Talented Mr. Ripley* seems more like a travelogue in which the characters are situated in front of beautiful landscapes for the sake of the film's scenic design. *Purple Noon* (*Plein Soleil*) is the real winner here, because the story mainly centers on the ménage à trois and the beautiful settings are integrated into the story line, not an excuse for telling it more beautifully!

PSYCHO (1960, 1998)

Psycho (1960), d. Alfred Hitchcock, Paramount, 109 min., b&w, sc. Joseph Stefano, from the novel by Robert Bloch, ph. John L. Russell, m. Bernard Herrmann, v. MCA/Universal.

Psycho is the first breakthrough Hitchcock movie in a style of horror/slasher/serial killer films that reintroduce noir stylistics but is conceived in a totally new and updated manner. Still not a genre, the new noir takes advantage of color and the latest in projection and sound techniques. Combined with a less restrictive rating system which allows for greater thematic freedom and truth, these post-1960 films contain more violence, and nudity, and harsher themes not tackled before. *Psycho* is the commercial black-and-white film that started it all, and from it re-emerged film noir, now the new noir or neo-noir with several new spins.

Marion Crane (Janet Leigh) has just stolen $40,000 from the real estate office where she works. She drives out of town and comes upon the Bates Motel. After having a sandwich with the owner's son, Norman (creepily played by Anthony Perkins), she decides to take a shower. In the shower, she is slashed to death—probably the most remarkable shower scene in American cinema. Her boyfriend, Sam Loomis (John Gavin), with her sister, Lila (Vera Miles), trace Marion to the Bates Motel. After Arbogast, a detective hot on the trail (Martin Balsam), disappears, Loomis and Lila search the house and find Norman's mother's skeleton in the basement, seated in a wicker chair. Norman, dressed in a dress and wig and wielding a gigantic knife, attempts to kill Lila. Sam Loomis stops him, and Norman is jailed for the murders of Marion and Arbogast. He sits in a padded cell, speaking in the voice of his mother as we hear a pat psychological explanation about how his mother took over Norman's personality. The closing shot shows Marion's car rental being pulled out of a swamp, in the trunk is the missing $40,000, wrapped in a newspaper.

With *Psycho*'s emphasis on gore and slasher murders, Hitchcock has turned a new corner in making the crime film. He leavens the heavy horror with humor sprinkled throughout the tale, then surprises us at the end with the identity of the murderer and all the Freudian reasons behind his crimes. Clearly the crime film of the 1950s headed in a new direction in the following decade.

Psycho (1998), d. Gus Van Sant, Universal, 109 min., color and wide screen, sc. Joseph Stefano, ph. Christopher Doyle, m. Bernard Herrmann's score adapted by Danny Elfman, v. Universal/MCA.

The second version of Hitchcock's film (not to be confused with the serial films *Psycho* II, III, and IV, all starring Anthony Perkins as an aging Norman Bates) is a scene-by-scene color remake of the original without the shocks. Vince Vaughn vainly tries to breathe life into the Norman Bates role. Except for the addition of a masturbatory scene, his portrait of the deranged Norman is vapid. Equally vapid is Anne Heche's playing of Marion Crane; Janet Leigh did it with aplomb and class. Although there is more nudity in this rendition of the famous slasher murder, Heche winds up lying on the side of the tub, not on the floor next to the drain. (It was said Saul Bass directed the original shower scene, with water and blood circling the drain as the camera pulls back and brilliantly photographs the iris of Janet Leigh's eye—bright concentric circles.) Van Sant's rendition of the shower scene is poor, not even faithful to Hitchcock's. The only true surprises in the film are William H. Macy's portrayal of Arbogast and Robert Forster in the role of the psychiatrist. The use of color seems to have destroyed the starkness of the original, although the brilliant music score restores some of the shock power lost in the visuals. This is one homage that should not have been filmed—a poor, poor neo-noir remake.

CAPE FEAR (1962, 1991)

Cape Fear (1962), d. J. Lee Thompson, Universal International, 105 min., b&w, CinemaScope, sc. James R. Webb, from John D. MacDonald's novel *The Executioners*, ph. Samuel Leavitt, m. Bernard Herrmann, v. Universal/MCA.

This new noir emphasizes the suspenseful, thriller aspect just as *Psycho*, two years earlier, emphasized gore and slashing, as well as uncovering the psychological reasons behind the murders. *Cape Fear* is not very concerned with psychological underpinnings. It is concerned with sadism.

The story is quite simple. Robert Mitchum plays Max Cady, a real baddie just released from the Georgia State Penitentiary after serving fourteen years for beating a bar girl. (He claims he was not guilty.) District Attorney Sam Bowden (Gregory Peck) proved the case against

Cady. Cady returns to the town where he was convicted and starts to harass Bowden, his wife, Peggy (Polly Bergen), and his daughter, Nancy (Lori Martin). First their dog disappears, then Cady beats up a local bar girl (played by dancer Barrie Chase), who refuses to testify against him. He has a fancy for Nancy Bowden, and menaces her and her mother. Gregory Peck plays Bowden with all the sincerity he can muster. When their maid is killed in a kitchen accident, and threats to Cady by a local detective (Telly Savalas) and the police chief (Martin Balsam) prove to no avail, the family decides to go on vacation—on their boat on the Cape Fear River. In the thrilling climax of the film, Bowden kills Cady on the river during a wild storm, and the family survives the ordeal. Soft-spoken Robert Mitchum—wearing a panama hat, chomping on a smelly cigar, and speaking in that slick Southern accent he used in *Night of the Hunter*—easily steals the film from its other stars. Peck is very good as Sam Bowden, stepping into another of the character roles he filmed in 1962 (e.g., the lawyer in Harper Lee's *To Kill a Mockingbird*). Certainly *Cape Fear* was a change of pace for Peck. It is also a terrific new noir thriller.

Cape Fear (1991), d. Martin Scorsese, Universal, 128 min., color and Panavision, sc. Wesley Strick, based on the 1962 screenplay and original novel by John D. MacDonald, ph. Freddie Francis, m. Elmer Bernstein, conducting the original Bernard Herrmann score, v. Universal/MCA.

Although it is much like the remake of *Psycho* in many aspects—same production company, same script with minor revisions, same music score with different conductor—*Cape Fear* (1991) is unlike its predecessor because it is the first really successful neo-noir remake of the early 1990s. Martin Scorsese takes the same story and opens it out beautifully. Yes, it is Robert de Niro as Max Cady—white trash, tattoos all over his body, frightening his fellow prisoners and the Bowden family with his visceral sadism. He lusts after Sam Bowden's daughter Danny (the nymphet tease Juliette Lewis). In fact, they have a scene together in the high school auditorium that is titillating but devoid of violence. Cady also lusts after Bowden's wife, Leigh (luscious Jessica Lange). In this version, the Bowdens are not the happily married couple they seem to be. In fact, Sam (macho actor Nick Nolte) is having a hot-blooded affair with one of his law clerks (Illeana Douglas). When Cady discovers this, he dates Sam's lover and beats her so badly that Bowden seeks revenge. The conclusion is far more visual, visceral, and startling than in the 1962 version. The special effects catch us in the vortex of a storm and the battle between Sam and Max on the Cape Fear River—good versus evil and, of course, good triumphs. But as in so many films of the era, there is that essential "red herring": once you think you have throttled the enemy, he rises up from the dead. Finally, De Niro drowns, and the family that kills together, stays together. One wonders if Bowden brought Cady's revenge upon his family by convicting him on such slim evidence. Or should he have let him go, so he could beat more women and get away with it? Whatever, *Cape Fear* is a terrific neo-noir remake, and De Niro's performance is absolutely stunning.

POINT BLANK (1967) AND *PAYBACK* (1999)

Point Blank (1967), d. John Boorman, Universal, 99 min., Metrocolor and Panavision, sc. Alexander Jacobs, David Newhouse, and Rafe Newhouse, from Richard Stark's novel *The Hunter*, ph. Philip H. Lathrop, m. Johnny Mandel, v. Universal/MCA.

Of all of the new crime noirs in color that came out in the mid-1960s, including *Harper* (1966) (and *Chinatown* [1974]), *Point Blank* is at the center of the neo-noir movement. It is a very, very violent film starring Lee Marvin as Walker, told in flashbacks. Walker is supposedly shot dead by his best friend, Mal Reese (played unctuously by John Vernon); his wife, Lynn (Sharon Acker), betrayed him to Mal after all three participated in a successful robbery. But Walker is alive, seeking vengeance and his share of the robbery proceeds. He kills everyone who gets in his way, including mob boss Brewster (Carroll O'Connor), and threatens Chris (Angie Dickinson), the girl Mal had taken up with after he dumped Lynn because of her drug habit. The real star, however, is the city of Los Angeles. English director John Boorman uses the city effectively—getting the pace, the architecture, even the smell of Los Angeles into the film—although some of the cutting is a bit convoluted. Walker triumphs over his would-be assassins, only to lose out to the police at the end. Typical of the new noir, the film is full of violence and sadism, and it also diminishes any moral sense the characters once possessed. Lee Marvin as Walker is the antihero, a killer who must kill or be killed. The film does establish one essential point: revenge is futile. But Marvin plays his role to the hilt, mowing down anyone in his way. He is vicious, vengeful, unstoppable. It is a bravura performance.

Payback (1999), d. Brian Helgeland, Paramount, 110 min., color and CinemaScope, sc. Brian Helgeland and Terry Hayes, on Richard Starks's novel *The Hunter*, m. Chris Boardman, v. Paramount.

Mel Gibson stars as Porter, who is left for dead by his wife, Lynn (Deborah Kara Younger), and her lover, Val (terrifically played by Gregg Henry). He only wants his "seventy grand"—nothing else. Val leaves Lynn, a drug addict, and moves up in Chicago's criminal society. Porter kills the mob head, Carter (William Devane), on a dare from a higher mob boss named Bronson (played convincingly by Kris Kristofferson). He then kidnaps Bronson's son but is caught and brutally beaten, losing some fingers. He even kills the mob kingpin (James Coburn) and, with his accomplice, Rosie (a hooker with a heart of gold whom he used to chauffeur in the old days, played by Maria Bello), succeeds in ripping off the mob, avenging himself with a bomb kills Bronson, and drives off with the new love of his life, $70,000 richer.

There are flashes of humor in the film—for example, Val's sadomasochistic sex with an Oriental girl named Pearl (played by Lucy Liu) and one-liners delivered by Gibson during some of his dialogues with mobsters. Otherwise, this is a happy neo-noir remake despite the cruelty to humans which is paramount in the script. Like *Point Blank*, this film is not for the weak of heart—probably more for the weak-minded. In his *New York Times* review of the film (February 5, 1999), Stephen Holden had one word for *Payback*—"loathsome." I cannot agree, because there is much cleverness and ingenuity in this remake. Nevertheless, it is a star vehicle for Mel Gibson, and without his presence the movie would not work. *Point Blank* is still the better original neo-noir.

THE THOMAS CROWN AFFAIR (1968, 1999)

The Thomas Crown Affair (1968), d. Norman Jewison, United Artists, 102 min., Color by Deluxe, CinemaScope, sc. Alan R. Trustman, ph. Haskell Wexler, m. Michel Legrand (song: "The Windmills of Your Mind"), v. United Artists.

Steve McQueen plays Thomas Crown, a financial wizard who masterminds a Boston bank robbery "for the fun of it" and gets away with it. Hot on his trail is Faye Dunaway as Vicki Anderson, an insurance investigator who suspects Crown of the theft. Paul Burke plays Det. Eddie Malone, who also tries to nail McQueen for the caper. But the unexpected happens, and Crown and Anderson fall in love. Taking a simple caper drama, and updating it, and using color and CinemaScope with split-screen technology showing what is happening at the same moment during the bank heist make this film one of the engaging new noirs of the 1960s. There is definite chemistry between McQueen and Dunaway, who get able assists from Jack Weston, Yaphet Kotto, and a large group of bank robbers who work with the utmost style and are perfectly synchronized. The film does not have a brain in its head—its only reason for being is pure, escapist entertainment.

The Thomas Crown Affair (1999), d. John McTiernan, MGM, 111 min., Color by Deluxe and Technicolor, sc. Leslie Dixon and Kurt Wimmer, based on the original screenplay by Alan R. Trustman, ph. Tom Priestly, m. Bill Conti, v. MGM.

This neo-noir remake of the 1968 film is superior in every way. Pierce

Brosnan plays Thomas Crown. We see him in the office of his psychiatrist (played, in homage to the original, by Faye Dunaway), stating that he can never trust anyone, especially a woman. That thought unravels through the entire film, adding both psychological and emotional motives to the mix of love, lust, and theft which is the predominant theme of the film. Instead of robbing a bank, this Thomas Crown goes after art—a particular Monet in a Boston museum. Rene Russo plays Catherine Banning, an insurance investigator who gets emotionally involved with Crown. Dennis Leary (a noir icon) plays Det. Michael McCann, who aids Banning in her entrapment of Crown. But the film turns us around completely, with a very sexual sequence between the lovers and the promise of wealth and marriage in the future. Yes, they get away with the loot after a cat-and-mouse game that is typical of caper films of the 1990s. This is one neo-noir remake that is very, very entertaining, fast, attractive, and mature. Brosnan and Russo should be teamed again in a film that suits their unique personalities.

THE GETAWAY (1972, 1994)

The Getaway (1972), d. Sam Peckinpah, National General/First Artists, 122 min., Technicolor, Todd-AO 35, sc. Walter Hill, based on the novel by Jim Thompson, ph. Lucien Ballard, m. Quincy Jones, v. Warner Bros.

Another neo-noir thriller, starring Steve McQueen as Doc McCoy, a master heist man and bank robber who is sprung from a Texas jail by Jack Benyon (Ben Johnson) after he has slept with Doc's wife, Carol (Ali McGraw). They form a gang of thieves that gets away with $500,000, but Jack intends to double-cross Doc and Carol by having Rudy Travis (Al Lettieri) kill them before the split. Doc gains the upper hand, apparently kills Rudy, and goes off to El Paso to join the rest of the robbers and split the money. But Rudy is alive and shows up to avenge himself against Doc. There is a huge shoot-out in a seedy El Paso hotel. (And in a subplot Sally Struthers comes on sexually to Rudy in spite of her husband's pleas to stop. Struthers's nymphet dominates the last third of the film and really brings down the action.) There are lots of explosions, killings, and car chases, and a wonderful escape by Doc and Carol in a garbage truck. At the end, Doc and Carol, unlike so many couples on the run (Bonnie and Clyde, Keechie and Bowie in *They Live by Night*), make it over the border into Mexico with their cool half-million. They give the truck driver (Slim Pickens) a sizable tip, and probably live happily ever after. *The Getaway* is a wonderful Peckinpah neo-noir, filled with enough blood and corruption to satisfy an audience hungry for violent escapist fare.

The Getaway **(1994),** d. Roger Donaldson, Universal, 115 min., DeLuxe Color and Panavision, sc. Walter Hill and Amy Jones, based on the Jim Thompson novel, ph. Peter Menzies, Jr., m. Mark Isham, v. Universal/ MCA.

This second version of *The Getaway* is a very, very good neo-noir remake, and heightens the criminal elements and the violence of the original. In this updated version Alec Baldwin plays Doc; his real-life wife, Kim Basinger, plays Carol; and James Woods is Jack Benyon. Michael Madsen plays Rudy Travis, the pathological thug Jack orders to kill Doc and Carol. Doc gets the drop on Rudy and thinks he has killed him. Rudy survives, however, and he and the rest of the gang hunt down the pair until they obtain the money from the robbery. When Doc goes to Jack's home to split the money, Jack tells him about his affair with Carol in such detail that Carol shoots him dead. The couple begin to run. They arrive in a border town hotel to split the money with the rest of the gang, but Rudy is determined to kill Doc, Carol, and the others, and take all the cash for himself. He meets a gruesome end with a shotgun blast. Carol and Doc cross into Mexico with the proceeds of the robbery, to start a new life.

The notable difference in this remake is the nude scenes featuring the Baldwins (a longer version, shown in Europe, featured explicit sex scenes) and the buildup of Carol's role. Originally seen as an auxiliary to McQueen's Doc, Carol now is a true partner in both sex and crime. This remake has an authentic feel of the American Southwest of the 1990s, and enough action, double crosses, and emotional octane to make it a top commercial crimer. As with *The Thomas Crown Affair*, another original McQueen vehicle, *The Getaway* transcends the original and establishes a good case for continuing to remake neo-noirs.

DAY OF THE JACKAL (1973) AND THE JACKAL (1997)

Day of the Jackal **(1973),** d. Fred Zinnemann, Universal, 143 min., sc. Kenneth Ross, based on the novel by Frederic Forsyth, ph. Jean Tournier, m. Georges Delerue, v. Universal/MCA.

Political suspense novels were always better in black-and-white. When Fred Zinnemann decided to add color and a tight editing style, an old-fashioned assassination film became far more exciting. Remember Alfred Hitchcock's *Foreign Correspondent* (1940)? There is an assassination attempt on the Dutch Prime Minister. The assassin is successful—but he shot a decoy; the real Prime Minister was spirited away by a group of pacifists, headed by Herbert Marshall, who wanted to stop a certain treaty from being signed. Hitchcock's mise-en-scène was certainly noir.

Zinnemann is most certainly neo-noir. Edward Fox, with his boyish good looks, does not appear to be an assassin; the film watches him go through many twists and turns until he lines up his target—Charles de Gaulle—in the crosshairs of his telescopic sight. His single rifle shot misses, of course, and he is caught by the French police. The suspense lies in watching Fox reach the ultimate moment, then fail. The band continues to play, the soldiers march to its strains, and De Gaulle momentarily stares into space, acknowledging the unsuccessful attempt on his life. It is Michel Lonsdale as Det. Claude Lebel who is the true hero, tracking down the most elusive man in the world, identifying and trailing him throughout France until the frantic conclusion of the film. Although the audience knows the ending (obviously De Gaulle did not die), director Zinnemann keeps the suspense of the film surging until the last moment. A wonderful color neo-noir.

The Jackal (1997), d. Michael Caton-Jones, Universal, 124 min., color and Panavision, sc. Chuck Pfarrer, based Frederick Forsyth's *The Day of the Jackal*, by ph. Karl Walter Lindenlaub, m. Carter Burwell, v. Universal/ MCA.

This is clearly not a remake of the fascinating Zinnemann film. In fact, the plot has been changed so thoroughly that one cannot recognize it as being faithful either to the film or to Forsyth's novel. Starring Richard Gere as the FBI agent and Bruce Willis as the assassin, this is a high-tech neo-noir with a different plot from the original. Someone is plotting to kill the head of America's FBI. Is it an IRA assassin, a Basque terrorist, or a former KGB agent? Willis plays the Jackal very well—he uses disguises and in one of the most terrifying scenes, he ingratiates himself with a gay Washington man and kills him in order to go under cover. (There is a more subtle but similar scene in the Zinnemann film.) The film ends with a double shoot-out, first at the assassination site, then in the Washington subway. Gere throttles Willis at the end. Much star power here, but it's still a neo-noir bastardization of little substance.

LA FEMME NIKITA (1990) AND *POINT OF NO RETURN* (1993)

La Femme Nikita (1990), d. Luc Besson, Gaumont, 117 min., color & Technovision, sc. Luc Besson, ph. Thierry Arbogast, m. Eric Serra, v. not available.

This French neo-noir thriller was a box-office champion in Paris because of its stunning performance by Anne Parillaud as Nikita and the wonderful special effects. Add to that the stunning cinematography by Thierry Arbogast and the soundtrack score by Eric Serra, and you have a commercial winner. The plot is deceptively simple: Parillaud is Nikita, an amoral druggie and killer. She commits murder with two friends, is convicted, and is sentenced to death. After supposedly being given a lethal injection, she wakes up in a "government school for special operatives." She is told her old identity is gone, and she will pay back society for what she has done as a spy/assassin. For two years she undergoes vigorous training with a fellow operative Bob (played winningly by Tcheky Karyo), and Amande (Jeanne Moreau) teaches her all the feminine things she should have learned to make her a fascinating woman, proud of herself and capable of love. It is the old "Pygmalion" story, but with an edge of violence. Nikita eventually meets Marco (Jean-Hugues Anglade), a sweet and affectionate supermarket cashier. They fall in love, but she must hide her government activities from him (this is what the rest of the film is about). The film began as a violent thriller, but transcends this and becomes a story about Nikita's transformation into a beautiful woman who has found real love. Nikita eventually gets involved with Victor the Cleaner (played by Jean Reno) and almost loses her life in a final shoot-out. But the director opts for a happy ending.

***Point of No Return* (1993),** d. John Badham, Warner Bros., 109 min., Technicolor and Panavision, sc. Robert Getchell, based on Luc Besson's 1990 script, ph. Michael W. Watkins, m. Hans Zimmer, v. Warner Bros.

This film must be the fastest neo-noir remake on record. *Nikita* was released in France in 1990 and was distributed in America in 1991. Warner Bros. recognized a hot property when they saw it, and starred Bridget Fonda as Maggie (the Nikita role); Gabriel Byrne as Bob, the Svengali who transforms her from amoral killer to government assassin; and Dermot Mulroney as J.P., the man Nikita learns to love. The story is exactly the same as the original neo-noir. Anne Bancroft takes over the Jeanne Moreau role, showing Maggie how to become a sexy woman. Harvey Keitel is ineffective as Victor the Cleaner—a gangster with no morals.

However this remake falls far from the intensity of the original. Anne Parillaud had a gamine sadness that was almost poetic. Bridget Fonda does not bring such an intensity to her moods or her identity change. Dermot Mulroney is lost in the role of her sweet photographer/lover who lives downstairs in their apartment building in Venice, California. For Americans, this location might be more hip, but the poignancy of the original is lost, especially in the relationships between Bob and Maggie (he loves her but cannot act on his feelings) and Maggie and J.P. (Nikita loved Marco's lack of aggression in the original, but J.P. does not come off as a sensitive lover in this remake). Once again, the neo-noir remake is definitely of less quality than the original. One anonymous critic called it "pathetic" and "trash" when you think of the original film.

Point of No Return does have some good moments, but it dims in comparison to *La Femme Nikita*.

ADDENDA

As this book is going to press, four additional sets of pre-noir films that became full-fledged noir films can be added to those in Appendix A:

M (1931), Fritz Lang's German Expressionist film starring Peter Lorre that was remade into Joseph Losey's *M* (1951), starring David Wayne in the child-killer role originated by Lorre.

The Last Mile (1932), Sam Bischoff's prison drama starring Preston Foster was remade into Howard W. Koch's 1951 film noir with the same title, starring Mickey Rooney.

The Mouthpiece (1933), Elliot Nugent's pre-noir starring Warren William as a shady lawyer was remade twice, first as the pre-noir *The Man Who Talked Too Much* (1940), directed by Vincent Sherman and starring George Brent, and then the full-fledged noir *Illegal* (1955), directed by Lewis Allen and starring Edward G. Robinson as the attorney who is ready to lay his life on the line in defense of his gangster client.

Pièges (aka *Personal Column*) (1939), a masterpiece of French poetic realism directed by Robert Siodmak and starring Maurice Chevalier, the film paved the way for the true noir entitled *Lured* (1947), starring George Sanders and Lucille Ball in the same story of a police inspector out to trap a murderer using attractive women as bait.

Two additional sets of films noirs, remakes of original noirs, can be added to Appendix B;

This Gun for Hire (1942), Frank Tuttle's noir version of Graham Greene's novel, starring Alan Ladd as the madly obsessed killer "Raven," out for vengeance. James Cagney played the same role in a Vista-vision version of the same plot in *Short Cut to Hell* (1957), the star's only venture in directing himself. Finally, Robert Wagner starred in a cable television version of the Greene novel in 1991, playing the role originated by Ladd.

Cornell Woolrich's story for the 1946 film noir *Black Angel*, directed by Roy William Neill and starring Dan Duryea as an alcoholic who believes he committed murder on a bender the night before, is the same plot of Roy Baker's 1952 film, *Night without Sleep*, starring Gary Merrill in the same role with Linda Darnell trying to disprove his self-blame as June Vincent did in the earlier version.

Nota bene: I am certain readers of *Noir, Now and Then* will find other originals and remakes of noir films that continue to tantalize and fascinate. Vale.

Selected Bibliography

Borde, Raymond, and Etienne Chaumenton. *Panorama du film noir américain*. Paris: Editions du Minuit, 1955.

Brion, Patric. *Le film noir*. Paris: Éditions Nathan, 1991.

Christopher, Nicholas. *Somewhere in the Night: Film Noir and the American City*. New York: Free Press, 1997.

Durgnat, Raymond. "Paint It Black: The Family Tree of Film Noir." In *Film Noir Reader*, ed. Alain Silver and James Ursini, pp. 37–51. New York: Limelight, 1996.

Hamilton, William L. "Style Noir." *New York Times*, September 14, 1997.

Hirsch, Foster. *The Dark Side of the Screen: Film Noir*. San Diego: A. S. Barnes, 1981.

———. *Detours and Lost Highways: A Map of Neo-Noir*. New York: Limelight, 1999.

Krutnik, Frank. *In a Lonely Street: Film Noir, Genre, and Masculinity*. London: Routledge, 1991.

Mitchell, Charles. "The Film Noir Alphabet." *Big Reel Magazine* (May 1999).

Muller, Eddie. *Dark City: The Lost World of Film Noir*. New York: St. Martin's/ Griffin, 1998.

Palmer, R. Barton. *Hollywood's Dark Cinema: The American Film Noir*. New York: Twayne, 1994.

Rafter, Nicole. *Shots in the Mirror: Crime Films and Society*. New York: Oxford University Press, 2000.

Russell, Lawrence. "Review of *The Asphalt Jungle*." www.fcourt.com. May 1999.

Schrader, Paul G. "Notes on Film Noir." In *Film Noir Reader*, ed. Alain Silver and James Ursini, pp. 53–63. New York: Limelight, 1996.

Silver, Alain, and James Ursini, eds. *Film Noir Reader*. New York: Limelight, 1996.

———. *Film Noir Reader 2*. New York: Limelight, 1998.

————. *The Noir Style*. Woodstock, NY: Overlook Press, 1999.

Silver, Alain, and Elizabeth Ward, eds. *Film Noir: An Encyclopedic Reference to the American Style*, 3rd ed. Woodstock, NY: Overlook Press, 1992.

Thompson, Peggy, and Saeko Usukawa. *The Little Black and White Book of Film Noir: Quotations from Films of the 40's and 50's*. San Francisco: Arsenal Pulp Press, 1992.

————. *Hard-Boiled: Great Lines from Classic Noir Films*. San Francisco: Chronicle Books, 1995.

ELECTRONIC SOURCES

Chicago Sun-Times. www.suntimes.com/ebert.

Internet Movie Database. www.imdb.com.

New York News. www.nynews.com.

New York Post. www.nypost.com.

New York Times. www.nytimes.com.

Variety. www.variety.com.

VIDEO SOURCES

The following is a list of video distributors who have large collections of noir films; they are in the VHS format (NTSC) and may have some films available in the new DVD format:

Darker Images Video, P.O. Box 479, Millinocket, ME 04460 (207) 723-4429. Charles and Roberta Mitchell are film noir specialists and have the largest range of titles at fair prices. They are the best source for rare films noirs and advertise in *Classic Images* regularly.

Evergreen Video, 37 Carmine St., New York, NY (212) 691–7632. Owner Steve Feites is very knowledgeable about noir and has a good collection.

Facet's Video, 1517 W. Fullerton Ave., Chicago, IL (800) 331–6197. Some rare titles available in their excellent catalogues which they publish regularly.

Kim's Underground, 144 Bleecker St., New York, NY (212) 260–1010. For New Yorkers looking for special titles.

Kino Video, 333 West 39th St., New York, NY (800) 562-3330. Owner Matt Krim has the finest selection of noir titles sold commercially. www.kino.com.

TLA Video, 521 4th St., Philadelphia, PA (215) 564–3838. Good film noir collection and wonderful, up-to-date, very readable catalogues on all genres.

Index

Page references for main entries appear in **boldface type**.

About the Author

RONALD SCHWARTZ is Professor of Romance Languages and Film at City University of New York. He is the author of six books on Spanish literature, Latin American literature, Spanish cinema and Latin American film.